GHOSTS OF THE SHANKILL

by

Simon Shaw

Grosvenor House
Publishing Limited

This book is published by
Grosvenor House Publishing Ltd
Link House
140 The Broadway, Tolworth, Surrey, KT6 7HT.
www.grosvenorhousepublishing.co.uk

A CIP record for this book
is available from the British Library

Paperback ISBN 978-1-83615-621-5
eBook ISBN 978-1-83615-622-2

DEDICATION

This book is dedicated to the memory of William Robert Lambe.

Born 16 June 1914 at 23 Tasmania Street, Belfast. Son of Robert and Jean Lambe. Married to Sadie Boal at Shankill Road Methodist Church 26 October 1935. Father of Jean. Captain 3rd Coventry Company (Heath Road Methodist) Boys' Brigade. Died at Jordan Well, Coventry, while on duty as a Police Special Constable attempting to rescue people trapped in a cellar being used as an air raid shelter during the Coventry Blitz on 14 November 1940.

His warfare is o'er, his battle is fought,
His victory won, though dearly bought.
His fresh, young life, could not be saved,
He slumbers now, in a hero's grave.

CONTENTS

INTRODUCTION

WARNING: This story contains some discriminatory, dehumanising, offensive and outdated language. No offence is intended on my part. This is reproduced from source material and is only used for historical accuracy and to illustrate a main theme of this work - the racial prejudice and stereotypes that existed and impacted on people of colour during the timeframe of this book. The story cannot accurately be told without including it. I have followed the guidance written in the landmark book *Irish People of Colour: A social history of mixed race Irish in Britain and Ireland between 1700 and 2000* by Conrad Koza Bryan and Chamion Caballero, and some of the most offensive words have been starred out.

First published in 1969, the book *Holy War in Belfast* (HWIB) by Andrew Boyd documents sectarian rioting in Belfast over the centuries. In the chapter dealing with the 'Lady Day' riots which began on 15 August 1872, there is an intriguing passage relating to a Black man. The book refers to him as a *negro* called George Henry Thompson. It tells us he led a mob of 2,000 Shankill Road Protestants that drove Catholic families from the area and spearheaded the attack on the home of 'Widow Donaghy,' where he was 'shouting like a man demented' about 'papists and Fenians.' The front door was kicked in and 'one of his followers seized the terrified widow and thrust a large black cockroach in her face.' She was ordered to curse the Pope, with the man threatening to make her swallow 'the bloody cockroach' if she refused. The widow fled and the mob immediately wrecked the house and burned everything in it.

In the afternoon Constable John Cresswell of the Royal Irish Constabulary witnessed a man being pursued and stoned by the mob. He managed to escape into the safety of a nearby house. Thompson was beating the door when Cresswell intervened and grabbed him by the collar of his coat. In an instant, 'the negro, a powerfully built man,' turned and struck Cresswell 'a stunning blow on the head.' As he lined up a second punch, a man rushed out from a nearby public house and grabbed his arm. Thompson tossed this man and the policeman aside and escaped into the crowd, who all then vanished into the side streets. He then lay low but was eventually arrested early the next month. He was found guilty of being the leader of a riotous mob and sentenced to two years with hard labour at the County Antrim Assizes in 1873.

By any stretch of the imagination it's a horrific account. George Henry Thompson appears to have been an out of control bigoted monster and the ordeal of 'Widow Donaghy' must have been truly awful. Boyd's book was a bestseller, and irrespective of whether one thought it was biased or not - his premise was that firebrand Protestant preachers were basically responsible for all sectarian disturbances that ever occurred in Belfast - a 'must read' for anyone trying to fathom the reasons for the political, religious and ethnic divisions in Northern Ireland. I first read it in the late 1980s and the brief story of George Henry Thompson always stuck with me as it was so unusual. Belfast is a far more diverse place nowadays, but I suspect if a Black person was to lead a riot on the present day Shankill Road it would still be regarded as out of the ordinary by some people, and probably send social media into a meltdown with a flood of racist comments.

With the advent of the internet and access to online records such as old newspapers, I decided to check out just how accurate Boyd's account of George and his alleged actions is, and also to see if I could find out more information about him. I was partly inspired to do this by how my home city of Coventry, had, in fairly recent times, reclaimed its incredible connection to the famous African American actor and playwright of the 19th century called Ira Frederick Aldridge (1807-1867). Aged just 20, using the name of Frederick William Keene, he became the Actor-Manager of Coventry's theatre for a short season in 1828, making him the first Black person to manage a theatre in the United Kingdom. He returned to perform again in 1857 and 1859, this time under his own name and as a well established and highly regarded actor.

In August 2017 a Blue Plaque was unveiled commemorating this historic event. This was followed in 2021 by a stunning mural of him in the role of Shakespeare's *Othello*, by the talented artist Dreph, and an award winning sculpture called *In Honour of Ira Frederick Aldridge* by Favour Jonathan. Prior to the Blue Plaque I had never even heard of him let alone his incredible connection with Coventry. What more could I learn about George Henry Thompson I wondered?

Initially this was more down to curiosity than any other motive, but having compared Boyd's account to what is actually written in the contemporary newspaper reports, I was stunned to discover just how different it is. While it is true that a Black man called George Henry Thompson was indeed sent to prison for being a ringleader of rioters on the Shankill Road, much of the rest of it is not an accurate version of what really happened, and of course there is no 'before and after' story or context given to why Thompson was there in the first place.

This inspired me to compose a blog piece to set the record straight. An overheard conversation in a local arts and creative hub called the LTB Showrooms then sparked the idea to commission a painting, something I had never done before in my life. I wanted this to be the focal point of the project and in the event that nothing else came of it, at least I would be the owner of a very unique piece of artwork - *The Ghosts of the Shankill* - from which the title of this book comes.

This features on the front cover and the artist is Jonny Nicholds, who proved to be the ideal choice. As my research progressed he was able to subtly incorporate other aspects of George Henry Thompson's life into the painting to represent far more than his astonishing appearance on the Shankill Road.

As I amassed more information, from prior to and going beyond the riots of 1872, it became clear that there was enough material for a book rather than a short blog piece. It has been a long held ambition of mine to write a book so I decided to go for it.

My other main motivation is a deep affection for Belfast and the Shankill in particular. Outside of Coventry, various parts of Belfast and Monkstown in Newtownabbey, are the only places I have ever lived, spending time there from late 1992 to mid 1995.

That adventure began on the Shankill Road, where a taxi driver dropped me off outside the imposing Shankill Road Mission building, which was a place of worship and outreach for the Presbyterian Church in Ireland. As I paid the fare and was about to open the door, he wished me luck and added a heartfelt "Céad míle fáilte," explaining to me that it meant 100,000 welcomes in Irish. Perhaps not a usual welcome to a road known throughout the world for its devotion to all things British but memorable nonetheless.

The Mission ran a hostel for the homeless a few streets away, which accepted me and was to put a roof over my head in the early months of my time in Belfast. The manager, John McFarlane, was a tough but fair gentleman and imparted much wisdom on my younger self. I recall him saying, "don't let your left hand know what your right hand is doing," which has its origins in the New Testament and essentially means don't do things for 'show' to impress others. He also advised that it was best not to bear grudges or look a gift horse in the mouth.

John was a Christian, and as such, he had shared his testimony (his life story and how he became a Christian) with the hostel residents. This included being a prominent member of the Shankill Defence Association when 'The Troubles' erupted in the late 1960s and later commanding a unit of the Ulster Volunteer Force (UVF) paramilitary group in the area. The demon drink then consumed his life and he became an alcoholic. Found drunk in a gutter, members of a church picked him up and took him into their place of worship where he found Christ and was Saved. From then on he was a 'soldier' for Christ, helping the homeless at the hostel, speaking at Christian gatherings and using his influence to intercede with paramilitary groups when young people were under the threat of punishment by them.

It may surprise some readers that Roman Catholics stayed at the Shankill Hostel. My first roommate was one, not that it mattered. It wasn't uncommon for John to take a phone call from the Morning Star hostel in Divis Street asking if he could accommodate someone they had asked to leave or had no room to put up. As soon as the receiver was put down, he would drive to this place of refuge located in the nearby Irish Republican stronghold to collect the person and bring them over to the two houses linked by a serving hatch that made up the hostel in Shankill Parade. Here they were totally safe and nobody inside or outside of the hostel bothered them on account of their faith.

The hostel was run like an army boot camp. Residents had to be up by 8 am, with beds made and the males clean shaven. During the week, Christian devotions would take place at 8.30 am, either led by Ministers from the Shankill Road Mission, guests, or by John himself. On Sunday you had to attend either the morning or evening church service at the

Mission building on the Shankill Road, which was known locally as the 'Albert Hall.' The hostel was a strictly alcohol free zone and if the smell of alcohol was on your breath you ran the risk of being kicked out. Meals were ample and plentiful with Thursday's 'Ulster fry' being my favourite.

Mr. McFarlane would also pay residents 'pocket money' for helping him with odd jobs, such as assisting him with the catering services that he provided for local community events. I recall helping lay the tables at the Rangers Club in Azamor Street and also tidying the yard of his home in Boundary Street. He also got me a job as Church Warden at the Mission which topped up my 'brew' (dole) money for a while. That was a creepy old building when you were the only person inside late at night and had to visit every floor to check everything was switched off before locking the main door on your way out!

John was an Orangeman and a proud loyalist, but I never once heard any bigotry from him. The way the hostel operated and its amazing staff were a credit to him and the Shankill Road Mission. Some of the rules may seem extreme but I wouldn't have lasted five minutes in any other of Belfast's hostels at that time which weren't so strict. I myself eventually fell foul of the rules - by not going to church one Sunday - and got the boot. I still smile about the exchange with him over this:

"So I hear you didn't go to church yesterday Simon?"
"That's right John."
"Were you ill son?"
"No."
"Ah, a conscientious objector. You're out!"

Blunt and direct as many Belfast folk are. Game over for me. Ironically enough I stayed that night at the Jaffa Street home of the Mission's Junior Minister, Rev. Graham Stockdale and his wife Janine. Later, well after they had left the Shankill area, this lovely couple had a son called Jacob who has grown up to be a top Rugby Union player, playing for Ulster and scoring a record seven tries for Ireland during the 2018 Six Nations tournament.

A few days later I visited the hostel to see a friend and there was no animosity or bearing of grudges; John even gave us a lift to where we were going chatting politely with us all the way there.

Nowadays neither the hostel or the Mission exist, and John sadly passed away in 2007. The Shankill Road Mission building does still stand though, and after many years of standing empty, at the time of writing, is now one of the homes of Vault Artist Studios - an innovative community driven not for profit arts charity.

I hope the people of the Shankill who read this will appreciate my attempts to bring an otherwise little known part of their rich history to light.

As well as highlighting a unique person and unique piece of history - especially Black Irish history - through my research I am also able to tell more of 'Widow Donaghy's' story. She was called Margaret Donaghy or Donegan. She went through an appalling ordeal in the riots but George's role in this was nowhere near as bad as what HWIB alleges. It was also her evidence in court that prevented him from getting a harsher sentence. The shocking cockroach incident involved another sort of beetle altogether as I will reveal, and George wasn't even present when it took place as HWIB erroneously states.

Other than what Andrew Boyd wrote about George Henry Thompson I could find very little mentions of him on the internet. When my own research was almost finished, I decided to try again and this time managed to find a much better and more detailed account of his exploits in Belfast written by Dr. Mark Doyle, Professor of History at Middle Tennessee State University. This was contained in a publication called *Ireland in an Imperial World*, with Mark's contribution entitled: *Those the Empire Washed Ashore: Uncovering Ireland's Multiracial Past.* I was relieved to see that my own findings and conclusions were very similar but also noted that I appeared to have uncovered much more information about George. So I reached out to him via email stating what I was up to and asking if he had done any further research since then. I received a very nice response from him encouraging me to continue as it seemed I had indeed uncovered further details about the life and times of this intriguing man.

Mark also told me that Conrad Koza Bryan was researching George for a book called *Irish People of Colour: A social history of mixed race Irish in Britain and Ireland between 1700 and 2000*, which he was co-authoring with Chamion Caballero. He encouraged me to get in touch and after this incredible book was published, I was lucky enough to meet Conrad and his daughter Anisha, who did many of the brilliant illustrations in it, at a talk he gave at the Coventry Irish Society in December 2024. Conrad had included Mark's work concerning George and added some further research of his own. Again, I realised on reading it that I had got much further down the road with who George was and what probably became of him.

This story also includes tangent tales of a number of other people, many of whom had some interactions with him and some who did not. I write a little about Joseph Wilson, a man of mixed heritage who was known as 'Black Joe.' He lived in Belfast at the same time as Thompson and also made newspaper headlines at various times. He too had strong connections with the Shankill. They include the twists and turns in the life of Edward Birnie and his family. This tale itself branches out in many directions to include an Italian artist whose religious artwork can still be seen to this day at St. Malachy's church in Belfast. He also made his mark in Cork and Omagh. His name was Felice Piccione, and he also once lived in the Shankill. Ina Galbraith Richmond was a talented harpist and singer from Scotland. From there, she followed her brother to Kilkenny and then became the first woman in the world to manage a gas works at Magherafelt in 1908.

I must stress, my telling of George's story is not intended to glamorise, gloss over or justify criminality. It is simply to give a more accurate account of him and reveal what life was like for a Black man at the margins of society in the United Kingdom during Victorian times.

I have transcribed many articles and excerpts from newspapers. For the most part, these are exactly as they were written, so some of the spellings, capitalisations and grammar are of their time and may seem a little odd nowadays.

- Simon Shaw,
November 2025.

ACKNOWLEDGEMENTS

Thank you to all that gave encouragement and support:

Jonny Nicholds, Dr. Mark Doyle, Conrad Koza Bryan, Adam Wood, Rob Orland, Maureen Cottle, Stephen Ryan, Mick McCullagh & Sheila Medlock. My dad, who had a deep love of history, and my mum, who introduced me to the joy of reading books. Lily Blair - who still has the nicest smile in all of Belfast; The Hamilton family circle who were so kind to me when I lived in and near Belfast - especially Adeline, Campbell, Irene and Sandy who are sadly no longer with us. Chris C. Suzypug, Maisy & Georgia for putting up with me x

Special thanks to members of the Belfast Forum:
https://www.belfastforum.co.uk

The British Newspaper Archive:
https://www.britishnewspaperarchive.co.uk
Ancestry.co.uk
Lennon-Wylie website https://www.lennonwylie.co.uk
PRONI & GRONI websites.
Grosvenor House Publishing.

PROLOGUE

... I believe myself that there is a great future for Africa in God's good time. The inner wildernesses and the ocean-depths will cease to be strewn with the bones of perishing captives on the route by sea or the slave cafila by land. You have heard of the horrors by sea, how men and women are packed between low decks, sitting in each other's lap, or as in Arab dhows actually placed in layers with mats between. I have visited the old slave barracoons and the now mouldering fort in Tasso Island, where clustering lime and guava and every beauty of nature contrasted with the prison-dens where the poor dark sufferers once were crammed. I have a high opinion of cultivated African intelligence, of which there is every grade, as among the natives there is almost every hue. They are in fact an innocent, confiding, loving, and loveable people, yet never were people so ill-used. Their intelligence in truth is arrested. Yet what was that of our forefathers when men and women were dressed in skins, when their bodies were painted, and when they lived in dens in the earth or holes in the trees. I have met negroes many, who were gracious, courteous, intelligent, masters of many tongues, Arabic, English, French, Spanish, and Portuguese, among the rest. Black men can and do extract iron, gold, and silver from the ore, and work these metals with much and various skill. They grow cotton and weave it into a long enduring web, prepare indigo and other dyes. They dye their garments and mats made from plaited fibres of various kinds. Excellent nets they make with the aloe fibre. They work utensils and ornaments in wood, in ivory, and even in gold. Leather they cure and stain, and adapt to an infinity of uses. They possess and grow the more valuable cereals, fruits of many kinds, pulse and leguumens (sic) too, and herbs for medicine or for food. They pursue and capture the beast in the forest, the fish in the sea.

Yes, there is a good future for Africa, at once of our doing and their own. Already the Musselman (Muslim) has penetrated far down the central wildes, and I doubt not will one day reach the confines of the Cape. His creed, no doubt, is not our creed, but he has borrowed largely from Christianity. He preaches one God, and only one. Every chapter of the Koran invokes with praise and blessings his most merciful name. It is surely a great advance on cannibalism, the worship of sticks and stones, and doubtless will pave the way for that truer Christianity which preaches amity to all men, the black man and the white, a yet more loving Creator, a loftier and more spiritual creed.

Part of a lecture entitled *Recollections of Travel* by Dr. Henry McCormac, which took place at the Victoria Hall, Belfast, on Saturday 29 November 1862.

- The Northern Whig, 1 December 1862.

1.
TALES FROM WALKER'S LANE

Walker's Lane was located off Frederick Street and was close to the North Queen Street end of it. It is not usually named on old maps, but was just up from Alexander Street and ran from Frederick Street to May's Lane. May's Lane ran from North Queen Street to Alexander Street, as did Constabulary Lane, which also intersected Walker's Lane. Frederick Street, then as now, runs between York Street and North Queen Street in the northern part of Belfast city centre. Alexander Street ran in a straight line between Frederick Street and Great George's Street - on a modern map, where McGurk's Way meets Great George's Street is approximately where part of it would have been.

In the 19th Century, Walker's Lane was one of the most notorious areas of Belfast for criminality and vice. *The Belfast and Province of Ulster Directory 1865* does not detail its inhabitants but says there were 38 small houses in it. The 1870 version of the same directory does list the principal inhabitants and the vast majority were women. 37 properties are listed, including four two story buildings that were vacant. Many of these were used as shebeens (illegal drinking dens), brothels and lodging houses.

Those familiar with the ways of the world and conscious of the risks involved would knowingly visit and enjoy what was on offer there. Others, less wise, would be lured in by pimps, with promises of whiskey and the company of amiable women. These people, sometimes when drunk and sometimes not, often found themselves relieved of their property - money, watches, clothing, boots, umbrellas etc. The non-monetary items then tended to make their way to nearby pawn shops. Sadly, as some of the stories below will illustrate, young ladies from the country who had made their way to Belfast and were in search of lodgings, also found themselves unwittingly taken to the 'houses of ill-repute' after being tricked by unscrupulous characters connected with them.

From time to time, Christians would also enter this veritable lion's den and preach the gospel to those who would listen. Their hope was to bring as many people to Christ as they could, particularly the sex workers of the brothels.

The area was subject to a redevelopment order in the late 1960s / early 1970s and the public right of way to it was extinguished on 15 January 1974. Nowadays, much of where it was located, appears to be a car park.

To give some idea of what it was like I have compiled the following stories from Easter Monday 1840 to 30 October 1866. Many of them make for desperately sad reading and some are horrific. I do not envy anyone that lived there, particularly the women, who were clearly exploited and faced many forms of abuse. The tales could have gone on well beyond 1866, but the last tale is, I believe, possibly relevant to the core story of this book.

EASTER MONDAY 1840

Easter Monday fell on 20 April and there was a disturbance in Walker's Lane in the evening. James Addison and his wife were at the heart of this. Addison was in a very excited state and throwing stones and whatever came to hand at a crowd that had gathered near his home. At around 8:30 pm, Eliza Fullerton, aged 33, left her house to buy sugar candy. As she emerged onto the lane, a crowd ran by which Addison was throwing things at. A woman told her she had been hit in the breast, and seconds later a brick launched by him hit Eliza on the left side of her head causing a deep cut and heavy bleeding. She staggered and fell, and despite trying to get up she could not. Eliza knew she was done for. Onlookers carried her home and despite medical attention, she died from her injuries some five weeks later on 24 May. Witnesses at Addison's trial said his wife had also been throwing stones prior to the incident when Eliza was mortally wounded, and that Addison had also been fighting people. One said that he came out of his house and said "he would have a life that night" even if he should be hanged for it.

His trial for manslaughter was held at the County Antrim Assizes at Carrickfergus on 23 July 1840. He was found guilty by the jury but with a recommendation of mercy due to the excited state he had been in. Three days later, on 26 July, James Addison was sentenced to 3 months in the house of correction with hard labour.[1]

ATTEMPT AT SUICIDE

On Saturday 19 June 1847 a young woman named Jane Edwards, aged about 22, was preparing to commit suicide by jumping off a parapet of the Queen's Bridge over the River Lagan. Constable Horner spotted her at the pump on the bridge and sensed she was about to launch herself into the waters below. She had removed her bonnet and shawl and was in the act of taking off her frock when he quickly ran over to her and intervened to arrest her. Jane was not happy about this and he took her to the police office with some difficulty.

She was from Birmingham in the English Midlands and had been living in Walker's Lane for about five or six months. At her court appearances she was described as being 'of an interesting and respectable appearance' and it was revealed that this was not her first suicide attempt. On another occasion a coal porter had witnessed similar scenes to Constable Horner and had also intervened. When asked why she was attempting to end her life she replied that she had "no particular reason."

The police had made enquiries and suggested she acted like this when under the influence of drink. Jane, who may have been pregnant at the time, promised she would not do it again and was discharged.[2]

SUNDAY MORNING RIOTS

Sabbath mornings could be quite feisty affairs in Walker's Lane. At the Belfast Police Court held on Monday 15 October 1849, John Patterson and his sister Mary were charged with assaulting two girls named O'Sullivan on the previous day - Sunday 14 October. John Patterson had battered the two girls - blackening their eyes in the process - but said this was in self defence as they and others were attempting to wreck his elderly mother's house. Mary Patterson produced a large handful of her own hair which she said one of the O'Sullivan's had pulled out of her head.

A Policeman belonging to the nearby North Queen Street station told the court that the people of Walker's Lane were very troublesome and disorderly, particularly on Sabbath mornings. The presence of the police was not a deterrent to this.

The magistrate was the Mayor of Belfast, Sir William Gillilan Johnson, who had been knighted by Queen Victoria during her visit to Belfast in August of that year. He said he would endeavour to put a stop to such behaviour and gave the Patterson's the option of paying fines (£4 for John; £2 for Mary) or going to prison for two months.[3]

A WOMAN AND A SAILOR DROWNED

On Wednesday 15 January 1851, at around 2 pm, the body of a young woman called Ellen Madden was found in Mr. Murphy's timber pond which adjoined the River Lagan on the Ballymacarrett side. Ellen, who was originally from the town of Antrim, was a sex worker in one of the brothels in Walker's Lane. Half an hour later, the body of Joseph Ewart, an Englishman who was the mate on a collier called *The Fisher* which was docked at the Queen's quay, was discovered near the bow of that vessel.

It appeared the two had hooked up together the previous night and partied until the early hours. They were last seen together on *The Fisher* where Ellen was apparently seen asleep in the collier's cabin at 2 o'clock in the morning.

An inquest was held which delivered a verdict of 'found drowned' on both bodies. It was speculated that both parties were drunk, may have quarrelled and had missed their footing when attempting to get on the boat or reach the quayside from the boat.[4]

A MOST DANGEROUS CHARACTER

At the Belfast Police Court on Thursday 29 June, 1854, a lad called William John McCormick charged William McKenna with assaulting him. McCormick said they had been drinking together in Walker's Lane and he had treated McKenna well by paying for his drinks. They left to play a game of skittles in Frederick Street and after this McKenna stole his coat. He followed him to a brothel in Walker's Lane and demanded that his coat was returned. McKenna responded by attacking him with a poker and inflicted several wounds on his head. McCormick admitted to being drunk himself but he recalled what happened perfectly. His account was corroborated by a girl named Susan Greenshields.

Constable Jamieson said that McKenna was "a most dangerous person" who was employed to induce drunken people to go into brothels where they would then be robbed of their clothes and money. He was found guilty and given the choice of a 30 shillings fine or six weeks in prison with hard labour.[5]

UNLICENSED LODGING HOUSES

Belfast Police Court, Tuesday 12 December, 1854:

Prosecutions of low lodging-house keepers for following that profession without being properly licensed for the purpose, according to the local acts. Mr. McKechnie, the Inspector of Lodging Houses, appointed by the Council, according to the provisions of the Act, was the witness examined for the prosecution.

The localities from which the defendants were brought are, Hudson's Entry, Smithfield Court, Ritchie's Place, Walker's Lane, and Caxton Street, places sufficiently notorious already, but in which few would have believed that there existed such hotbeds of misery, desolation, and disease as appeared from the revelations of the Inspector.

Mary McAdam, of Hudson's Entry, had five lodgers in her house, besides two adult persons of a family, and for the accommodation of these she is the occupier of one front room 8 feet long by 7 broad and 6 high, thus containing a cubic area of 366 feet, and one back room, which contained three beds, and was only 10 feet long by 8 feet broad and 6 feet high, thus having a cubic area of 480 feet. There was no back yard to the premises, and scarcely any ventilation.

Surgeon Browne said the Council did not wish to impose the full fine, but that they only wished it to be known that the most vigorous measures would be taken henceforth in the matter, and the full fine of 40s would be prayed for if any of these parties should be brought up again.

Mr. TRACY (Magistrate) said that he would now impose the fine of 2s 6d and costs, and if the present defendant, or any of the others, were brought up again, he certainly would impose the full amount. Sarah Brown, Esther McGoogan, and Jas. Sweeny, denizens of the same locality, were fined in similar sums for similar offences.

William Hamill, of Hudson's Entry, was also fined in 2s 6d and costs for refusing to admit the inspector when he knocked at his door, and threatening to put a ball through him.

Mary Adams, Smithfield Court, was fined for having crammed five lodgers, three adult members of the family and one child, into a house containing one back room, ten feet long by eight broad and six high, in which there were no beds, but only a few wisps of straw, and a half-loft of still less dimensions. The house had no yard attached to it, and scarcely any ventilation.

In Ritchie's Place, Arthur Doherty had a house containing three rooms, one of which was nine feet long by six feet broad, and six high, and another ten feet long, by nine broad and six high. In these he had five beds. He had nine lodgers, besides two adults of a family; and he had no yard, and scarcely any ventilation.

In Walker's Lane, Richard Gorman had one room, 12 feet long by 8 broad, and 6 high, containing three beds, having no yard, and very bad ventilation, and in this he stowed 5 lodgers, and 2 adult members of his family!

Rose Ann O'Neill* and Ann Smith, of the same locality, were the owners of similar dens.

In Caxton Street, Eliza McLarkey had two rooms, one 12 feet long by 7 broad and 7 high, containing two beds, and the other 12 feet long by 7 broad and 7 high, containing three beds; had a very small yard, and very bad ventilations, but yet managed to accommodate six lodgers, and three adult members of the family. Margaret Logan and Mary Logan, also of Caxton Street, were fined for similar offences.

- The Belfast News-Letter, 13 December 1854.

* The 1870 *Belfast and Province of Ulster Directory* lists a Rose Ann O'Neill living at 13 Walker's Lane.

ASSAULT WITH A SMOOTHING IRON

Belfast Police Court - Wednesday 3 January, 1855:

Harriet Drew, a young woman of abandoned habits, was charged by Ellen McAreavy, the proprietress of a house of bad repute in Walker's-lane, with assault. The complainant's head was bandaged, and the attack was stated to have been made with a smoothing iron, which the defendant caught up during an altercation. Mr. Tracy said that the prisoner was incorrigible and irreclaimable. Her father was willing and anxious to bring her back to her home, but she chose rather to adhere to the abandoned life she was leading. Efforts also had been made to procure her admission to the Penitentiary, but owing to her own unwillingness they were fruitless. She was sentenced to be imprisoned for three months.

- The Belfast Daily Mercury, 4 January 1855.

A GRIZZLY BITE

Two damsels of Walker's-lane, off North Queen-street, proceeded, on yesterday, (Friday 4 May) to decide a dispute of theirs by a match at fisticuffing; and, possibly, heated by the blows of her antagonist, one of the amazons caught the other's ear in her mouth, and severed the end of it, which she immediately dropped on the ground, and which proceeding, consequently, must have decided the combat in the other's favour.

The wounded party proceeded with the piece to the General Hospital, where she had it tacked, by six stitches, to the part from which had been severed.

- The Ulsterman, 5 May 1855

SEAMAN WHISKER

Belfast Police Court - Tuesday 28 December, 1858:

Mary McGuiggan was charged by a seaman named John Whisker with taking a sum of money out of his pocket. The complainant's story was the usual one of having been decoyed by the girl to a house in Walker's Lane, and while there she put her hand in his pocket, but he called out for the watchman. Constable Hendren said he happened to be passing, heard the call, and went into the house, when he found the prisoner with her hand in the complainant's pocket. He immediately caught her hand and shook out of it silver and copper to the amount of 5s 3d. The Prisoner was sent to jail for one month.

- The Belfast Morning News, 30 December 1858.

MOVEMENT AMONG THE OUTCASTS

Of the many and notable effects of the Spirit's work which we have to chronicle from time to time, the most astounding are those which it is our duty to notice today, as among the latest. The light has begun to dawn in the darkest and most degraded spots within our civic boundaries.

In the neighbourhood of the infantry barracks* exists a network of low and miserable streets, lanes and courts, inhabited by a class of persons of the most profligate character. Among these places are the infamous Walker's Lane and the bad localities adjoining. Cases of disorderly conduct have been for some time past on the decrease there, and the constabulary of North Queen Street station, as well as the local police, began to feel somewhat surprised at this. On Saturday evening, however, a number of the unfortunate females in those lanes left their old haunts of vice and professed a desire to become reformed in character and conduct. Seven or eight of them were received into the house of a charitably minded woman residing in Hardinge Street where some praying persons remained with them, advising them and endeavouring to lead them not only to reform their lives, but to "repent and be converted." There are about a dozen others in the same lanes all desirous of changing their mode of life, and steps are being taken to send them into the Penitentiary and places of industrial employment. Others have been sent home to the country. Some outcasts are anxious to get employment in mills or elsewhere, so that they may earn a livelihood; but all of them give evidence of a sincere wish to forsake their evil ways, and lead a better life in future.

A person who kept one of the dens of vice in Walker's Lane has closed it up; and she and the other inmates are following the path of the penitent. On Sabbath night till a late hour, religious services were conducted in a house in that wretched quarter, where no sound or thought of holiness found entrance or utterance before.

- The Banner of Ulster, 2 August 1859.

* The barracks were on North Queen Street.

DESPERATE ASSAULT

Belfast Police Court - Monday 5 December, 1859:

Ann Watt and Mary Watt, mother and daughter, were brought up for having committed an aggravated assault on Sarah Bullock.

The prosecutrix stated that the old woman, Ann Watt, kept a house of ill-fame in Walker's Lane, and her two daughters and a child of one of them lived with her; witness had lived there about a month; on Sunday morning, about two o'clock, she went in, and they all attacked her; the old woman beat her with a poker, and they knocked her down and pulled the hair out of her head; another daughter of Ann Watt's held the arms of witness while the others were beating her.

Constable McAlister stated that he was on duty in North Queen Street, when two young men came to him, and told him that they were murdering a girl in a house in Walker's Lane. He went to the place where he heard the noise proceed from, and there found four women, besides the prosecutrix, whose face was covered with blood. It was a customary thing for the old woman to abuse girls with a poker. The prisoners caught his cape, and would not come to the Police-office till he got assistance.

Mr TRACY (Magistrate) - Ann Watt, I am very sorry I have not the power to send you to jail for twelve months. You are far advanced in life, and you keep a house of ill-fame, and have your daughters living in it. You are a very wicked old woman, and I feel it would be a waste of time to say a word of advice to you. I award you two months at hard labour, and the same to your daughter, and if the third is brought here, I will send her after you.

- The Belfast News-Letter, 6 December 1859.

ROBBERY

Belfast Police Court - Friday 21 September, 1860:

Margaret McLaughlin, of Walker's Lane, was brought up on remand charged with having, last Sunday night, stolen the entire clothing of a girl named Jane McWhitter, of Ballyclare, whom she entrapped into a house of ill-fame in Walker's Lane, on the representation that it was a lodging-house; and, after the young woman had retired to bed, her clothes were all stolen, and she left without anything to dress herself the next morning.

The BENCH sentenced the prisoner to be imprisoned for six months, and directed Chief-Constable McKittrick to provide clothes for McWhitter.

- The Belfast Weekly News, 22 September 1860.

A DEGRADED MOTHER AND HER DAUGHTERS

Belfast Police Court - Tuesday 11 November, 1862:

Anne Watt and her two daughters, Alice Watt and Mary Watt, and Margaret McCormick, four improper females, who reside in a house of ill-fame kept by Anne Watt in Walker's Lane, were brought up in custody; Alice Watt being charged with having stolen and pawned a Balmoral cape, the property of John McKeown, of 16 Boyd Street, off Peter's Hill, and also with having assaulted him; and Mary Watt, Anne Watt, and Margaret McCormick with having also assaulted complainant. Mr. SEEDS, who appeared for the prosecution, withdrew the charge of theft.

John McKeown deposed that he paid a visit the previous day to the house of the prisoners, in Walker's Lane. Alice Watt took his Balmoral cape from him and was going to pawn it. When he attempted to prevent her, she struck him with a poker. Mary Watt also struck him, and the old mother took him by the legs and attempted to take his boots off. Margaret McCormick also assaulted him.

His WORSHIP (Dr. McGee, J.P.) sentenced the old mother to be imprisoned for two months. Her daughters and McCormick were imprisoned for one month each.

- The Belfast News-Letter, 12 November 1862.

CANNIBALISM IN WALKER'S LANE

Belfast Police Court - Monday 4 May, 1863:

Mary Lynas, apparently about nineteen or twenty years of age, was charged by Margaret Ashcroft with having bitten part of the forefinger off one of her (complainant's) hands on Sunday night.

The parties are women of improper character, belonging to that infamous locality, Walker's Lane. Prosecutrix went to a house of which the prisoner was mistress for the purpose of getting a knife which she claimed, and which she said she lent some days before to the prisoner. She saw the knife on a table, and she lifted it without any remark. The prisoner, who was drunk, ran at her, and caught hold of the knife. She pulled it from Ashcroft, and in doing so inflicted a deep wound on the hand of the latter. Both again took hold of the knife; the prisoner seized one of Aschcroft's fingers in her mouth, and after chewing it for some minutes, bit it off by the first joint.

The prisoner admitted the charge, and implored the Court to deal mercifully with her. She was sentenced to six months' imprisonment with hard labour. At the end of that term she will be further imprisoned for six months unless she can give bail for her good behavior, which she will, as a matter of course, be unable to give.

- The Belfast News-Letter, 5 May 1863.

BETTER THAN EATING THEM DRY

Belfast Police Court - Tuesday 14 June, 1864:

Ann Daly, a woman of desperate character, was charged with disorderly conduct in Walker's Lane, and with having committed several assaults on a constable. When arrested she managed to divest herself of a great part of her clothes, and acted in a most outrageous manner. She kicked the constable severely.

Mr. LYONS (Justice of the Peace)- Daly, you are to go to jail for two months.

Prisoner - Thank (you) your worship. That's better than eating them dry, and a couple of months is only a sleep for me.

- The Belfast Weekly News, 18 June 1864.

ATTEMPTED RAPE AND ASSAULT

In the early hours of Wednesday 8 February 1865, two policemen found a woman in the street who was in a very distressed state. She was bleeding from her mouth and nose, her dress was torn and tears were flowing from her eyes. Her name was Margaret Hinds and at North Queen Street police station she told a harrowing tale to Constable McAlister, one of the two peelers who came to her aid.

On the night of Tuesday 7 February 1865, Margaret, who was about 23 years old, boarded the last train from Antrim to Belfast on the Northern Counties Railway. It left at 9 pm. She was a domestic servant who worked near Antrim and was suffering from smallpox. On reaching Belfast, her intention was to catch the last train to Newtownards, and from there, make her way to her hometown of Portaferry where she planned to recuperate from her illness. Travelling in the same carriage were two men. One of them was called John or Thomas McCusker. At some point the men had a conversation about a cow that one of them had purchased. Margaret recognised that the name of the man who had sold it was her employer or previous employer, so a friendly conversation between the three followed.

When they got to Belfast, she discovered that the last train to Newtownards had already departed. Being a stranger to Belfast, she asked McCusker if he knew of decent lodgings in the town. He said he did and would take her to his Aunt's house.

McCusker, who reports stated was a butcher and resided in Hudson's Entry, which was off North Street, first took Margaret to one or possibly two public houses where he attempted to ply her with punch and other liquors. Then he took her to his 'Aunt's' place where she was to stay for the night. This was a brothel in Walker's Lane. They were let in by Alice Watt who was there with her sister. Watt locked the front door and ordered some drinks. McCusker went upstairs. Margaret knew something was seriously amiss and asked to be let out. Watt refused and she was taken upstairs to a room where McCusker was lying in a bed. She asked the women if this was where she was to stay for the night, and they replied that it was and that there was no other place for her. One of the women then placed her back against the room's door to stop her escaping. Margaret said if she was not allowed to leave she would jump out of the window. McCusker, who newspaper reports say was 'stripped' so presumably was naked or partially naked, got up out of the bed and began to indecently assault her. She fiercely resisted and he dragged her about the room and punched her in the face, giving her a bloody nose and knocking out two of her teeth. She was then forced onto the bed, and with Alice Watt holding her down and cursing her, McCusker attempted to rape her. However, despite her injuries, Margaret was no pushover and continued to resist both of them. Somehow, before McCusker succeeded in violating her, she managed to summon the strength to free herself and bolted down the stairs and escaped into the street where the policemen found her. From the descriptions she gave of her assailants, McCusker and Alice Watt were quickly apprehended.

At the initial court hearing, due to having smallpox, Margaret gave evidence through a window from outside the courtroom. She then spent a number of weeks in hospital recovering from both smallpox and the injuries sustained in her ordeal at the hands of McCusker and the women who aided and abetted him. McCusker and Watt were remanded a number of times until she had recovered sufficiently enough for their trial to take place.

On 10 April, McCusker was convicted of common assault; indecent assault and intent to commit rape. His Worship J. Hastings Otway, Q.C., sentenced him to eighteen months in jail and remarked that the prisoner had been convicted of about as brutal an offence as had ever been proved in criminal court. He also revealed that McCusker had previously been jailed for assaulting a woman called Mary McCusker and for selling beef that was unfit for human consumption.[6] I could find no record of Alice Watt being convicted so possibly the charges against her were dropped.

* The 1870 *Belfast and Province of Ulster Directory* lists Ann Watt as living at 16 Walker's Lane so there is a good chance that this is where the various assaults took place.

MAGGIE AND THE PENSIONER

Belfast Police Court - Saturday 24 June, 1865:

Matthew Felix, a member of the veteran force called local pensioners, and hailing from Lurgan, said he came on business to Belfast, where he is a stranger, and was spending last night with a cousin. He was returning between two and three o'clock in the morning through North Queen Street, and wandered into Walker's Lane. He did not explain how such an extravagant topographical error as straying into a parallel street took place. But he found a house open, and went in to light his pipe - nothing more.

In the house were Margaret McMullan and two other women, and, as soon as he entered, Maggie, giving the lie to all ideas of Irish hospitality, ran and locked the door, and swore that she would have his life or the price of some whiskey. The alarmed warrior took to his feet, and charged the door. Maggie arrested his course, charged him in return, and tore his watch from him. The other two women were round him, and he lost a handkerchief and a pair of gloves.

He called for help; a constable came and bade the women release their prisoner. McMullan kept the watch till in the Police Office. The policeman, 93, stated that when he heard the voice, and went up, the prosecutor gave the prisoner in charge for robbing him of his watch. She said he had given it to her to keep till he should return with 5s, to pay for his entertainment. The prisoner persisted in denying her guilt, and was committed for trial.

- The Belfast Morning News, 26 June 1865.

SAUCY MRS. MARTIN

Belfast Police Court - Monday 29 January, 1866:

Ann Cunningham was charged by Sub-Constable Smith with being drunk in Walker's Lane, and proclaiming herself "Saucy Mrs. Martin, the pride of the Orangemen of Sandy Row." The prisoner was fined 40s and costs.

- The Belfast News-Letter, 30 January 1866.

A BLACK FROM NEW YORK

Belfast Police Court - Monday 29 October, 1866:

Henry Thompson, a black, from New York; Benjamin Hunter, and Mary Jane Brown were charged by Constable Drought under the following circumstances :- The constable stated that he heard a great noise proceeding out of a house in Walker's Lane, and when he went to the place he found the prisoners acting in a very disorderly manner. The black was choking the female prisoner, who was struggling with him, and Hunter was also acting in a very violent manner, and he charged the woman and the black with attempting to strip and rob him in the house. When he (the constable) went forward to arrest the black man, the woman then turned round and tried to rescue the black from custody. Drought stated that every time the black man is in the town he takes up in this house in Walker's Lane, and helps the woman to rob people who go into the house. On Saturday night two people had been robbed of their watches in this house. Hunter was discharged, and Thompson and Brown were each sent to jail for one month at hard labour.

- The Northern Whig, 30 October 1866.

* In the *Belfast and Province of Ulster Street Directory 1870*, a Mary Brown is listed as living at 37 Walker's Lane.

2.
THE ATHENS OF IRELAND

Without going into a detailed account of Irish history - or rather my interpretation of other people's interpretations of Irish history - I will try to briefly turn the clock back to give a flavour of the time and set the scene for when George Henry Thompson enters centre stage into a maelstrom.

In 1872 Belfast was a rapidly expanding town, being one of the fastest growing in the United Kingdom and most certainly in Ireland. It was the only heavily industrialised part of Ireland and regarded as its commercial capital. Linen mills, foundries and shipyards such as Harland and Wolff provided employment for many. Newspapers of the time described it as being 'the Athens of Ireland' and gave it the nickname of 'Linenopolis' - in the 1840s and 1850s Belfast was often called 'the Manchester of Ireland.'

A few years earlier, on Saturday 28 May 1870, the guest of honour at the *Belfast and North of Ireland Workmen's Exhibition*, which was a major cross-community event held at the Ulster Hall, was the Lord Chancellor of Ireland, the Right Honourable Thomas O'Hagan. He was a Belfast born Roman Catholic. Prior to distributing prizes for competition winners, he gave a speech which included the following:

> *... The best proof of the value of this Exhibition to the working man is this, that it would be impossible for him without it to have an opportunity of demonstrating and showing to the world what virtue, what strength, what intelligence there are among the working people of this province in the way of art and industry. (Applause.)*
>
> *I shall not go into detail, but I may say this, that, in the great industries of this town, I believe it stands at least on a par with any other portion of the British Empire. (Cheers.) I know that in one of its great industries, which has been a great industry of the world since the Pyramids were founded - the linen industry - Belfast is famed all the world over. (Loud cheers.) I believe I may say that, although not geographically so, yet this is the greatest centre of that industry in the world - (cheers) - and it is impossible to observe what I have observed within the last hour without seeing that the working people of this community are able to prosecute every branch of that industry through all its parts, from the green fibre to the preparation of the*

flax, until you come up to the snowy cambric and those marvellous creations of Ardoyne and Lisburn, which are, I believe, without a parallel in the palaces of the world. (Cheers.) This is one of your industries of which I cannot say more and should not say less. Another is this - that industry which enables you to contribute to the navy of the British Empire. (Hear, hear.) You have a trade here, as I believe, and is demonstrated, of iron shipbuilding, which may bear comparison with that of any other city in the world - (cheers) - and I believe the working people in that trade are deriving great advantages from the contracts of the Government, which have been given, not from any desire to favour, not from any desire to foster a common industry, but simply because the real value of anything is just as much as it would bring, and because you can do the work best you are preferred - (applause.)

And so, I may say, I believe that it is with reference to everything in this town of Belfast; for if there be one matter in which I, as a citizen of this town - a citizen that was, a citizen that is, though my local habitation may be elsewhere - can rejoice, it is in this - that the people of Belfast have advanced, not by reliance on Government, not be reliance on party, not be reliance on the public purse, but by self-reliance and self-exertion. I trust it will ever be so; and, if it be, your prosperity, great as it is, is great only in its infancy. You have reached to that stage of progression at which retrogression is not to be feared, save through your own defect. (Cheers.)

I will only say one word more, because I do not think it would be fair if I did not say it. In addition to these two industries of which you have every reason to be proud, there is a third, which has grown up since I was a boy, and resided in Belfast, and which, I believe, is also as good of its kind as any in the world - I allude to the machine-making trade. (Cheers.) Nobody can go through the Exhibition here and observe what the working men have done in this respect, and nobody having seen the inventiveness and ingenuity and originality they exhibit, and afterwards having visited the great establishments that are in Belfast, could come to any other conclusion than that in that industry you may hold your heads as high as any people in the world. (Applause.) The name of Belfast is a name well known on the steppes of Russia and the banks of the old Nile; and you are able, in the fair fields of competition, to beat down the foremost of the nations of the world. (Cheers.)[1]

The census of 1871 put the population of the Borough of Belfast at 174,412, with 55,575 of those being Roman Catholics. Therefore, the town - which was to become a city in 1888 - had a large Protestant majority; of these 60,249 were Presbyterians, 46,423 were Episcopolians (Church of Ireland) and 6,775 were Methodists. A wide variety of 'other denominations' were recorded which among others included:

24 Mormons, 21 Jews, 8 Freethinkers, 7 Christian Israelites, 5 Non-sectarian, 1 Confuscianist, 1 Deist, 1 Eclectic, 1 Materialist, 1 Prussian Protestant, 1 Greek Church, 1 French Catholic and 1 Swiss Protestant.

The census also recorded the birthplaces of the inhabitants of the borough from outside the UK which gives an indication of the diversity of the town:

Europe 283, America 257, Asia 22, Africa 9 and Tahiti 1.

There were 97 vessels docked with 542 people onboard, 71 of whom were foreign.

158,515 people were born in Ulster, 3,617 in Leinster, 1,297 in Munster and 743 in Connaught. (The numbers of English, Welsh and Scottish people are not recorded for the Borough of Belfast but the figures for County Antrim were 5,911 English and Welsh, with 4,917 from Scotland. The figures for this county also included: British Colonies and East Indies, 587, foreign parts, 758 and born at sea 46.)

In terms of literacy, 95,986 people could read and write, 31,700 could read only and 46,726 were illiterate.[2] Not a single person was able to speak the Irish language only, but 294 were recorded as being able to speak Irish and English. In the 1861 census, 325 could speak both languages and 4 people spoke Irish only. The 1831 census recorded the population as 28,739 which gives some indication of the massive growth of the town.[3]

It is also worth giving some census statistics for County Down relating to diversity. Part of Belfast was in, and indeed still is, in this county. *The Downpatrick Recorder* of 12 September 1874 stated:

> *There were in the county at the time the return was taken 367 foreigners, and of these 113 were born in Europe, 1 in Asia (Burmah*), 4 in Africa, and 249 in America. Their occupations are also given, and it would appear that 35 were professionally engaged, 19 domestically, 17 commercially, 24 agriculturally, 61 industrially, and 211 indefinitely and non-productively.*
>
> * Burma, now known as Myanmar.

And a little further afield, the *Ulster Examiner and Northern Star* reported in its edition of 21 April 1873, that the population figure for the capital city of Dublin was 246,326, with 158,936 recorded for the County of Dublin. It also went on to give an indication of the diversity of the population for that area:

> *As may be expected the foreigners resident in Dublin are less numerous in proportion than they are in London. Still even in the county there were 461 persons born in other European countries, eleven Chinese, eighty-three Africans, and 280 Americans. The number of foreigners in the city was 1,176.*

Whilst Belfast had a substantial Protestant majority, Ireland was an overwhelmingly Roman Catholic country. The Act of Union of 1800 - which came into effect on 1 January 1801 - had joined Great Britain and Ireland together to form the United Kingdom. This meant Ireland no longer had a parliament of its own and elected MPs to Westminster.

One of the drawbacks with the Act of Union was that Roman Catholics were not allowed to serve as MPs at Westminster. Clearly this was not acceptable to the majority of the Irish people. It wasn't until 1829, when the Roman Catholic Relief Act was passed, that this was rectified. This change was largely achieved through the efforts of Daniel O'Connell - the political leader of Ireland's Catholics in the first half of the 19th century and known as 'The Liberator.'

By the 1870s, a major cause of friction for the majority community was the lack of a devolved Irish parliament, and they were demanding 'Home Rule' to rectify this. This would have meant Ireland staying within the UK but effectively being ruled by its own government and making its own laws. Attempts to achieve this were being carried out through democratic means, with the Home Rule Association and the Home Government Association to the fore. A letter published in *The Daily Examiner* on 16 January gives an indication of this desire for Home Rule and the authors frustration with Ulster's Protestants who are often branded as 'planters':

NATIONAL DEGENERACY

TO THE EDITOR OF THE DAILY EXAMINER.

SIR,

What a degenerate and unpatriotic spectacle the Protestant population of Belfast and the whole province of Ulster presents today when compared with the glorious and successful efforts of their forefathers ninety-three years ago in favour of Ireland and her native legislature! Then Protestants, Presbyterians, and Catholics united in a common phalanx for the express purpose of raising volunteers, in order to maintain, if necessary, the independence of their country vie et armis; *and Mr. Haverty in his "History of Ireland" says that "to the men of Belfast is to be attributed the glory of having originated the volunteers - p.706.*

In May, 1779, the volunteer movement was so successful that it had begun to attract the attention of the Government; and in September the number of men enrolled in the counties of Down and Antrim and in and about Coleraine, amounted to 3,925. It is stated that in the first year 42,000 volunteers were, including all parts of the country, enrolled for the defence of their country and the rights of their native Parliament.

The Planter population of this town and province have sadly changed and degenerated in their political principles and policy. They have forsaken the grand old principles which were once so characteristic of the Dissenting - the Presbyterian body, especially in the North. There are no Orrs or McCrackens to be found in Ulster now. Dr. Madden says that the Society of United Irishmen was composed of 106 Protestants or Presbyterians, and only 56 Catholics. So that the Planter and Protestant or Dissenting element vastly preponderated the Celtic and Catholic in the last great effort that was made to rescue our country from the thraldom of foreign oppression.

It must, however, be conceded that there are still some really patriotic men to be found among the Protestant and Dissenting population in the North; but like angels visits they are few, very few indeed.

At the present time what is the conduct of eminently-civilised Protestants and Presbyterians, in the North of Ireland especially? Are they not the inveterate foes of everything that would tend to resuscitate the nationality of their country and ameliorate the condition of her people? Are they not working might and main to prevent the discontinuance of a denationalising system of education for rising and unborn generations of Irishmen. It is sad to know there are so many calling themselves Irishmen, and yet they are really more English than the English themselves. Men born in Ireland, reared, educated, and become prosperous in the various avocations they happen to pursue in the country, and yet, as Mr. D. C. Heron said in the Monaghan Court House, they are "living as foreigners in the land of their birth."

It is beyond a question of doubt that Home Rule and denominational education will eventually be obtained, notwithstanding the efforts of some recreants to impede the success of these great questions, and the recently discovered defection from the national ranks of one who was formerly looked upon as being in eloquence and patriotism second only to the great liberator himself.

Now the question arises, can those measures be obtained without the aid and co-operation of the Northern Planters. Certainly they can, for, after all, what are the Protestants of Ireland, the Black North included, but a mere fraction of the population. There are some honourable exceptions whose influence will be on our side, and victory must be ours.

It is the duty, and it should be the policy at least, of the English Government to give Ireland her rights in restoring to the Irish people the management of their own affairs, their own Parliament, as it existed from 1782 to 1800, when the country prospered at an unexampled rate for eighteen years. The Alabama claims are yet unsettled, Russia is watching to be revenged for Sebastopol, Germany recollects the importation of arms to France and may at any time make a Luxemburg question a pretext to open a quarrel with John Bull. The Irish are dissatisfied with sham and imperfect Land Bills, and the impertinent vapouring of the Whig Chief Secretary. Were England to go to war at present with America or any other great power, the Irish, from rising to the setting sun, would be found on the side of her enemies.

Yours etc.
M.
Belfast, 11th Jan, 1872.

Others, such as the Irish Republican Brotherhood (IRB), better known as Fenians, sought to get rid of the British connection altogether and wanted a completely independent Ireland. One of their founders was James Stephens. The Fenians were prepared to use any means necessary to achieve their aims. At Manchester, in September 1867, a policeman, Sergeant Charles Brett, was shot dead by them in a violent rescue of two of their prisoners from a prison transport van. Three men - William Philip Allen, Michael Larkin, and Michael O'Brien (alias William Gould) - were convicted of Brett's murder in early November and from the dock in unison exclaimed, "God Save Ireland!" as the death sentence was pronounced on them by Justice John Mellor.

They were hanged on 23 November at Salford Prison, becoming known to Irish Nationalists as the *Manchester Martyrs.* A few weeks later, the influential Nationalist leader, Timothy Daniel Sullivan, who we shall hear more about later, composed a song called 'God Save Ireland' to commemorate them. For years afterwards this served as the unofficial Irish national anthem and is still to this day a well known 'rebel' song. He published the lyrics in his Dublin based newspaper, *The Nation*, on 7 December 1867. The words were set to the tune of an American civil war song called 'Tramp, Tramp, Tramp, (the boys are marching)' with a chorus of:

"God save Ireland," said the heroes,
"God save Ireland," said they all;
"Whether on the scaffold high,
Or the battle-field, we die,
Oh, what matter, when for Erin dear we fall!"

Six days after the song lyrics were published, on 13 December, at Clerkenwell, London, the Fenians bombed a prison in an attempt to free another of their prisoners. The barrel of gunpowder that was used severely damaged houses on the opposite side of the road, killing 12 innocent people and injuring up to 120. It was the worst atrocity of their campaign and hardened British public opinion against them.

In North America, Fenians based in the United States carried out a number of armed raids and fought battles against British soldiers and locally recruited volunteers in Canada - which included substantial numbers of Orangemen and also men from the First Nations who were staunchly loyal to the Crown.

Belfast's Roman Catholic population, although a minority, was growing in number, confidence and assertiveness. It was also more educated than previous generations. New churches and associated buildings were springing up, along with organisations such as the Catholic Young Men's Society. The nine counties of Ulster and its principal town Belfast, were often portrayed as a Protestant Loyalist pro-British stronghold. This clearly annoyed the intellectuals, influencers and leaders among them. They were keen to show that this was not entirely true, and that many in Ulster supported the nationwide efforts to secure Home Rule and/or a total independence from Great Britain.

While the restrictive and repressive laws applied to Catholics of previous times had been removed, the memory of them burned brightly, as did the various failed uprisings and rebellions by earlier generations of Irish people.

A more recent source of grievance was the woefully inadequate response of the British government to the Great Famine of 1845-1852, which resulted in the deaths of around a million people from starvation and associated diseases. Another million emigrated - many of them leaving from Belfast, which was then a main port for emigration. Others who were in distress moved from the countryside to Belfast itself to try and find work and simply survive. The working class areas were already overcrowded and suffered from poor housing. All of this, combined with other factors, resulted in the deaths of thousands of people from all traditions in Belfast from famine related illnesses such as dysentery, typhus and cholera.

Many died in the workhouse, which opened in 1841, and various hospitals in the town. A lot of the victims lie in unmarked graves. Some of these were buried in the Shankill Graveyard on the Shankill Road. In May 2025, a memorial stone was unveiled there thanks to the hard work of the Shankill Area Social History Group and the National Famine Commemoration Committee. Dr Robyn Atcheson was among those who spoke at the event, and she has done, and is doing, sterling work about the impact of the famine on Belfast.

The following poem is another example of the yearning to 'get their country back' that Belfast's Nationalists were feeling. It was published in a local newspaper, *The Weekly Examiner*, on Saturday 18 May 1872:

THE HARP OF ERIN

IN the days of Erin's splendour,
Ere wild storms around her raged,
Ere the fierce and ruthless stranger
O'er her fields victorious strayed -
In the days of wealth and grandeur,
When her sons shone bright around her,
Loud her minstrel harp was heard.

In the great hall of the nation,
Where each spotless law was made,
There, amid the heart's emotion,
Lays of love and valour strayed.
There, 'mid Erin's rank and fashion,
There in Tara was its station,
There her minstrel harp was heard.

There enraptured sat each chieftain,
There his state the monarch held,
And amid their exultation
Loud its matchless accents swelled.
There the poets of the nation,
Bards of learning and devotion,
Came the minstrel harp to hear.

Thus, through years of wealth and plenty,
Minstrels waked its lays sublime,
Sang the songs of love and duty,
Songs that live throughout all time.
Not alone the proud and wealthy,
But the peasant, hale and hearty,
Loved its symphony to hear.

Now forgotten, ah, for ever!
Low the bards and minstrels lie,
And that harp's sweet strains for ever,
Ah ! for ever, ever lie!
Yet no hand the bond can sever,
None can break the tie asunder
That fast binds its memory dear.

In a Northern city slumbers
Amid wealth, from year to year -
In Belfast, a harp, whose numbers,
Once a king had loved to hear.

Yes, unstrung, it meekly slumbers;
There, unknown its magic numbers,
There forgotten lowly lies.

"Is there yet a soul in Ireland"
Left intact, untouched by time?
Is there yet a love for Ireland
That would wake its strains sublime?
That would waken through this fair land
The once glorious lays of Ireland,
The old harp that slumbering lies?

Yes, I see, as in a vision,
The old harp awake again;
Hear its accents through the nation,
Hear again its magic strain.
Yes, once more it takes its station
In each home, 'mid exultation,
Peer and peasant list its strains.

- E. J., Belfast, 14 May.

The largest concentration of Protestants in Ireland was in the province of Ulster. Most saw themselves as Irish *and* British, cherishing the link with Great Britain and being steadfastly loyal to the Crown. Many had further ties to Great Britain through their Scottish & English ancestry, with a lot of them being descended from the British people that migrated to Ireland as part of the 'Plantation of Ulster' in the early 1600s during the reign of King James I. A key remit for the new arrivals was to maintain their British way of life and Protestant faith. In their eyes, the plantation, which saw new towns built and old towns rebuilt, land cleared for farming etc., had resulted in the province becoming the most advanced, prosperous and civilised part of Ireland. This was achieved in the face of a hostile native population that viewed them as invaders who had stolen their land from them and were imposing an alien culture in Ireland.

In 1872, the vast majority of the Protestant community was totally opposed to the violent activities of the Fenians. Likewise, Home Rule, though it did have some influential Protestant advocates, was massively opposed by them. It was viewed as a stepping stone to an independent Ireland, which, with the loosening of ties to the British Empire, would jeopardise the economic prosperity of Ireland, particularly in places like Belfast.

They also feared that an Irish parliament would be dominated by the Roman Catholic church and the country would effectively be run by the Vatican - 'Home rule is Rome rule!' If this happened, they believed there would potentially be a return to the dark days of 1641, when the native Irish rebelled against British rule. This uprising included the massacre of thousands of British migrants in Ulster, with particularly horrific atrocities carried out at the River Bann in Portadown, County Armagh. For the Protestant British settlers, it was a watershed moment that highlighted the insecurity of their tenure as a minority in Catholic Ireland, and the memory of it ran deep.

Less than fifty years later, thousands more Protestants died of starvation and associated illnesses during the Siege of Derry (1688-1689) as they held the city for the new King of England, William III, in defiance of the deposed king, the Catholic James II. James' army, including French soldiers, lay encamped outside its famous walls, but when they called on those inside to surrender, they were met with the response of 'No Surrender!' which remains the watchword of the Protestant Unionist Loyalist community to this day.

One of the most vocal opponents of Home Rule and teachings of the Roman Catholic church in Belfast at this time was an evangelical Presbyterian Minister called the Reverend Hugh Hanna. He viewed the Pope as the Antichrist. Due to his fiery and loud style of oration, he was known as 'Roaring Hanna' and other epithets. He felt it was part of his Christian duty to inform all and sundry about the perils of 'Romanism' and did so through sermons, street preaching and lectures. The street preaching in particular was not appreciated by Belfast's growing Roman Catholic population who found some of it offensive; nor were the processions through the streets of children belonging to his Sabbath schools. They and some others described him as a rabble rouser.

To the working class Protestants of Belfast, he was regarded as a champion of the British constitution and defender of their faith. Through his revival meetings and preaching of the gospel among them, he had brought many to God and his flock also included Roman Catholic converts. He was also noted favourably for his contributions to education, both religious and secular. He always stressed that he had no issue with individual Roman Catholics, his problem was with the church itself, and what he viewed as its unscriptural teachings. In modern day terms, you could say that he was a key influencer.

On Sunday 9 June 1872, Rev. Hanna's new church, St. Enoch's, which had seating for 2,500 worshippers, formally opened for worship at Carlisle Circus. It was an impressive building in the gothic style that many thought resembled a cathedral. Its name was chosen as a nod to Scotland, and honoured the people from there that brought the Presbyterian faith to Ireland. It was built as a replacement for Rev. Hanna's church in Berry Street, which was too small for his vast congregation and Sabbath schools.

That Sunday morning, despite inclement weather, it was full to the brim and several hundred people had to be turned away. The Rev. James Oswald Dykes, M.A., the Scottish born Minister of the English Presbyterian Church, Regent Square, London, conducted the first service at 11.30 a.m. After the preliminary prayers had been completed, he took the beatitude 'Blessed are the poor in spirit, for theirs is the kingdom of heaven' (Matthew 5:3) as the theme for his sermon.[4]

3.
THE ROAD TO RIOT

1872 also marked the repeal of the Party Processions Act (1850). This legislation had been designed to prevent processions taking place that were likely to offend other parties and cause a breach of the peace. Belfast had suffered many sectarian disturbances as its population grew in the 19th century, with, prior to 1872, rioting taking place in the years 1829, 1843, 1857 and 1864.[1] It is worth noting that Catholic Nationalists and some others held Rev. Hugh Hanna directly responsible for being the cause of the disturbances in 1857 and 1864.

The act had varying degrees of success and was often ignored. It had been opposed for years and the campaign against it was led by a Protestant MP and Orangeman called William Johnston, but its repeal in May saw celebratory processions held by Nationalists in Coalisland and Maghera.[2]

The first big test after the repeal of the act came on Friday 12 July, when processions by the Loyal Orange Institution of Ireland took place to commemorate the anniversary of the Battle of the Boyne, which was fought on that day in 1690. These celebrated - and to this day still do - the victory of the Protestant King William III, Prince of Orange, over his Roman Catholic father-in-law, King James II. The confrontation, which was a significant event in British, Irish and European history, took place on Irish soil near Oldbridge in County Meath where the River Boyne flows. In the eyes of the Protestant Irish, the victory of 'King Billy' at this battle followed by the triumph of his forces at Aughrim in 1691, secured their 'freedom, religion and laws,' while in the eyes of the Catholic Irish, the defeat of James II diminished all of those things and immensely damaged their hopes of restoring a Gaelic Roman Catholic Ireland.

In Belfast, as a precaution, wooden barricades, guarded by the police, were erected near Christ Church in College Square and at a corner of Hercules Street. The residents here and in some other mainly Catholic streets erected Green arches (an equivalent to Orange arches) and temporary police barracks were set up in streets near to where the authorities feared trouble might break out. Some 350 extra police were drafted into the city from all over Ireland.

Orangemen from Belfast took part in three different processions and meetings. A large number gathered at Carlisle Circus before marching to the Northern Counties Railway station. Here they boarded trains to Antrim and joined the meeting at Massereene Park. Conn's Water Bridge in Ballymacarrett was the meeting point for those who headed off to take part in the celebrations in Bangor and the fountain in Great Victoria Street was the starting point for those who stayed in the town and marched to the meeting at Belvoir Park.[3]

At Belvoir Park, a scuffle broke out in the crowd and a man received minor injuries when he was stabbed. The attacker was assumed to be a Roman Catholic and was quickly surrounded. Rev. Hugh Hanna and other clergymen rushed down from the speaker's platform to protect him and formed a human shield to ensure he was not beaten up or worse. They did this until the police arrived. It turned out that the attacker was not a Roman Catholic and the fight had no sectarian connotations. Rev. Hanna's actions in protecting a man whom he thought to be a Roman Catholic even drew grudging praise from Belfast's leading Nationalist newspaper.

The stoning in Donegall Street of some Orangemen who were returning home after a parade was seemingly the only noteworthy incident of a sectarian nature.[4]

On Sunday 3 August some 1,700 scholars and teachers from St. Enoch's Sabbath Schools gathered at Carlisle Circus. Led by the band and pipers of the 78th Highlanders and with a hundred banners on display, they processed through the principal streets of Belfast to the Ulster Railway Station. Here they boarded a special excursion train that took them to Lurgan in County Armagh. At Brownlow Demesne, which Lord Lurgan had kindly granted permission for them to use, they enjoyed picnics, listened to music from the band and prior to leaving, listened to an address from the Rev. Hugh Hanna. He praised them for their conduct and called for cheers for the Prince of Wales and the Lord Lieutenant of Ireland, who was due to visit Lurgan shortly. Thanks were also given to Lord Lurgan. The 'gallant and handsome Highlanders' were applauded and there were cheers for the teachers. People from Lurgan lined the streets as they made their way back to the station and large numbers of people did likewise in Belfast as they arrived back in the town and headed to the dispersal point at the Linen Hall. The event passed off peacefully.[5]

Just six days after the Sabbath School procession, it was announced that another parade of a very different kind would commence from Carlisle Circus. To celebrate the repeal of the Party Processions Act and create a Roman Catholic and Nationalist procession to rival and 'out-do' the Protestant Twelfth, Nationalist leaders selected the 15 August for a number of 'monster' demonstrations in Ireland. This date was a holiday known as 'Lady Day in Harvest.' In the Roman Catholic faith it is an important feast day that marks the Assumption of the Virgin Mary into Heaven. *The Daily Examiner* published this advert for it on Friday 9 August:

TO THE NATIONALISTS OF BELFAST AND SURROUNDING DISTRICTS

A MONSTER MEETING WILL BE HELD AT HANNAHSTOWN, ON THURSDAY, 15th AUGUST, FOR THE PURPOSE OF UNITING IRISHMEN of all Creeds and Classes.

A Procession will be formed at CARLISLE CIRCUS at TEN o'clock.

Any Association wishing to join the Procession will please send a Deputation to meet the Committee in the FORESTER'S HALL, *on* SATURDAY *Evening next, 10th inst, at Eight o'clock.*

BY ORDER OF COMMITTEE.

It is worth briefly looking at Lady Day in Harvest, also often called simply Lady Day, and its significance to Irish Roman Catholics in the 19th Century. This will give a little insight into why it was chosen for what was going to be the biggest ever procession by Nationalists in Belfast. It was a popular holiday, particularly for agricultural workers in the rural parts of the country. An account in the *Limerick Chronicle* from 18 August 1832 gives an insight to how it was celebrated at that time:

> *Some apprehension was felt at the appearance of lights in various parts of the country on Wednesday night, but it should be observed that* Lady Day in Harvest *is one of the greatest holidays in the year with the peasantry, and on the evening of this day, they light fires, and burn wisps which they carry on*

poles through the country at a rapid rate. We believe there was nothing of a political or insurrectionary nature in the exhibition.

Lady Day in Harvest 1843 saw a huge demonstration on the Hill of Tara in County Meath. Daniel O'Connell, the man who was largely responsible for the emancipation of Roman Catholics in the late 1820s, was now on another mission, and here, where the High Kings of Ireland were once crowned, he addressed a crowd of anything up to half a million people. While still professing loyalty to the Queen of England, he was seeking the repeal of the Union between Great Britain and Ireland. His speech was principally about the merits of repeal, but he did include reference to the religious significance of the day:

This is a holy festival in the Catholic church. It is the anniversary of the blessed day when the mother of the Redeemer ascended from earth to meet her son and reign with him forever. Oh! on such a day I would not tell a falsehood. I hope I am under her protection. I hope that our sacred cause has her prayers for its success (loud cheers).

On 5 October 1844, *The Vindicator* (Belfast) reproduced a 'hymn' by 'J.K.' that was originally published in *The Nation* (Dublin):

THE IRISH EMIGRANT REAPER'S HARVEST HYMN TO THE VIRGIN

(Lady-day in Harvest - 1844.)

ALL HAIL! holy Mary, our hope and our joy -
Smile down, blessed Queen, on the "Wild Irish Boy,"
Who wanders far, far from his dear-beloved home -
Oh! Mary, be with me wherever I roam -
Be with me, oh! Mary;
Forsake me not, Mary,
But guide me, and guard me wherever I roam.

From the home of my fathers' in anguish I go,
To toil for the dark-livered, cold hearted foe,
Who mocks me, and hates me, and calls me "a slave,"

An "alien," a "savage," all names but a "knave;"
But, blessed be Mary,
My sweet, holy Mary,
The Boddagh, he never dare call me a "knave."

From my mother's mud sheeling an outcast I fly,
With a cloud on my heart, and a tear in my eye;
Oh! I blaze as I think how - if SOME ONE *would say -*
"Revenge on your tyrants" - but Mary, I pray
From my soul's depth, oh! Mary,
And hear me, sweet Mary,
For union and peace to old Ireland, I pray.

The land that I fly from is fertile and fair,
And more than I ask for, or wish for, is there;
But I must not taste the good things that I see,
"There's nothing but rags and green rushes for me."
Oh! mild Virgin Mary,
Oh! sweet mother Mary,

Who keeps my rough hand from red murder but thee?
There's gold for the Saxon, and silver galore,
And riches in piles on the banks of the Nore;
But I scorn his pelf, and his ill-gotten store -
Give their own to the Irish - we ask for no more.
You see, blessed Mary -
You know, blessed Mary -
You know in your heart that we covet no more.

Then on, lads - "no shrinking" - and freedom we'll gain,
And wipe from the green flag each Sassenagh stain;
And, now, holy Mary, your blessing we crave,
Give hearts to the timid, and hands to the brave;
And, then, mother Mary,
Our own holy Mary,
Light liberty's lamp in the hut of the slave.

In addition to the faithful attending church services, cattle markets and fairs took place and railway companies laid on excursion trains to the seaside. People let their hair down and generally had a good time. An account from *The Waterford Mail* of 16 August 1867 tells us of the festivities that took place in that area that year:

LADY DAY IN HARVEST

An immense number of people arrived in this city yesterday from all parts. There were excursion trains from Kilkenny and intermediate stations, Limerick and intermediate stations, and from Ross and Dunncannon by the river steamers.

The greater portion of the people proceeded at once to Tramore, where at one period of the day they could be numbered by thousands. The weather was very fine all day in Tramore, and in addition to the many natural attractions already possessed by this "Brighton of Ireland," the brass band of the 67th Regiment was present on the Atlantic Terrace, and performed some select music. The terrace and field adjoining were crowded, and everyone seemed to thoroughly enjoy the treat.

The officials on the Tramore railway had a busy time of it all day. Their arrangements for the transit of the crowds of pleasure seekers to and from Tramore were very efficient, and gave great satisfaction. Not a few of the excursionists went to Dunmore on cars, and returned in the evening much pleased with their trip.

The following year, newspapers reported that there were fears of trouble in Downpatrick and Banbridge on Lady Day in Harvest. It was said Catholics planned to hold demonstrations displaying party colours which was likely to provoke a reaction from local Protestants. Police and army reinforcements were drafted in but the intervention of magistrates and Catholic priests is said to have averted any chance of conflict.

On 15 August 1871, a meeting in favour of Home Rule for Ireland took place at the Fair Green in Dundalk. A report in *The Belfast News-Letter* of 16 August said that 6,000 to 8,000 people attended; a report in *The Flag of Ireland* from 19 August states 15,000 were present and Belfast's *The Daily Examiner* of 16 August said 20,000. *The Belfast News-Letter* account describes houses being decorated with evergreens and flags that were principally green and orange. One of these, which was in a conspicuous position, had 'Erin-go-Bragh' (and) 'Ireland for the Irish' inscribed on it and a harp in the middle. Their reporter noted that the harp *was* surmounted by a crown though. People wore green or green and orange sashes, scarfs, rosettes and some hats which had a strip of green paper around them with the words 'Home Rule' on it. A procession around the town took place before the meeting which was accompanied by the fife and drum band and brass bands from Dundalk, and also a brass band from Newry, from where a large number of people had travelled to be part of proceedings.

The meeting itself began around 2.30pm. The platform for the speakers featured mottoes painted in green which included 'Home Rule, United we stand - divided we fall, Orange and Green will carry the day,' and over the entrance steps, 'Cead Mille Failthe.' (sic) Two flags floated from the platform, one was inscribed with 'Erin-go-Bragh - Home Rule,' and the other, 'Home Rule - God Save Ireland.'

Although not all the advertised speakers were able to attend, one of whom was a leading Home Rule advocate from Belfast, Isaac Butt, Q.C., it was still a high profile line-up from both religious traditions that sat on the stage including Members of Parliament, clergymen, solicitors, Justices of the Peace and a delegation from Dublin which included the prominent Nationalist leader Alexander Martin Sullivan. John Martin, another leading Nationalist and the M.P. for Meath, was one of the speakers. *The Daily Examiner* recorded his words, part of which were as follows:

> *My friends, this meeting, this demonstration of so many thousands of good Irishmen and good Irishwomen, is a glad omen in my eyes. It is a sign to me that that cause for which I, in an humble way, have laboured so long - that cause which has been adopted now already through the three provinces of Ireland, enlisting the support of all that is virtuous and all that is good, and which is now spreading around the frontier of Ulster, is irresistible in its might. I saw among the flags borne through Dundalk in this procession one that had "the flag of Newry" inscribed upon it. I am rejoiced at that, for it leads me to hope that the cause of Home Rule will make a step in advance in Newry, and from Newry to Belfast, and from Belfast to Derry, and round by Donegal till there is not a lake in Ireland whose shores will not resound to the cry of Home Rule, until every Irishman throughout the length and breadth of our land will be resolved to sink all minor differences, and stand by the rights of their own dear country. (Cheers.)*
>
> *I know that in Ulster a majority, and a large majority, of the population are as wedded in their hearts to Home Rule as I am, but it is necessary that we*

> *should take up a bold and decisive position in regard to England, we must show England that there can be no doubt as to the great want that exists in Ireland, we must show our rulers that public declaration is the deliberate wish, the indispensable requirement of the Irish people. Already the people in the other three provinces have the fire of freedom burning in their hearts, it was warm there when no public demonstration called it forth, and now that the time has come for them to express their views they have done so with an alacrity and a manly spirit which shows how eagerly they desire the blessings of freedom, and yearn to raise their country from the condition of a mere province to her fitting place among the nations of the earth.*

So we can see that Lady Day in Harvest was a very important holiday for Ireland's Roman Catholics, combining religious observation with recreational activities, but from time to time politics was added into the mix. The Home Rule meeting in Dundalk may have provided a template for what was to come in Belfast the following year, which would see John Martin's wish come true. His belief that Ulster's Protestants would join their Roman Catholic neighbours in support of Home Rule was to prove well wide of the mark though.

4.
FAITH AND FATHERLAND

As we have seen from the newspaper advert in the previous chapter, the starting place for the procession in Belfast that would wind its way to Hannahstown was to be Carlisle Circus. This was the very place where the church of the Nationalist's *nemesis*, the Rev. Hugh Hanna, now stood. Despite the Orange processions the previous month having been left alone by Catholics, it was fairly obvious that this was going to be a major test of the fair play principle which they expected in return from the majority Protestant loyalist community of Belfast. This was not lost on the local press. As the big day approached, newspapers with a mainly Protestant readership asked for the Nationalist parades across Ulster to be left unmolested.

At the end of the 'Ulster Scot's Letters To His Friends At Home And Abroad' column published in the *Belfast Weekly News* on Saturday 10 August, the author wrote:

> *On the 15th instant - Lady Day - there will, it is stated, be Roman Catholic processions. I appeal to my Orange and Protestant brethren to remember that any interference with such processions would be disastrous. Act, my dear brethren, on that day in such a way as that your bitterest enemies shall not be able to point the finger of condemnation at you. Be peaceable; give no offence, and take no offence.*

Other publications highlighted that the Relief of Derry celebrations by the (Protestant) Apprentice Boys organisation on 12 August in Londonderry had not been attacked or interfered with.[1]

While the route of the parade would see it pass through parts of central Belfast and then on to Hannahstown via mainly Catholic populated streets in the west of the town, the starting place of Carlisle Circus, despite the appeals for tolerance to be shown, was indeed to prove contentious. A letter published in the morning edition of *The Belfast News-Letter* on 13 August read:

THE APPROACHING 15TH OF AUGUST

TO THE EDITOR OF THE BELFAST NEWS-LETTER

SIR - As the parties who intend celebrating "Lady Day," by marching in procession with questionable emblems, have selected Carlisle Circus as the place of starting from, I hope they will see the proprierty of selecting some other locality, as the neighbourhood of Carlisle Circus is entirely Protestant. On the 12th of July the Orangemen selected Protestant localities to assemble in. Surely the Roman Catholics ought to select a Roman Catholic locality, if only for peace sake, and out of consideration for the feelings of the Protestant inhabitants of the locality. Hercules Street, Durham Street, and Barrack Street were closed against even individuals passing on the 12th of July, and, by the same rule of law, the authorities should not allow Carlisle Circus to be made the starting point on the 15th of August. If the Roman Catholics mean no offence let them select some other neighbourhood.

(signed) CARLISLE CIRCUS.

Another letter published by the same newspaper in a later edition the same day reinforced this message:

THE DEMONSTRATION ON THURSDAY

TO THE EDITOR OF THE BELFAST NEWS-LETTER

SIR - I entirely agree with your correspondent in today's paper that the authorities should not allow the proposed meeting on Thursday, to assemble at the Carlisle Circus, or to pass that way. The whole locality is loyal and Protestant, and the meeting would be extremely offensive to the respectable inhabitants. Besides, property there would certainly suffer, and the value of it would be much depreciated if the locality was identified with such a meeting as proposed. There can be no doubt that the loyal men on the Shankhill, (Old) Lodge, and Crumlin Roads would look on such a meeting as a piece of wanton provocation.

August 13, 1872. - (signed) LOYALIST.

On the day of the actual procession, the morning edition of *The Belfast News-Letter* contained more correspondence echoing the above sentiments:

LADY DAY AND ITS PROCESSIONISTS

TO THE EDITOR OF THE BELFAST NEWS-LETTER

SIR- Will you allow me to offer one other earnest word of warning to the authorities and the processionists in regard to the threatened proceedings on tomorrow? The proposed assembly at the Carlisle Circus is in the highest degree repugnant to the Protestant and loyal feeling of that respectable district. Such an assembly must exasperate public feeling to a very serious extent, and imperil the peace of the town. If the processionists desire to have peace, they will keep at a respectable distance from the Carlisle Circus. If the authorities would effectually maintain order, they will certainly prevent the processionists from appearing in that quarter of the town. If, however, this should not be done, it may be understood by all whom it may concern, that no such outrage on loyal feeling will be tolerated on any other occasion. Great sacrifices should be made in the interests of public order, but there are, also, still higher interests occasionally to be maintained.

(Signed) LOYALIST.
August 14, 1872.

The newspaper itself also published a lengthy appeal for the procession to be left alone in the same issue - but it *was* highly critical of such a march taking place in Belfast and the likelihood of what it termed offensive emblems being displayed and offensive tunes being played.

To suggest that Carlisle Circus and its locality was entirely Protestant wasn't quite true as many Catholics lived near it too - not least those who resided in the Shankill - and there was a convent nearby. Also, it was used as an assembly point for other processions with no political connotations and for day trips out to the countryside by factory workers. The previous year, in April, a spectacular cross-community parade began there and made its way to Ormeau Park to celebrate the opening of that famous green space.

However, most of the nearby streets definitely *were* mainly Protestant, and with Rev. Hanna's church now open, it was clearly a hugely provocative decision by the march organisers to opt for this starting point if they truly were intent on 'uniting Irishmen of all creeds and classes.' They had after all blamed him for being the cause of previous riots and surely knew there would be a reaction to this decision. Perhaps it was a calculated move by them; knowing that when the procession was inevitably attacked they could take the moral high ground and tell the world, "We did not interfere with the Orange gatherings, which we find offensive, but look what they have done to our parade!"

On 15 August, it was therefore no surprise to anyone when thousands of Protestants gathered outside St. Enoch's church to, in their eyes, defend it. A line of police and several magistrates, one being Sir John Savage who was also the Mayor, separated them and the Nationalists making their way up Clifton Street. In its edition published that morning before the march began, *The Daily Examiner* claimed that this was down to the Rev. Hugh Hanna. According to them, he had sworn to the local magistrates that a breach of the peace would occur should the parade begin near his church. It also inferred that Roman Catholic magistrates had visited Roman Catholic clergy in Belfast urging them to persuade the organisers not to start the procession at Carlisle Circus but this was to no avail. (It was true that two of Belfast's magistrates who were Roman Catholics - Mr. Bernard Hughes and Dr. Henry Murney - had met some organisers of the procession and asked them to change the starting point to the Linen Hall; nothing was agreed but the magistrates mistakenly believed their appeal would be successful.[2])

For this newspaper, the deployment of the police to prevent a lawful parade starting at its advertised place was further proof of institutional bias against the Roman Catholic population of the city.

However, after stone throwing between the rival factions threatened to get out of hand, the march organisers were either persuaded by the magistrates, or simply chose not to force the issue, and the procession began further down Clifton Street and headed off into the town centre via Donegall Street.

It was an impressive spectacle by any stretch of the imagination. The 'wearing of the green' was much in evidence with an abundance of sashes, rosettes, neckties, ribbons and scarves. In an otherwise condescending article, the *The Belfast News-Letter*, a partisan Protestant publication, said; 'The display of Green was amazing.'[3] Banners with slogans including 'God Save Ireland,' 'Erin Go Bragh,' 'Remember Limerick,' 'Amnesty for Political Prisoners,' 'Let Erin Remember' and 'Sons of St Patrick' were carried, and another featured Patrick Sarsfield, the commander of the Jacobite forces that fought against King William III in Ireland. A flag of Robert Emmet, who led a rebellion against British rule in 1803, was said to be particularly eye-catching. The crownless harp flag was flown prominently along with the French tricolour, and marching bands, including St. Peter's, St. Joseph's and St. Patrick's, played Irish tunes including 'St Patrick's Day,' 'Garryowen,' 'God Save Ireland' and 'O'Donnell Abu,' as well as the French national anthem, 'La Marseillaise'.

There had been some minor stone throwing incidents in the town centre, but it was not until the procession made its way up Divis Street and reached its junction with Dover Street, which was a connecting road to the Shankill, that it came under a brief but serious attack. Here a Protestant mob was gathered at James Wallace's brick works - known as the brickfields - and they launched brickbats, stones and anything else they could get their hands on at the marchers. Of course, those in green did not take this lying down and fought back with equal ferocity, ripping up palings (fencing) to use as staves and strike their assailants. One man was reportedly shot in the shoulder by a man in the procession. The speedy intervention of the police stopped the violence and prevented more injuries.

The march, which was led by a boy on a horse who was dressed in a long green cloak bound with white and wearing a buff-coloured felt hat with gold trimming, then made its way to the 'monster' meeting at Hannahstown, where anything up to 30,000 people listened to music and speeches that called for Home Rule and the release of Fenian prisoners.

Back in Belfast, some 500 Protestant rivetters and labourers from the shipyards headed into town and tried to make their way to the Catholic stronghold of Hercules Street.* It is possible they were provoked into doing this after being challenged by a 150 strong mob of Catholics armed with oak staves that had taunted them at Queen's Island earlier. After traversing through a number of streets they were checked by the police who fixed bayonets and charged at them. Across the city people gathered at various locations and some minor trouble broke out as people finished work at the linen mills.[4]

When the meeting concluded at Hannahstown, a car driver called William Millen was accidentally shot dead while conveying some of the processionists home. A 'car' was the name for a horse drawn cab or carriage which was used like a modern day taxi or bus. Before the procession left the field, those taking part who had pistols had been advised to load them in anticipation of further attacks on the way back. William had two female passengers and was in the dickey seat of his car, which was the last one in the return procession. He was hit in the back when a pistol was discharged by an unknown person. "William John, I am killed!" were reportedly the last words he uttered, which were addressed to a friend close-by[5]

The procession returned to Belfast, with young men armed with sticks in the vanguard, but it was blocked by the police from going anywhere near Carlisle Circus. The authorities had heard it was to be attacked again. The town briefly appeared to be calm but by early evening thousands of people were on the streets and soon rival mobs were clashing. The Athens of Ireland rapidly descended into chaos.

As with many Belfast riots over the centuries, it was a brutal and savage affair, with at least two more people killed and a third who died due to the stress caused when his property was attacked.

James McSorley, aged 19, a Catholic, who lived at 37, Lincoln Street, died in contentious circumstances at 9, Lincoln Street, shortly after 11 p.m. on Friday 16 August. He was stabbed with a bayonet sword by a policeman after police charged down the street to clear what they said was a mob of stone throwers. Police were dispatched to the area after receiving reports that houses in nearby Leeson Street were being wrecked. Witnesses from the street said the stone throwing had ceased some minutes before the charge and that James had not been one of those engaged in this. When the police charged he tried to take refuge at No. 9 where the door was open, but had barely got inside when a pursuing policeman thrust his bayonet into the side of the defenceless young man. The policeman could not be identified and none came forward at the inquest in October to admit responsibility, so a verdict was recorded that: 'That some unknown member of the police force did feloniously kill and slay James McSorley.'[6]

Sub Constable Joseph Morton, a policeman drafted into Belfast from Thurles, North Tipperary, to reinforce the local force, was shot dead in Norfolk Street, off the Falls Road, by a gunman on 20 August. The gunman was believed to be a Protestant but ultimately no one was ever convicted for his murder.[7,8] Joseph was also a Catholic and was buried far from the hills of Tipperary in Belfast after being given a full police funeral on 24 August. All officers not on riot duty attended. A thousand or more people, mainly women and children, lined the Falls Road and joined the cortege as it made its way to Milltown Cemetery. Six of his colleagues from Tipperary bore his coffin from Queen Street to his final resting place, and a hundred others from that county were the chief mourners. Father Cahill and Father Walsh read prayers for the dead at the gates and Father Walsh conducted the burial service.[9,10]

One person who was not there was his heavily pregnant widow, Anne. While attempting to reach Belfast from Thurles, she gave birth to a son at a railway station in Dublin.[11,12] He would be named Joseph after his father, and like his father, he too would serve in the Royal Irish Constabulary and be killed on duty in another tumultuous period of Irish history which is now known as the War of Independence. In the early hours of Friday 28 May 1920, the police barrack at Kilmallock, County Limerick, came under sustained attack from fifty to several hundred I.R.A. members - who were described as 'Sinn Feiners' in contemporary newspaper reports. Prior to launching their assault, telephone lines had been cut and the railway line sabotaged. Properties overlooking the barracks were commandeered and sentries were posted on all entrances and exits to and from the small town. Ten policemen were inside and refused to surrender when called on to do so. A fierce battle then ensued for around five hours - with guns, grenades and other bombs being used.

The attackers eventually succeeded in setting the barrack ablaze leaving its defenders with no option but to evacuate as the fire spread. Eight of them, many of whom were injured, fixed bayonets and made their exit onto Lord Edward Street, expecting to meet their doom. Fortunately for them, the I.R.A. was withdrawing at this point, content that the building was destroyed. However, two of the policemen who had been posted to the part of the building that was ablaze were missing. These were Sergeant Thomas Kane and Constable Joseph Morton. The burning roof had collapsed onto them and their charred remains - which were hardly recognisable - were recovered later. Whether they had been killed prior to this could not be determined but some reports suggested they may have been shot dead or died in a bomb blast prior to the roof collapsing.[13]

Constable Morton, aged 48, was given a funeral in the town with military honours. Sixty policemen followed the band of the Royal Welsh Fusiliers in the procession as they played the 'Dead March' to the churchyard. Three volleys of shots were fired over the grave after which the 'Last Post' was played by the band. When the procession returned, it halted outside the ruined barracks and the surviving eight policemen were given promotions. The band then played 'God Save The King'.[14]

Back to Belfast in 1872 and on the same night that James McSorley lost his life, another Catholic, Owen Brannigan, reportedly died from 'excitement' when his home in Lettuce Hill off Barrack Street was assaulted by the wreckers. Many newspaper reports suggested the death toll from the riots was a lot higher than officially recorded. These implied that people were buried in secret at night to avoid the attention of the authorities.

In addition to the fatalities, hundreds were injured. Both sides used firearms, knives, swords, bayonets, meat cleavers, bludgeons, shillelagh sticks, knuckle dusters, cudgels, pokers, paving stones, bricks, bare fists and any other thing that came to hand as weapons - *The Belfast Weekly News* of 24 August even claimed that a dead cat had been thrown at Sub Constable Hasley, who we shall hear more from later, in Divis Street. A spear and some cannons were also confiscated by the police. Alcohol played an important role in sustaining the ferocity of the rioters.

The principal combatants were men, but women and children also joined in. At the Assizes in 1873, Ellen Burns, a Catholic, received a four month prison sentence with hard labour for riot.[15] At Hercules Street, on 15 August, when most of the men were taking part in the procession and were therefore away from the area, it is said the women of the district, led by a 'stout lady of undisputed gallantry,' took up positions to keep out the approaching Protestant mob from the shipyard should they have broken through police lines.[16] Hercules Street was home to many butchers so it goes without saying a bloodbath would have followed with all the tools of that trade that were to hand. Women and girls also took part in the house wreckings and also played a key role in supplying a steady supply of beer, stones and other missiles to the men. *The Daily Examiner* of 19 August, in an account of rioting on the Shankill Road the previous day, included this:

> *...The women, whose gentler nature might have been expected to revolt at the scenes of bloodshed and violence perpetrated in their presence, seemed to have for the time dispensed with all the attributes of their sex, and given themselves up entirely to the fiendish frenzy of the occasion. They dug up the pavement, and filling their aprons full of stones, followed the male rioters in their assaults, and when the latter appeared to hesitate, urged them on with imprecations and taunts of cowardice to prosecute their aggression, and to show no mercy to those whom they called the "bloody rebels." Even children contributed to swell the*

ranks of the rioters on the Shankhill Road, and one could not help despairing for the future peace of the town, and wondering what sort of training they had got, when witnessing their infantine efforts to second the attacks of their elders.

And in its reporting of the riots, *The Belfast News-Letter*, published on the same day, included this:

> ... *A more appalling scene than that which presented itself on the Falls Road could not be conceived. Vast numbers of wild-looking women and ferocious-looking men came out of the bye streets leading into the Pound, and thronged the thoroughfare in front of the Model School. The shrieks which the women were setting up when they saw any of those engaged in the fight in a critical position were frightful, and they ran about crying to the men who had refrained from taking an active part in the riot to go forward and assist those who were fighting. Through the mud on the road and the mire in the field they ran, heedless of the danger, inciting the men to fight, and when they were not always successful they bewailed the decay of courage amongst the men of the "Loney," and called down imprecations on their heads for cowards.*

Both reports suggest that women were not conforming to the expected gender stereotypes of the age. It is also important to note that both publications are clearly mimicking each other - Protestant women being the worst offenders according to the Catholic publication and Catholic women the worst offenders according to the Protestant publication. This was a common trait of *The Daily Examiner* and *The Belfast News-Letter* at that time.

Looting of shops and public houses was widespread; places of worship and schools were attacked and of course one of the saddest and cruellest things was the forcing out of people of the opposite faith from areas where they were in the minority - with homes being wrecked and furniture burned for good measure. (Upwards of 250 homes were wrecked and 837 families forced out according to Justice Lawson in an address to the County Antrim Assizes in March 1873.[17]) Some Catholics in Protestant areas would be challenged to curse the Pope, and Protestants in Catholic areas forced onto their knees and told to bless themselves or ordered to curse King William. Failure to do so was likely to result in a savage beating. Of course, in amongst all the hatred, others *were* looking out for their neighbours of the opposite faith - either by ensuring their property was not attacked or by taking in their belongings for safekeeping when it was. Some even arranged house exchanges. *The Daily Examiner*, on 24 August included this example of good neighbourliness:

TERRORISM IN LIME STREET

The instances we have heard of the terrorism in which Catholics were placed under the orange regime are too numerous for detail, but we are glad to mention an instance in which Protestants showed a kindly and Christian feeling towards the Catholics driven from their homes. A family who resided in Lime Street, after receiving "notice to quit," found it difficult to get away and safety, but three respectable Protestants volunteered their assistance, and rescued them and their furniture.

There was little respect for the forces of law and order nor fear of them. The disturbances only abated through a combination of depleting supplies of alcohol, sheer fatigue, heavy rain and the police and army being massively reinforced so they could swamp the streets in huge numbers. The 78th Highlanders, who had arrived in Belfast from Nova Scotia via Queenstown (Cobh, County Cork) on 20 December of the previous year, were one of the army regiments deployed to restore order. One of their soldiers, who were nicknamed 'Kilties,' sent a letter home to relatives in Kirkcaldy, Scotland, which *The Fife Free Press* published on 24 August:

Belfast, 19 August.

There is a great row here at present between the Catholics and the Protestants, and they have carried it on to such an extent that the soldiers had to be called upon to put it down, which is no easy matter.

We have been kept in readiness to turn out at any time for the last three days past. I never saw before the like of what I have seen for the last few days - people just killing each other; others breaking into public-houses and drinking until they were mad with it, and of course they would fall, and the mob would just trample over them.

I was out on Saturday night along with the regiment, and I saw five people shot dead and others very sorely hurt, and that was only one part of the town - some other parts were worse. And I suspect the worst of it is yet to come, for both parties are determined not to go to their work until they meet each other. You must understand that they live in two different parts of the town, and that we are posted right in the centre, so that they can't get at each other.

I can't say any more at present, for we have to go out this afternoon, every man of us, and we have got men from all parts of Ireland. I am in good health at present, but I was thinking on Saturday night that I might not be long that way, for the air was quite black with the stones they threw at each other, and we had to go and separate them.

It goes without saying that the majority of people in Belfast were utterly horrified at what went on in their home town. Many felt that the authorities could have done more in the early part of the disturbances to nip it in the bud. This opinion was expressed at a meeting of Orangemen held on the evening of 21 August at the Agnes Street Orange Hall in the Shankill. They condemned the wrecking and violence and said it was nothing to do with Orangemen. In their opinion, the police, with proper leadership, could have had things under control in 12 hours. A resolution at the meeting was passed that said that if the authorities did not put an end to the mayhem they would form a 'vigilance committee' to suppress the mobs without distinction to creed or party.[18]

Some London based newspapers went on to produce illustrations of the riots which are easy enough to find online. It's worth pointing out a couple of things about these. None were actually drawn in Belfast; some have captions with words such as 'Orangemen attacking the procession' when in fact the Orange Order did not hold any counter procession or attack it; and last but not least, the sketches, and particularly the depiction of the people in them, was ridiculed by Belfast's leading Catholic and Protestant newspapers. The Nationalist publication, *The Daily Examiner*, on Monday 2 September, had this to say:

THE Belfast people who see themselves represented in several English papers this week in connexion with the riots, which have sent our name far over the world, will be considerably amused at the original figures and costumes which are made to do duty in giving the "intelligent foreigner" an idea of "ye manners and customs of ye inhabitants of ye Northern Athens."

It must, indeed, be admitted that nothing could exceed in atrocity the deeds which found perpetration in many parts of Belfast during the disturbances now happily past, but anything more ludicrous or grotesque than this English attempt to illustrate the several scenes of disorder could scarcely find conception.

From these pictures persons unacquainted with Belfast would conclude that the prevailing fashion in dress was long-tailed coats, knee breeches, and brogues; tall hats abridged of their brims, the inevitable "Barcelona" of the stage Irishman, and of course, the conventional sprig of shillelagh. Just as a French crowd would be represented in blouses, or a gathering of English labourers in smock-frocks, so have the artists in this case made us all Myles na Copaleens *or* Shawn the Posts, *the only model, no doubt, their experience enabled them to study. There could be no more convincing proof of the misconceptions regarding the people of this country prevailing in England than these wretched attempts to represent leading scenes in the Belfast riots. They are laughable in the extreme, and about as faithful as it would be to picture all the residents within the sound of St. Mungo's bells as wearing kilts, and carrying skian dhus (sic) and claymores without number in their belts.*

(*Myles Na Copaleen* was a character in the play *The Colleen Bawn* or *Bride of Garryowen* and *Shawn the Post* was in *Arrah na Pogue* or *The Wicklow Wedding*. This is what the article is referring to in relation to 'Stage Irishmen.')

The following day, a letter appeared in *The Belfast News-Letter* along similar lines:

LONDON IDEAS OF THE BELFAST RIOTS

TO THE EDITOR OF THE BELFAST NEWS-LETTER.

SIR - Some of the most exaggerated illustrations were noticeable in two of the London *papers in reference to the late riots. One of these was the* Police News, *and the other the* Illustrated London News.

In the former several plates were given, the artist's conception being totally at variance with the reality. The most striking one of these was - "A policeman shot dead." Here we have both men face to face on the street, *with the companions of the unfortunate victim in the distance, wearing the costume as is exactly used by the fire brigade. The other representations are equally comic, the "rowdies" in the different scenes attired as the ancient "Paddy." The illustrations given by the latter are not so bad, though a great mistake exists in each representation by the introduction of several able-bodied men. The notes explanatory of the pictures involve some peculiarities, "The poor Catholics of Sandy Row" forming a chief subject for comment.*

What ideas must be formed of us abroad when our neighbours hold such extravagant views!

W. L.

(Constable Morton, the policeman who was shot dead, was hit from a distance and not in a cowboy style gunfight; Sandy Row was the most Protestant and loyalist area of Belfast - Protestants evicted from mainly Catholic areas nearby went there for sanctuary during the riots - which is why the author draws attention to an illustration of Catholics being there which would appear to be fanciful.)

Last but not least, an article by 'Ulster Scot' in *The Belfast Weekly News* of 7 September included:

> *... The manner in which the London Radical Press, especially the illustrated journals, has dealt with these sad riots affords extraordinary evidence of the incurable and loathsome ignorance of the generality of the Cockney writers of everything pertaining to Ireland ... The same ignorance represents five-storied houses as having been wrecked and gutted during the late riots? - Sketches of offices in, 5, Tavistock Street, Covent Garden, London.*

* Hercules Street was demolished in the 1880s and replaced by Royal Avenue.

5.
DISTINCTIONS IN COLOUR

The riots were reported widely across the rest of the UK and throughout the English speaking world. In the reports that covered them when they were actually taking place and immediately after (15-30 August) I have not found a single reference to a Black man leading any of the mobs despite the Shankill Road - which was commonly spelled Shankhill Road back then - being mentioned prominently many times. Many English newspapers voiced their opinions on the riots and what caused them in their editorial columns. *The Leeds Times* published a lengthy one on 24 August 1872 and the opening paragraph read:

THE RIOTS IN BELFAST

We really ought to beg pardon of the pagans and savages - whom, from the height of our civilisation, we look down upon as little better than wild beasts - for the gross injustice we have done them. There is nothing in the fights of rival tribes of blacks in Africa more senseless and brutish than the riots which have for a week past disgraced the commercial capital of Ireland. No pagan worshippers of hideous and blood-stained idols ever exhibited their fanaticism in more barbarous acts than have been perpetrated by the rival sects of Christians who have just been contending for mastery in Belfast.

That paragraph gives an indication of how African people were sometimes portrayed in U.K. newspapers of the 19th century - uncivilised, pagan and basically savages. The Belfast rioters - white and Christians - had somehow managed to sink below this level of 'barbarity' which *The Leeds Times* evidently found astonishing and deplorable.

Applying labels and stereotypes to people of colour had gone on throughout the century. The title of this chapter is taken from a piece which appeared in *The Birmingham Journal and General Advertiser* of

29 March 1828. It is describing terminology applied to people of mixed heritage:

DISTINCTIONS IN COLOUR

*A S**bo is the nighest remove from black, being the child of a mulatto father, and negro woman, or vice versa. A mulatto is the child of a white man by a negress. A Quadroon is the child of a mulatto mother by a white father. The child of a Quadroon by a white man is a Mustee. The child of a white man by a Mustee woman is a Mustiphini. The child of a Mustiphini by a white father is a Quintroon; and the child of a Quintroon woman by a white is free by law.*

Before detailing the involvement of George Henry Thompson in the riots, his time in Belfast and how we come to know of this, it is worth building on the above to provide some further examples of how Black people were portrayed in print media in the United Kingdom in 1872.

At this time the press had a particular interest and fascination with African Americans. Slavery had been abolished in the United States in the previous decade. Stories from American newspapers were frequently reproduced in British and Irish newspapers. These often related to political advances, the progress of the various Christian churches in gaining adherents among the 'freedmen,' education, racially motivated attacks and the activities of the *Ku Klux Klan* - a white supremacist terror organisation. One such item was this printed by *The Belfast News-Letter* on 30 March:

KU-KLUX IN MONTGOMERY COUNTY

A PUBLIC SCHOOL BROKEN UP AND THE TEACHERS DRIVEN OFF.

THE Houston (Texas) Daily Union *gives the following, which is possessed of local as well as general interest, the Mr. Murray referred to being a Belfast man, who left our town about eighteen months ago, where he had been employed for some years previous as assistant in a highly-respectable mercantile establishment:-*

"Just before going to press we received the communication which we publish below. The public school which has been broken up in Montgomery County by a well-known organisation of the Ku-Klux, was a coloured one, in Danville; it had 140 pupils, and has been taught for the last month and a week by Messrs. Swain and Murray, whose names are signed to the communication. They are quiet gentlemen and excellent teachers,

the same of whom Principal Cline spoke so highly after his recent visit to the schools of that county. They are Englishmen, but lately come to this country, and have no connection with our politics. Neither of them are naturalised citizens. They escaped for their lives, and do not intend to return. They are now in the city, and all that we here say can be verified by interviewing them. Their daily school register, neatly and excellently kept, is before us. They are excellent teachers, the school was very prosperous, and the coloured people were delighted.The Ku-Klux Giddings Democracy have now broken it up. A year or two since, in the same region, a band of men took a white man, who was teaching a coloured school, strapped him to a log, gave him two hundred lashes, and made him leave, declaring that they would hang him if he ever came back.

Yet, the poor, malignantly imbecile Telegraph *of this city, took great offence at the* Union, *a few days since, for giving the Montgomery County Democracy the credit (now clearly undeserved) of giving up their prejudices against public schools. There is a regularly organised band of the Ku-Klux Klan in Montgomery county, and their history is one of midnight violence, bloodshed, and murder. They whipped one school teacher, they murdered the brothers, William and Edward Jones, they kept several hundred coloured men from voting at the last election, they have now driven off two quiet and excellent foreign teachers, and broken up one of the finest schools in the State. It is all of a piece with the opposition to the school tax, the effort to frighten the judges into granting injunctions against its collection, and the bribing of the grand jury to indict the Governor. There is a conspiracy in Texas against both the Federal and State Governments inspired by damnable treason:-*

On Monday morning, 26th February, 1872, we received a strap, similar to those used in the time of slavery, by the hand of a coloured boy, said to be sent from Gary's store. In the evening, we took the unusual precaution in fastening the windows and locking the door.

On going to school the next morning, the 27th, we found the school house had been broken into, and could not open the door, on account of three benches being placed against it - one window being open, by which we suppose the parties had entered. A table belonging to the school we saw on the top of a tree near Thomson's old store. The blackboard was standing outside the school house with "K K K" in one corner, Ku Klux Klan, written across, and a head with the word "Death" in the opposite corner. One of the water buckets we found hung to a joist, and a joint of the stove pipe removed and placed in the stove.

[Signed]
HENRY SWAIN, Teacher.
THOS. N. MURRAY, Assistant.
Danville, Montgomery county, Texas. Tuesday evening, 27th February 1872.

Wednesday morning, 28th February. - We are informed this morning by some of the pupils that they found the school-door open and the benches scattered about in every direction, on their arrival there.

Other items were frivolous and intended to amuse readers, often featuring in columns featuring other 'funnies.' The following sample of articles and adverts from that year is small but representative of language that was permissible, acceptable and in common usage. They are frequently highly offensive, discriminatory and dehumanising. It will hopefully give an insight into the prejudice that George Henry Thompson suffered and the names that he was called, as this did not appear out of thin air. The prevalence of such words and stereotypes clearly filtered down to all sections of society whether people were literate or not. Of course, not all Black people were referred to in this manner, but the press clearly had free reign to use whatever terminology it liked in relation to them. This served to reinforce the idea of white racial supremacy which was the norm back then, and planted the seeds for ongoing racial prejudice and stereotypes in later times.

For the other examples from 1872 I will start with an English publication from my own city, the *Coventry Herald & Free Press*, dated 24 May. This featured in a column entitled *Varieties* which was intended to amuse its readers:

> *A negro woman was relating her experience to a gaping congregation of colour, and among other things she said she had been in heaven. One of the ladies of colour asked her, "Sister, did you see any black folks in heaven ?" - "Oh, get out, you s'pose I go in de kitchen when I was dar !" This reminds us of the anecdote of a coloured man, who was so convinced of the lowliness of his position, and that labour was his natural lot, that he was even indifferent as to a future state, believing that "dey'll make n****r work eben if he go to hebben." A clergyman tried to argue him out of this opinion, by representing that this could not be the case, inasmuch as there was absolutely no work for him to do in heaven. His answer was- "Oh, you g'way, massa; I know better. If dare's no work for culled folks up dare, dey'll make some fur 'em, and if dare's nothing better to do, dey'll make 'em shub de clouds along. You can't fool dis chile, massa."*

(Columns like this appeared in many newspapers across the U.K. often sharing the same 'amusing' tales.)

From Wales, we have this from the *South Wales Evening Telegram* of 17 July:

> *ON SUNDAY, at the registry office, Tredegar, two black men were united to a couple of Welsh maidens, and the novel ceremonial attracted large crowds, and all kinds of comments. The Cambrian lasses must be hard up indeed for husbands, if they were compelled to unite themselves to S**bos, because their own countrymen would not come forward to the rescue. We presume that if this practice be continued, we shall shortly have a race of Creoles, Quadroons, and Octoroons at Tredegar. Our American cousins recently burnt a woman alive in one of the Southern States, for marrying a black man, lynching the n****r to death. But the time is rapidly approaching when growing intelligence will banish forever all the differences of race, caste, and colour, and when the inhabitants of the world shall be all cosmopolitans.*

From Scotland, the *Greenock Telegraph and Clyde Shipping Gazette* printed this on 4 March:

> *A negro, passing along the street, was astonished to hear a voice call out, "How d'ye do, Massa Mungo? How d'ye do Snowball?" and, on looking, observed it proceeded from a parrot in a splendid gilt cage. "Ah Massa Parrot," said blackee, "you great man here - you lib in a great house now; but me know your fader very well; he lib in de bush."*

(As an aside, I was also able to find an almost identical version of this so-called 'funny' some 46 years earlier in the 30 June 1826 edition of the *Coventry Herald and Weekly Advertiser.* Mungo was the name of a character from an operatic play called *The Padlock* that dates back to 1768. He was a caricature of a Black servant in the West Indies based on racial stereotypes and Mungo itself was yet another term used for a Black person.)

From Ireland, published on 6 April in *The Nation*, which was Dublin's leading Catholic Nationalist newspaper:

With creditable rapidity "the master race" in the Southern States of America are providing themselves with a literature of their own, written of course from their own point of view. The following is extracted from a "Coloured Folk's Hymn Book" used in South Carolina :-

We's be nearer to de Lard
Den de white folks, and dey knows it;
See de glory-gate unbarred-
Walk in darkeys past de guard,
Bet yer dollar He won't close it!

Walk in darkey troo de gate,
Hark de kullered angels holler;
Go away, white folks, you're too late,
We's de winning kuller! Wait
Till the trumpet blow to foller!

Halleloojah! tanks to praise!
Long enuff we've borne our crosses;
Now we's de superior race,
And, wid Gorramighty's grace,
We's gwine to hebben afore de bosses.

(This 'song' was widely published in newspapers across the United Kingdom from 1865 onwards. The original version, with slightly different words, appears to have made its way over here from the *New York Tribune.* By 1869 it had been adapted to the words printed above, and the last time I could find it was in July 1887 when *The Dublin Weekly News* printed it.)

From the *The Waterford Citizen* of 5 January:

> *That the skin of the Ethiopian is tolerably secure from change has ever been an undisputed fact; yet, according to the most recent revelations of science, such is the case no longer. A San Francisco doctor has discovered a process by which a white man can be transformed into a negro, which is certainly no less remarkable than that the African should be converted into a white man. The surgical operation, that has become so common since its recent discovery, of transplanting a portion of skin from some other part of the body, or even from some other person, to an ulcer, for the purpose of starting a new growth*

> *of cuticle, was performed upon the arm of a white man of 25 years, and a ruddy complexion, the borrowed cuticle having been taken from the arm of a full blooded negro. The experiment was a success, so far as the ulcer was concerned; but to the horror of the victim, the black skin is spreading rapidly, and the pleasing probability is that he will soon become a negro. Of course a corresponding operation on a negro might go far toward making him what our Southern friends call "Caucasian."*

From a Dublin newspaper, *The Evening Telegraph* of 24 December, we also learn of a 'toy' that was on sale:

> *STANLEY'S DANCING N****R (by Steam) - (Causes Roars of Laughter)- Selling by Thousands. - This ingenious and laughable contrivance is very unique, the n****r-dancer being worked by a novel steam-engine constructed entirely of metal, and with polished brass works. When in motion the n****r dances in various graceful attitudes for one hour at each operation. Packed in boxes, with directions and carriage paid, for Four Shillings and Sixpence in stamps. From B. and E. McHugh and Co., 6,8,10 and 12 Rosemary-street, Belfast. N.B.- None genuine that does not bear our name in full.*

In music halls, theatres and circuses, troupes of professional minstrels performed. While some of these *were* Black people, others were white people in blackface, as were a host of 'n****r comedians' that also 'entertained' the crowds. In May, *Price's Christy Minstrels*, described as 'The only Ethiopian Troupe in existence that have had the distinguished honour of performing in front of H.R.H. the Prince of Wales,' were engaged for six nights at the Theatre Royal in Belfast. At the same time, a rival establishment, The Royal Alhambra in North Street, had *Dan Lowery's Troupe of Black Minstrels* performing as part of a variety show. *The Queen's Minstrels* performed at the Ulster Hall in July. They were managed by two of the original Christy Minstrels. According to the advertisements in local newspapers, they had performed for and delighted Queen Victoria and were hence termed the 'Queen's servants.' For one performance in Belfast they were accompanied by the band and pipers of the 78th Highlanders. The Victoria Hall hosted *Sam Hague's*

Minstrels in December. They were described as 'The original and only American Slave Troupe.'

Those engaged in amateur dramatics in towns and villages across the United Kingdom also performed as minstrels in community venues and gave their take on how they perceived Black people lived their lives and entertained themselves. An example of this from Ireland was reported in the *Mayo Examiner* of 1 January 1872. It gave a long account of a performance by *The Ballina Amateur Minstrels* in Castlebar a few days earlier on 26 December. The show was for the benefit of the poor relieved by the Sisters of Mercy in the town.

It included various songs, one of which was 'The Ten Little N****rs'. Mr. Tambo, played by Mr. Purcell, and Mr. Bones, played by Mr. Huie, were a big hit with the audience. Purcell played the tambourine 'in as grotesque and amusing a style as if he were initiated amongst the veritable 'n****rs.' His acting was undoubtedly first class.' As for Mr. Huie, '...delivery of the puns and dialogues, his "bones" accompaniment, and his general "make up," were refreshing, exhilarating and enjoyable.'

The account goes on to tell us, 'The N****r Interlude,' called 'Miss Lucy's Tea Party,' was highly amusing. The heroine of the piece was represented by Mr. J. R. Dudgeon, who made a dashing Ethiopian beauty - 'she had a highly polished ebony complexion, her hair done up in the latest fashion, and her dress panniered, flounced, and pinked to perfection. She was all smiles, suavity and gracefulness.' It seems that Miss Lucy had numerous admirers who she flirted with - Mr. Dudgeon's acting skills in this department were highly praised. This piece climaxed when *S**bo*, who was Miss Lucy's servant, comedically tumbled onto the stage and smashed some chinaware. This caused Miss Lucy to faint. The audience lapped this up, cheering and repeatedly applauding Mr. Dudgeon for his acting prowess.

The 'highly amusing entertainment' was concluded by a 'n****r break-down', with Messrs. Fleming and Huie 'doing the dance and walk round in capital style.'

The article ended by stating, 'The audience were so well pleased, that at any future time the Ballina Amateur Minstrels may visit us, they will get a hearty reception.'

This leads me on to a bizarre court case in Belfast. This was heard before J. C. O'Donnell, Esq., Resident Magistrate on Monday 8 January, and was reported in *The Northern Whig* the following day as:

AN "AMATEUR N****R" IN TROUBLE

Archibald Allison, a respectably-dressed young man, with one of his eyes closed up and swollen, and Anne Bond, a gaily dressed female, were brought up in the custody of Sub-Constable Adam Pickett, the former charged with having assaulted Robert H. Brown, and the latter with having assaulted Archibald Allison.

Mr. Harper appeared for Bond. Robert H. Browne (sic) on being called, did not appear. Mr. Harper said that the complainant, Brown, not appearing to prosecute, the prisoner Allison was entitled to his discharge. He understood that Allison did not intend to prosecute Bond, and therefore she was entitled to her discharge also.

*Mr. O'DONNELL wished to know the circumstances under which the arrests were made. Sub-Constable Adam Pickett deposed that on Sunday night the prisoner Allison drove on a car to the Donegall Street Police Barrack, and stated that his coat was in a house in Talbot Street and that it would not be given up to him. He stated that he had taken off his clothes in the house and dressed himself in a n****r's suit, and that when he went to put on his coat he could not find it. Witness went with him to the house in Talbot Street. Allison asked Bond for his coat, and she said she knew nothing about it. A young man named Robert H. Brown came down stairs. Allison asked him if he knew anything about his coat, and he said not. Allison then struck Brown, and the female prisoner struck Allison.*

*Mr. O'DONNELL - What is this n****r's dress you talk about?*

Mr. Coulter - The dress worn by persons on the stage who perform "darkey" characters.

Sub-Constable Pickett produced the wig and collar for his Worship's inspection, and said the head-dress, trousers, and long-tailed coat were in the police barrack.

Margaret Stewart said she kept the house in Talbot Street where the assaults were committed. She knew nothing about the prisoner until she came down stairs and saw him dressed like a black man. His face was blackened. He was carrying-on through the house, and she directed him to leave the place.

Allison - You assaulted me too.

Stewart - I gave you a slap with my hand and told you to get out.

*Allison - This girl (Bond) had on the n*****'s dress too. (Laughter.)*

Mr. O'DONNELL - Was it Annie Bond gave you that black eye?

Allison - It was.

Mr. O'DONNELL *-You don't wish to prosecute her?*

Allison - No.

Mr. O'DONNELL *said that as these assaults took place inside a house, even although in presence of a policeman, they were not to be treated as public offences; and the parties making the complaints declining to prosecute, he would discharge the prisoners.*

A car-man here came into the box, and said that Allison engaged him to drive him about the town on the previous evening. He had him upwards for three hours, and he had not yet been paid his fare. He had also lost time in attending the court that morning. Mr. O'DONNELL *directed Allison to pay the car-man 7s.*

As alluded to in some of the above accounts, another term used for Black people was Ethiopian, regardless of whether they were born there or not. This dated back many years, but the British had fought a military campaign there in the late 1860s, so the comings and goings of this country seemed to be of particular interest to the press during this period. At the Carlingford Lough Regatta of September 1872, held at Warrenpoint, *The Belfast Weekly News* reported that a 'Punt race by Ethiopians' took place, where a number of youths represented 'the sons of ebony.' It was a 'novel' competition and the boys on *The Alice* worked hard to win the first prize of £1.

The travels and travails in Africa of the famous missionary and explorer Dr. David Livingstone were also widely reported in the press at this time. I will end with a letter published on 25 October 1872 by *The Belfast News-Letter.*

THE SLAVE TRADE IS NOT YET ABOLISHED - IT STILL FLOURISHES - AND WHY?

TO THE EDITOR OF THE BELFAST NEWS-LETTER

Sir,

I herewith send you some extracts from the journal of Commander Hugh McNeile Dyer, of her Majesty's ship Torch, now cruising on the West Coast of Africa, whose statements I am sure will interest your intelligent readers, not only on account of the horrible doings of their native chiefs, and the terrible traffic in slaves being still carried on there in spite of the vigilance of our cruisers, but also on account of the civilising influence of good Bishop Crowther, who is himself a native African, and was released from a slave-ship on the middle passage, and carried back and educated in the colony of Sierra Leone by the Church Missionary Society, within my own memory.

On the 15th June he writes:- "We passed close to the dominions of the King of Dahomey - he resides at Abomey, about 100 miles inland. He is good enough to invite all Europeans residing in his territory to his annual 'custom' or 'festival.' At this 'custom' last year he sacrificed 1,500 human beings, most of them in a very cruel manner. The Europeans dare not disobey his order to appear, and they are expected, also, to show themselves pleased with his Majesty's attention to ornamenting their door-posts each morning with fresh cut human heads. There have been some vessels wrecked lately on his coasts, and Dahomey has appropriated all the cargoes, giving one half to his chiefs, and then asked for, and has received, a present for liberating the crews.

"June 18th. - The people who inhabit the country we are now passing are cannibals. Last year, Capt. Chapman, of H.M.S. Dido, got the great rival tribes of Bonney and New Calabar to promise to make peace and give up cannibalism. He impressed on Kings Ja Ja and Oko Jumbo that, if they wanted meat for food, bullocks were very cheap at Lagos, and could easily be brought to their rivers by the trading steamers. 'Ah! I know beefee, beefee.' said Oko Jumbo, 'him very good, but man beefee more better!' and he smacked his lips as if he longed for a little then and there. Oko Jumbo's men caught a man and his wife belonging to Ja Ja's tribe in a canoe with a cargo of yams. The canoe was instantly broken up, a fire made of her, at which the united pair were roasted, the yams boiled, and the Oko Jumbians enjoyed their picnic as a great joke!"

On the other hand he writes:- "Lagos, June 22nd.- Once inside the bar, a magnificent harbour opens before us, large enough and deep enough for all the ships in the world. The town of Lagos is built on an island on the right side of the river as you enter. From the water it has a very picturesque appearance. None but the European portion is to be seen at first. This consists principally of stuccoed houses - two and three stories high - shingled and slated, surrounded with verandas, and standing in separate gardens or compounds. These houses extend along the river bank for about a mile and a half and have a broad road in front of them, bordered with shady trees. There are several wharfs running out from this road. On the Marina, alongside which several vessels were loading palm oil, kernels, and other produce, I saw several well-stocked stores or shops, two churches, and one large one in course of construction (to hold 1,500 people), and some substantial public offices. I went to the place where my brother John was killed, a gallant youth, an officer in Her Majesty's Navy, who was shot through the head while leading his men in a storming party against Lagos, which was then in possession of slave-dealers. The spot was pointed out to me by Captain Davies, who was on board the Volcano at the time of the action. He is now a wealthy merchant, living in comfortable style. He is married to Bonetta Forbes, a young lady who was brought to England by Capt. Forbes, of H.M.S. Bonetta, and taken under our Queen's protection. Her Majesty had her educated, and, after she married, became godmother to her eldest child. Her face bears the marks of the knife, which ornaments all Dahomians. I called on Bishop Crowther and had a most interesting conversation with him relative to the Niger. He says he is everywhere well received in that territory, as he knows their different dialects; that his settlements and mission stations were prosperous, and his schools full. He showed me several oil mills he is going to take with him up the Niger in July, and called them his civilisers. I was glad to learn from the Bishop that the Church Missionary Society, under which he works, teach all their pupils how to employ themselves usefully after they have received their religious and secular education. There are 35,000 inhabitants in the native town of Lagos, yet it is very quiet and orderly. One magistrate disposes of all the cases brought before him in less than an hour each day, and the police are very few. There is no doubt that Lagos will be the Liverpool of West Africa in the prosperous days that are evidently in store for this great country. It has internal water communication with an immense tract of oil producing country. One of the branches of the Niger enters the Lagoon, and already forwards British produce to Timbuctoo and the distant interior. And this place twenty years ago was a mangrove swamp, on which not a European resided. The native town was then about half its present size, and the hotbed of slavery.

Now, what is it, do you think, that continues to support the slavery and cannibalism described by Capt. Dyer, and that also retards the civilisation of the country by the good bishop; Mr. Laird, M.P., of Birkenhead; and others ? Nothing but our continuing to purchase, to import, and to use the slave-made sugar from Cuba and other Spanish and Portuguese West Indian colonies. The simple measure of prohibiting this importation would at once put down this infamous and murderous traffic; for, if we would only cease to buy the sugar, slavery must become unprofitable, and, of course, die a natural death. I remember the agitation that was kept up against the use of slave sugar, before Britain had consented to emancipate her slaves, at the expense to the nation of £20,000,000 sterling. But our legislators, after expending this large sum, have persisted in compelling us to buy the sugar ever since, by their allowing it to be mixed and imported, with the free sugar of our own West Indian colonies.

The Society of Friends took a leading part at the time in getting up petitions, and Presbyterians, Methodists, and Episcopalians heartily joined them in the good work; and, as we now find that the slavers are as actively at work as they ever were, a renewed agitation is required to put a stop to it. And which of all the above parties will now be first to take it up, and immortalise themselves by prosecuting it to a successful issue ?

*I was told, on undoubted authority, that the Messrs. Bewley, the eminent sugar refiners of Dublin, actually turned out a dead negro from one of their imported hogsheads!** I am quite sure that Jamaica never produced that sample of their manufacture.*

Yours truly,
JAMES HART.
27, Franklin Street, Oct. 18, 1872.

** A Hogshead was the name of a large barrel that was filled with sugar.

(After leaving the navy, Captain Hugh McNeile Dyer was appointed Governor of Kilmainham Gaol, Dublin, in April 1874. He was not long in the job when he died from inflammation of the lungs on 3 January 1875, aged 42. James Hart was a Belfast Town Councillor for Cromac Ward at the time he wrote this letter.)

6.
DICK TURPIN'S RIDE TO YORK

Prior to the rioting, is there any recorded evidence of George Henry Thompson being in Belfast? The answer is yes. The first definite account that I was able to find in the newspapers is from the *The Belfast News-Letter* and appeared on Tuesday 27 February 1872. The name is given as George Thompson, but given the location and the year that it took place, this is clearly the same person as George Henry Thompson:

CUSTODY COURT - Yesterday

Before DAVID TAYLOR Esq., J.P., and Dr. McGEE, J.P.

A COLOURED FIGHT

Arthur McIntyre, a white man, and George Thompson, a black man, were brought up in custody, charged by Sub-Constable Forbes with fighting on Saturday evening in Townsend Street.

Complainant proved the charge, and deposed that the prisoners' conduct being so disorderly, a large crowd was collected round them.

Thompson stated that McIntyre struck him first. McIntyre, who had been previously convicted twice, was fined 20s and costs, or 14 days in jail, and Thompson was discharged.

As we can see, the colour of George's skin was sufficient to induce the 'A Coloured Fight' headline but compared to some of the examples of how newspapers referred to Black people in this period it is tame by comparison. The account suggests he had a fair hearing as he was discharged. One can only speculate as to why he was involved in a street fight, but from the account given it seems he reacted to an unprovoked attack. The presence of a large crowd gathered round them possibly suggests it may have been a fight for money but we will never know for certain; neither party would have ever admitted that to the police or court if this was the case. Much more must have been said in the courtroom but sadly the report is just a summary of proceedings.

Townsend Street was and still is a road that links the Shankill and Falls districts. Nowadays a security gate divides it in two and the dominant landmark is the imposing former Townsend Street Presbyterian Church. This closed for worship in 2022, with the final sermon being preached on 11 September. A farewell message posted on its facebook page on 14 September of that year reads:

The Lord be with your spirit. Grace be with you.
(2 Timothy 4:22).

At the time of writing, the building is being used by the Ulster Orchestra. The Shankill side of the gate no longer has any residential properties. Where homes and businesses once stood in a street that was filled with the hustle and bustle of daily life, there are large patches of wasteland, and sadly, in an area that is crying out for much needed social housing, this has been the case for decades. The other side of the gate is mainly business premises with some homes along it near to its junction with Divis Street.

For the next account of George Henry Thompson in Belfast before his appearances in the dock related to the riots, we will jump forward in time to 1933; but before doing that we first have to travel back nearly 100 years prior to that - 1833 - to give some context to what unfolds. In May of that year, a book called 'Rookwood, A romance,' was published. It was written by William Harrison Ainsworth. Part of it, 'Dick Turpin's Ride to York,' was published in many newspapers not long afterwards. This related to the legendary highwayman Richard Turpin - better known to history as Dick Turpin, who was a notorious criminal in the 1700s and is most well-known for robbing people on highways as they travelled in horse drawn carriages. These would be held-up at gunpoint and the occupants robbed of their valuables. He was eventually caught, convicted and hanged at York in April 1739. His antics soon became legendary and were romanticised by later generations.

Ainsworth's fictionalised account, has Dick Turpin riding his horse, 'Black Bess,' on an epic almost non-stop 200 mile journey from London to York. All the time they were being closely pursued. After narrow escapes and overcoming many obstacles, they eventually made it to within sight of York, but as the new day dawned and the bell of the Minster tolled out the hour of six, the heroic horse breathed her last and died of exhaustion. She was a pure black horse without a white hair on her body and the star of the story.

The widespread coverage meant it became hugely popular and it wasn't long before the tale was converted into an equestrian show of the same name that was performed at amphitheatres and travelling circuses - *Astley's Amphitheatre* in London appears to have been the first to do this in June 1834. Ten years later there are accounts of *Batty's Olympic Circus* performing 'Dick Turpin's Ride to York' in Ireland at places such as Cork. Over the following decades it became a staple of circus performances across the British Isles. The star of the show was always Black Bess, or Bonny Black Bess, which was played by a highly trained horse.

In April 1871, *Batty's Model Circus* staged its first production of it in Belfast, and it was again part of their show in the town in February 1872. In early July of 1872, the prestigious new Theatre Royal in Belfast, which had opened in September of the previous year, was the venue for yet another version of this clearly popular story. (This theatre was the second of three Theatre Royal's that once stood at the corner of Arthur Square and Castle Lane.)

These performances were by Mr. Henry Powell and his *London Dramatic Company*. The proprietor and manager of the theatre, Mr. J. F. Warden, engaged Powell and his company for eleven nights which began on 25 June. They performed various pieces during this time, with 'Dick Turpin's Ride to York' - starring a thoroughbred mare appropriately enough called Black Bess, playing the part of her namesake and Powell himself in the role of the highwayman - making its appearance in July as the engagement came to an end. Admission prices were: Private Boxes, 40 and 30 shilling; Lower Boxes, 4 shillings; Upper Boxes, 2 shillings; Pit, 1 shilling; Gallery, 6d.

Our story now fast forwards to Saturday 25 March 1933 and a remarkable article that was published in *Ireland's Saturday Night*:

A BELFAST SHOW OF THE SEVENTIES

1^D^ TO GALLERY: 2^D^ TO PIT.

AN AUSTRALIAN'S MEMORIES.

Writing from the Bendigo district of Victoria, Australia, W. B., a Belfastman (who in a postscript confesses that he is still hunting for the pot of gold at the end of the rainbow), recalls in an amusing fashion one of the entertainments in his home town in the 'seventies. He writes:-

Sir,

On reading the article in your paper about Stage Ghosts, I wondered how many of the boys are left in Belfast who used to go to McCormick's Show. It was a little caravan that travelled through the country, but had settled in an empty allotment for the winter and built a temporary theatre, with a gallery like steps and stairs where the audience stood. It must have held 100 or more. Then there was the pit - a few hard benches to sit on. The admission fee was 1d for the gallery; 2d for the pit. It was in the middle 'seventies. They showed two houses each night and three on Saturday.

The principal performers were Mrs. McCormick, all the time in knee breeches, long stockings, short tailed coat, and soft hat. Her stage name was "Aul' Andrew Mucklestone," and it was a good thing to see her clearing out the first house to make room for the second. Any laggards were told "to get out or I'll shift ye." Her man played the dulcimer.

The leading lady had a very hoarse voice, so she was christened "Rusty Thrapple." Then there was the stage-manager, who had left a show called The Minor. He made a speech, telling us all he intended to make McCormick's Show better than The Minor. He strutted on stage with long yellow boots turned down at the top, tight knit breeches, doublet and hat with a feather.*

There was, in 1872, a West Indian negro in the show. His name was George Thompson. Poor George got 9 months for leading in the riots, and died shortly after he came out of the "clink." But the play was the thing - Hamlet, and the Death of Maria Marten. When poor Maria came out as a ghost, with a semi-white sheet around her and blood on it, too, the audience held their breaths and were afraid to go home - those of them who lived near Springfield for fear of the ghost.

The night that Dick Turpin and His Ride to York was put on, the house was crowded. Mrs. McCormick was Dick Turpin and the negro, George Thompson, was Black Bess. When they galloped on to the stage, with Dick on the back of the negro, Black Bess, it brought the house down; also when they stuck up the lady and gentleman travelling on the highway and Dick robbed them of their gold repeaters, but gave the lady back her purse - the chivalry was boisterously applauded. Of course the lady and gentleman were old "Rusty Thrapple" and the stage-manager. Sometimes the negro gave a plantation break down and some of the big fellows sang a song, and everyone was happy. The only trouble was to raise the penny to get into the show.

* *The Minor* was another theatre that was located nearby which seems to have been located between the Old Lodge Road and Peter's Hill. It operated very much like McCormick's Show with a similar audience and admission prices.

There is a lot to unpack in that letter. The author is recalling what was known as a 'Penny Theatre,' and little is recorded of these establishments in contemporary press articles. What information there is, generally labels them as low brow dens of infamy which attracted crowds of very rough people and exerted a bad influence on young people. Children, according to the detractors, often formed a large part of the audience and stole the pennies needed to get in.

Another way of describing them would be to say they were a cheaper alternative to the established theatres which enabled the working class population to see well known plays and the like - albeit with much lower production values, a handful of actors and a lot of improvisation.

How George Thompson came to be part of this particular theatre one can only speculate, but he seems to have had acting and dancing skills and could command an audience. If there were limited opportunities for him as a Black man in Belfast, taking up such a role would be one way of earning money, and as we have seen, minstrel shows were extremely popular. Learning routines from these and playing up to the stereotypes of Black people that the white audiences of Belfast expected to see probably wasn't too difficult for him, and he could have just improvised by devising his own routines - who in the audience would have known any different? He also had the huge advantage of actually being a Black person which would have added authenticity to his performances. Literally playing the role of a black horse because he was a Black man was admittedly a deviation from singing and dancing, but it wasn't much of one for back then when anything was permissible. It also suggests George had a great sense of humour. The audience lapped it up and it was clearly memorable for those who witnessed the spectacle. It also suggests he was a physically strong person if Mrs. McCormick was on his back.

The letter writer states that George was a West Indian. His nationality will come up again later, as will the prison sentence he actually received and whether he died or not after leaving the 'clink'.

Can we accurately date this performance? Not precisely, but if the same show was being performed in Belfast during February and again in early July, it probably indicates this approximation of it was taking place at the same time as either of these. What more can we learn about McCormick's Show ?

On Saturday 28 December 1872, a very disturbing case of domestic violence was reported in the *The Belfast News-Letter:*

POLICE NEWS
CUSTODY COURT - YESTERDAY
[Before J. C. O'DONNELL, Esq., R. M.]
A MUSICIAN AND HIS WIFE
John McCormack, a wandering minstrel, was put forward at the suit of his wife, Mary Ann McCormack, on the charge of ill-using and assaulting her.
The prosecutrix appeared in the witness-box with a black eye, and with her features so disfigured otherwise that further evidence was unnecessary to establish the charge. She stated that she had been married six years, during which time she had been a faithful attendant on the steps of her husband, whose profession led him about from place to place. Their earnings were not stationary, but depended on the impression created on the public by the Orphean powers of her partner. They had four of a family.
The COURT deprived the public of the privilege of listening to the musician for a while again, by sentencing him to four months' imprisonment with hard labour.

In all probability this must have been the couple who ran McCormick's Show. McCormick, McCormac and McCormack are all variations of the same surname and used interchangeably in relation to this theatre / travelling show.

It is highly probable that this improvised theatre was located in the Shankill district. Later accounts recalling it certainly place it there. *Ireland's Saturday Night*, known as 'The Pink' gives many of these. On 21 April 1928, in an article called *THE GOLDEN AGE: MEMORIES OF OLD BELFAST*, this was included:

> *… But give me "McCormack's Show" every time. It was situate about Townsend Street. Ye gods! That was some entertainment. The orchestra consisted of a piano and a violin - alas! poor Gusty - virtuoso! (he was the violinist). You are gone this many a day. You did your very utmost. I know, to keep the peace between the audience and the performers. It was a hard job. Those were the days of "mashers" and the peak-and-muffler brigade, and it was the danger of your life to enter "McCormack's Show" wearing a collar and tie!*

Townsend Street is of course where George Thompson was arrested for fighting with Arthur McIntyre in February 1872. Later it seems to have found a more permanent home in Conlon Street which was off the Old Lodge Road.

As an aside, I will try and shed some light on the 'Springfield ghost' mentioned in the letter from Australia. I suspect this ghost may be the same one as the 'Falls Road ghost' which is mentioned in some newspaper accounts in late 1872.

In its edition published on Thursday 5 December, *The Daily Examiner* tells us in a light-hearted way that the Falls Road ghost had been the subject of conversation for many weeks and young people in particular were convinced it existed; they believed it was the ghost of a rioter that wore a sou'wester hat, clutched paving stones in its bony hands, had a blood-besmeared aspect and made wild gesticulations. The writer of the piece joked that the Royal Irish Constabulary were terrified of it, but that on the whole, most reports suggested it was a well behaved ghost. Its movements were uncertain and eccentric but it usually operated from the brickfields at the Model School up to the Springfield Road. It concluded by saying:

> *It is consoling that, at all events in the matter of ghosts, we are no longer to be outdone by England.*

This was probably a reference to sensational stories about a ghost in the Peckham area of London which were circulating in 1871 and again from June 1872 until early December when a man was arrested. It seems he dressed in white and had been scaring people in lonely places by throwing his arms up and making strange noises. Additionally this 'ghost' threw peas at windows and generally made a nuisance of himself.

The next mention of the Falls Road ghost was in *The Belfast Weekly News* of Saturday 21 December:

CUSTODY COURT - THURSDAY
[Before EDWARD ORME, Esq., R.M.]
THE FALLS ROAD GHOST
A man named Alexander McGlone was charged by Sub-Constable Murphy with being disorderly on the Falls Road on the previous evening.
The constable said that he was brandishing a putty knife in front of some girls who were passing.

Prisoner - I am a glazier, and when I was going home I heard the girls say something about the Falls Road ghost coming, and I just had the knife in my hand.
Mr. ORME - You were going to fight the ghost with a putty knife. You are a gallant fellow. (Laughter.) You must pay 20s and costs.

This was the last mention I could find of the ghost.

7.
THE SONS OF WILLIAM

In September 1872, George Henry Thompson was arrested in Ligoniel, which was then an expanding mill village and townland just outside the north western edge of Belfast. He was brought before the Custody Court on 12 September, and appeared in front of Mr. J. C. O'Donnell, Resident Magistrate. He was charged with being one of a riotous mob and house wrecking on Sunday 18 August. Alongside him in the dock was a William Watkins or Wilkins (who becomes William Waterworth in reports of later hearings.)

Many of the newspaper reports about this first appearance in court mention the colour of his skin in their headlines, using expressions such as 'a man of colour' or 'a coloured man'.

Mr. McLean, Junior, conducted the prosecution and Mr. Steele the defence for George and also Watkins. Sub-Constables Andrew Doherty and Gilbert Hasley gave evidence stating that they both saw him on 18 August. He was at the head of a mob of 2,000 people in both Crimea Street and the Shankill Road. On the road, Doherty alleged he was waving a stick over his head. Hasley made no mention of a stick but said George was shouting "Come on ye sons of William!"* The magistrate asked who the 'sons of William' were and was told they were 'low roughs' (hooligans of the worst order), and in the opinion of the police they were out to create terror rather than defend the area from rival Catholic mobs. The police also said that in Crimea Street, he was seen entering a number of houses where after being visited, the occupants promptly left.

Margaret Donaghy (also called Donegan in reports) stated that on 18 August she lived in Crimea Street and now resided in Inkerman Street, Falls Road. A Black man and two other men had entered her house in Crimea Street and the Black man stated that he was looking for Fenians - or in some accounts five Fenians. Mrs. Donaghy replied she had nothing to make Fenians of but her young daughters. The man went to go upstairs to conduct a search but ultimately didn't and he and the others left the house.

Although she said she was "near frightened to death" by the intrusion, she stated that the Black man had not threatened her, told her the house would be wrecked or told her to leave. She was asked if the prisoner in the dock was the man who had entered her home. She wasn't certain but said she thought so. She was then asked if he was a chimney sweep or a man of colour. This question had previously been asked of one of the police constables - Andrew Doherty - who had replied that he was a man of colour and not a sweep. Mrs. Donaghy replied that the constable had said it was a man of colour. Asked if she had left her house after the Black man had visited she replied "no", but stated that afterwards, another "respectable looking" man had come in and informed her that the house was to be wrecked and that she had two hours to leave. At 2 o'clock in the morning on 19 August, the mob arrived and Margaret and her family fled over the yard wall into the safety of a neighbours house. Asked when she had returned home after this she said she had no home to go back to - it was all wrecked with everything broken and smashed.

At this point George's solicitor Mr. Steele clearly realised the arguments to have him convicted or put on trial for house wrecking didn't have a leg to stand on based on the evidence presented so far. So, for good measure, he got Margaret to confirm:

> *"The prisoner was not the man that wanted me to leave my house because it was to be wrecked. I cannot say for certain if the prisoner is the man who came into my house, but it is very like him. It might have been a sweep, but I am almost sure it was a black man. When he came into the house there was no one in the house but myself and my two little girls."*

A boy named Keatley was then called to give evidence. On 18 August he said he saw the Black man go into Mrs. Donaghy's but that he came out again quietly. In his opinion he was under the influence of drink. When he came out she threw a grape at him and swore. This is the first we hear of a grape** which was the local name for a three or four pronged fork or pitchfork. It was commonly used for cultivating potatoes and could also be used as a weapon. Mr. O'Donnell interjected to ask Margaret if the grape had been wrung from her hand. He is told that she took up the grape to defend her home and some of the men had taken it from her and threw it over the railings outside the door.

Constable Doherty is asked how many homes have been wrecked in Crimea Street and replies twenty. Another report has him saying twenty families have been put out so this could be a mix up with the reporting for one or the other statements.

No account is given of the 'defence' to the allegations but we can assume everything was denied. I will hazard a guess that his solicitor said something along the lines of that he was walking from Ligoniel to Millfield and was not involved with any mob. That he did not enter Margaret Donaghy's house or any other abode, and had been confused with a chimney sweep. The chimney sweep defence may sound ridiculous and offensive to modern ears, but given the lack of other Black people in the town, it probably made sense from a defence point of view. Mr. Steele also told the court of a letter received from his employer, a Mr. Martin of Ligoniel, which stated that George was an 'exceedingly well conducted man' and 'must have been labouring under some excitement if he committed the acts charged against him.'

So we have another little clue about George Henry Thompson's life in Belfast - at the time of his arrest he worked in the mill village just outside the town - or somewhere in the area that was classed as Ligoniel at that time. Mr. Martin either genuinely thought very highly of him or was simply doing his best to lessen the impact of any potential sentence should he be found guilty.

Why was he going to Millfield? Did he live there? Was it part of his work duties? Was he on an errand? If it was work related would he really have been sent out by his employer when a state of chaos existed in Belfast? Answering a question from George's solicitor, Constable Doherty had stated that in his opinion the direct route from Ligoniel to Millfield had not been taken, and George had gone considerably out of his way to be in Crimea Street. While it may be true that loitering in Crimea Street was certainly off the beaten track for that journey, coming down the Shankill Road or cutting across that area from Crumlin Road as part of that journey was a perfectly viable option to reach Millfield at that time.

Who was this Mr. Martin? Was he another theatrical impresario? Or could it have been a John Martin who was a spirit grocer and beer dealer who can be found in newspaper reports from roughly the same period? At the Belfast Police Court on Thursday 14 November 1867, John Martin,

Beer Dealer, of Ligoniel, was summoned by Sub-Constable Hawe for having harboured on his premises a number of people for the purpose of drinking. He was fined £2 which was mitigated to 10 shillings and 10 shillings costs.[1]

The same person appears to have been routinely turned down by the courts in Belfast whenever he did apply for a full licence to become a legitimate public house - an example being a refusal of a 'new licence' for a John Martin, Ligoniel, which was heard at the Belfast Quarter Sessions on Thursday 21 October 1869.[2] He was refused again at the next Quarter Sessions held in early January 1870,[3] and also at the Quarter Sessions held in April[4] and July[5] of the same year. In November 1872 another application for the same venue was made, albeit this time the applicant was a man called James Begg, who stated that he had previously been a messman in the 78th Regiment and was always of good character. Constable Hawe made another appearance and stated:

> *I am stationed in Ligoniel. I know this house. An application has been frequently made to this Court by a person named Martin. It was refused about three times… We have got three public houses in Ligoniel. There are three between Ligoniel and Belfast, and two on the other side of Ligoniel.*

The application was refused.[6] Interestingly, a Mr. Harper represented James Begg. He makes an appearance at George's second hearing as part of the defence team.

I also found a Mary Martin being involved in two court cases for drunkenness on and near the premises. The first was heard at the Ligoniel Petty Sessions on 25 September 1872 before Dr. McGee, J.P. and Samuel Archer, Esq., J.P. The *Belfast Evening Telegraph* reported the proceedings as follows:

A BEER CASE

Mary Martin was brought before the magistrates by the police on two charges, one of harbouring persons in her house in Ligoniel, and the other with having permitted drunkenness in her house in Ligoniel on the 15th inst.

Mr. Harper appeared for the defendant.

The evidence for the prosecution went to show that a woman named McCormack had been arrested for drunkenness on the streets, and it was reported that she got the drink in Martin's house.

Mr. HARPER *argued for the defence that there was no case if it could not be proved that the police actually found the persons in the house or saw them coming out of it. They had not done so in this case.*

Dr. McGEE *suggested the withdrawal of this charge, but would proceed with the next, the police not being able to sustain it with facility. On the suggestion of* Dr. McGee *both charges were withdrawn, and the defendant cautioned.*

DRUNK IN THE HOUSE.

Two women named Mary Bouter and Dorothea Riddel were summoned for having been drunk while on the premises of the last defendant on the same date.

Dr. McGEE *considered that it would be hardly fair to them to convict them alone on the evidence of a woman (Mrs. McCormack) who was along with them and was as bad themselves, and discharged them on paying the costs.*

Some things to note from this are that the date is in the right time frame for George possibly working at the same place, Mr. Harper is representing her and intriguingly we have a Mrs. McCormack - could this be Mrs. McCormack from the Penny Theatre that George performed at ? Were the Martin's and the McCormack's acquainted with each other and was George working for both of them? Or had the proprietors of the Penny Theatre recommended him to the Martin's or vice versa? This case was only three days after his first court appearance on 12 September. Sadly we will probably never know and can only speculate.

Mary Martin made another appearance at the Ligoniel Petty Sessions on 26 February 1873, where she was described as a Spirit Grocer and had been summoned for 'permitting drunkenness and quarrelsome and riotous behaviour on her premises' on 14 February. She was again represented by Mr. Harper, and soldiers from the 78th Highlanders were on the premises during this incident.[7]

A 'Spirit Grocery' was effectively a public house which may also have sold regular grocery provisions as well as beer and spirits. I am not totally sure of the differences between them and a licensed public house but it seems many of them flaunted whatever rules applied to them - the licensing laws changed in 1872 as well to add confusion to this matter. A court case from

3 June 1870, which was reported in *The Belfast Morning News* on 6 June 1870, illustrates how Justice O'Donnell felt about spirit grocers:

SPIRIT-GROCERS AND BAD WHISKEY

Sophia Short was charged with having been drunk and disorderly on the public street at an early hour on that morning.

Head-Constable Lamb said that, after the prisoner was lodged in the Police Office, she became so ill that he was obliged to send for a doctor to examine her. She was suffering from the effects of bad whiskey, which she had obtained in some of the night houses.

Mr. O'DONNELL said he had been making inquiries lately, and he had ascertained that the result of restricting the granting of licences to public houses had been a great increase of spirit-groceries and shebeens, which were kept open all night, and were the cause of a great deal of misery to those who frequented them. It was also a matter of fact that, when the licensed publican was seldom summoned for breaches of the Spirit Act, the magistrates were engaged every Thursday in investigating the cases, numbering, on an average, about twenty, which were weekly bought by the police against the beer retailers and night-house keepers. He believed that, just as licensed public houses decreased in any locality the number of night-houses increased. As an instance of this, he might mention that in Union Street, a short time since, there were six public houses, no spirit-grocers, and only one or two houses of ill-fame. Now, there were only three public houses; but there were also seven or eight spirit-grocers, and seventeen houses of ill-fame; so the constabulary had informed him.

The publicans generally obeyed the law, and were under the control of the police, and must close their houses at a certain hour. The spirit-grocers constantly violated the law, defied the police, and kept their houses open - many of them all night; besides, they sold the most deleterious stuff, as he (Mr. O'Donnell) was often told, there - drink that maddened rather than intoxicated men's brains. He was not to be understood, however, as desirous of seeing the number of public houses increased as a matter of abstract opinion, but when he saw that the restriction of those licences led to the increase of spirit-grocers and beer-dealers, he preferred the lesser of two evils.

The Prisoner was discharged with a caution.

If George *was* employed at what was effectively a public house then what was his role? I suspect it may well have been to primarily provide amusement to the customers - this being the stereotyped Black 'entertainment' that people had been conditioned to expect from the minstrel shows at regular theatres and George's own performances at McCormick's Show, which was just down the road from Ligoniel. So he could have been singing, dancing, giving comedic stump speeches etc. He probably carried out more conventional duties such as serving people, moving beer barrels and the like, and if he *was* a physically imposing person, then he may also have acted as security for the premises - turfing out drunkards and other problem customers.

Returning to his hearing, Mr. John Charles O'Donnell,[8] was not impressed with the police's evidence and criticised how they had put the case forward. Like George's solicitor, he had noted the abject failure to prove the house wrecking charge. He was satisfied there was a case against him for 'heading a tumultuous assembly' and 'terrifying the poor woman.' He said he would remand him in custody to give the police more time to build a case. The police told him it was difficult to get witnesses to come forward in cases like this. Constable Doherty claimed that "he saw people obliged to hide from the prisoner, as they were afraid of their lives of him." O'Donnell said they could compel witnesses to come forward and if they didn't there was a serious penalty for refusal.

The magistrate then went on a tirade about house wreckers which included "a fellow like that (George) encouraging the 'sons of William' to come on and wreck houses, thus dragging a historic name in the dust! More crime of that nature - loss of life, loss of property - has been committed in a week than was committed all over the country by those laws in nine or ten years. It has got so common that people seem to notice it as anything but extraordinary. If such a thing as this occurred in Westmeath, what would be said?"

So much for the impartiality of the bench! It seems he had clearly already decided that George Henry Thompson *was* guilty of ordering people to quit their homes and what did 'a fellow like that' mean exactly? Was it related to the colour of his skin maybe? Also it has to be noted that no independent witnesses appeared at this stage to corroborate the police claims that George was leading the mob; shouting "Come on ye sons of William" and waving a stick in the air. No claim is made at this hearing that he was being carried on the shoulders of two men at the head of the mob either.

* Also reported as "Come on sons of William" and "Come on my sons of William."

** A more common spelling for this is graip or graipe.

8.
THE WOODEN COCKROACH

There was an old woman
Who lived in a lamp,
She had no room
To beetle her champ.

So she up'd with the beetle
And broke the lamp,
And now she has room
To beetle her champ

Traditional Irish nursery rhyme.

'Champ' is a popular mashed potato dish in Ulster usually made with butter and scallions (spring onions). Nettles can be used instead of scallions and other versions mentioned in old newspaper articles include recipes for parsley, green pea and also broad-bean champ.

The custody court proceedings then continued and this is where we first hear about the infamous 'cockroach' incident mentioned in HWIB. Or rather we don't. No cockroach - bloody or otherwise - was actually involved. Exactly where Andrew Boyd got this information from one can only speculate. It certainly isn't in any of the contemporary newspapers that reported the case - Catholic, Protestant or non-partisan.

The young boy Keatley gave evidence again and said that on Monday 19 August he saw some parties about Mrs. Donaghy's house and heard some shouting about a beetle but could not tell the nature of it as he went away to assist a man removing furniture from the Shankill Road. We then hear again from Margaret who in the forenoon (morning) of 19 August, is surveying the scene of her wrecked home. A man forced his way in, seized a beetle and said he would make her swallow it if she did not curse the Pope.

To quote *The Daily Examiner* report about this, which remember was a Catholic Nationalist publication:

> *She would not do so, and* ***he then commenced and smashed with the beetle everything which had escaped the previous wrecking*** *(my emphasis). The constable said that he had that morning arrested a man on a charge of being concerned in the matter. The man being in court, he was put into the dock.*

The Belfast News-Letter, a publication aimed at a Protestant readership, printed an identical account. Let's take a moment to ponder on this: how on earth could you smash anything up with a cockroach or any other beetle of the insect variety?!

Throughout the reports concerning this incident, a beetle is *always* mentioned. So could the beetle have been something other than an insect? Well, a beetle was the well known name in Ireland for a large wooden potato pounder / masher which was shaped like a club. Another term for mashing potatoes was 'beetling'. It could of course be used for pounding other food too. The fact that there are reports stating it was used to smash up anything that had survived the house wrecking confirms that it was in fact a wooden beetle and definitely *not* an insect. It actually featured regularly in court cases of that period when it had been used as a weapon. Here are some examples:

The Belfast News-Letter, 6 September 1867:
"Anne Arthurs, a respectable-looking dame, of Samuel Street, charged James Conway, a pensioner, with assaulting her in her own house. By way of "a set-off," Charlotte Mercer, daughter-in-law of Conway, charged Isabella Arthurs, daughter of Anne Arthurs, with striking her on the eye with a ***beetle****."*

The Newry Reporter, 20 January 1870:
"...Bridget Crommie was next called by Mr. Browne. She proved that Tom Colligan struck McGuigan with a ***beetle*** *three or four times. Mrs. Colligan attacked her, and attempted to stop her from shouting for assistance."*

The Belfast News-Letter, 23 November 1870:
'Ellen Markey was brought up in custody of Sub-Constable Scott, charged with assaulting a woman named Sophia McLenaghan, in Nerney's Place, off Cromac Street.

Sophia McLenaghan deposed that the prisoner struck her violently on the head with a ***beetle****. The prisoner was remanded for a week."*

The Belfast News-Letter, 8 December 1882:

"...The woman who was afterwards shot was a daughter of McCormack's. Condy McCormack did all he could to effect a rescue before we saw Mary Doherty, and then, after we drove the cow on for some distance, we saw that woman. She had a stick in her hand, and she stood before us and said she would not give up the cow. She then drew a ***beetle*** *from her under her jacket and endeavoured to attract the neighbours. Bridget McCormack, who was also present, said, "We will kill him; he is long enough serving processes and executing decrees, and we are long enough expecting to get him in this place." Mary Doherty then commenced to strike my brother with the* ***beetle*** *and stick. He said, "I am giving you a warning to stand out. I will serve a process for the landlord and everybody else in spite of you." I then drove down the cow, and when my back was turned I heard the report of a shot. I turned round and saw the two scolding and she battering him with the* ***beetle****."*

Of course, it would have been a far more *horrific* experience for Margaret if this potato mashing 'beetle' *had* been forced down her throat - an insect would have been more preferable in those circumstances I suspect! She would have likely choked to death.

The person accused of being responsible, who is named as 'William Watkins' (William Waterworth) is discharged through a lack of evidence. Although he was discharged for this crime, he was remanded in custody on the charge of being part of a riotous mob on 18 August. He appeared again directly after George's next appearance in court on 19 September. It seems he and Thompson were in the dock together at these hearings because of separate events at Margaret's house which the police had incorrectly thought involved the same culprits. Watkins/Waterworth was not with George when he entered her home on 18 August and George was not with Watkins/Waterworth when he entered her home on 19 August.

In the newspaper reports about this next appearance, William Watkins is now named as George Waterwork in the *The Daily Examiner*, John Waterworth in the *Belfast Evening Telegraph* and William Waterworth in the *The Northern Whig* and *The Belfast News-Letter*. So I will call him William Waterworth from now on.

This time, Rose McKelvey, who we will hear from again at George's next hearing in Chapter 8, gave evidence about the incident. She said that on 19 August the prisoner went in through the window and came out with a book which he tore. He then went in and got a beetle and caught Mrs. Donaghy by her neck. He threatened to put the beetle down her throat if she would not curse the Pope. Under cross-examination she said she lived next door to Mrs. Donaghy in Crimea Street. She saw nothing in the prisoner's hand but a beetle. Mrs. Donaghy's house was wrecked and the furniture burned.

She must have been asked how she was able to witness the beetle incident as her house was on the same side of the street. She said she had come out from her own door when she saw Waterworth lift the book in the back part of the kitchen. He then lifted the beetle near the stairs. To confirm this she said, "I swear that I could see the foot of the stairs from where I was standing." She concluded by saying the prisoner was still in the house when she left to go to Agnes Street.

Margaret Donaghy, the victim, was next to give evidence and she said, "The prisoner came into my house, and he said he would make me curse the Pope or eat the beetle, or put it down my throat, or he would get it down any way."

Mr. Steele, for the defence, had obviously picked up on a legal issue and under his cross-examination Margaret confirms she had 'summoned' the prisoner in the dock and been examined against him last week in the 'other court.' She had failed to identify him on that occasion but had now come to the conclusion that he was the man that was going to force her to eat the beetle. Mr. Ward then pointed out that the man had been discharged last week as the witness (Margaret) would not swear that it was him who had held a beetle to her nose. After some consideration the case was then adjourned.

Rose McKelvey doesn't mention a cockroach in her evidence and if the beetle was indeed an insect, would she have really been able to clearly see something so small being picked up near the stairs? She would have of course have been able to see a much larger wooden beetle being picked up though. There is no mention of the beetle being used to smash anything up this time around.

Waterworth appeared in court again and for the last time on 23 September. The Magistrate, who was Mr. O'Donnell, said he could not send the case before a jury because Mrs. Donaghy had failed to identify the prisoner when he was first in the dock. Mr. Ward, representing Waterworth, asked him to discharge his client. Mr. McLean, for the prosecution, requested that he be bound over to keep the peace for six months and this is what happened. He was ordered to find bail of £10 himself and two sureties of £5 each. While that was a lot of money back then, assuming he was the perpetrator, he clearly got off lightly for doing such a horrible thing to this woman who had already suffered so much.

The actual account of all this in HWIB states:

> *He (George) kicked open the front door and as he did so one of his followers seized the widow and thrust a large black cockroach into her face. This man said he would make her swallow "the bloody cockroach" if she did not curse the Pope.*

I think it is safe to say that apart from George *not* kicking 'Widow Donaghy's' door in, the beetle incident, which took place the following day, without him being present, clearly had nothing to do with him and no cockroach was involved. Of course, irrespective of the seeming use of 'creative license' by Andrew Boyd, none of this detracts from the horrific ordeal that Margaret went through.

Can we shed any light on who William Waterworth was? Not with any certainty but the Belfast and Province of Ulster Directory 1870 which can be viewed on the Public Records of Northern Ireland (PRONI) website, lists a William John Waterworth as living at 10 North King Street. It says he is a Staff Sergeant in the Antrim Rifles. North King Street was/is in the Brown Square area of the Shankill. Thomas Waterworth, Laborer (sic), is recorded as living at 87 Westmoreland Street. That address was also in the Shankill and much closer to Crimea Street.

Thomas Waterworth is again listed at the same address in the 1877 directory which also records a John Waterworth, Tenter, residing at 129 Westmoreland Street. The 1880 directory records a W.J. Waterworth, Antrim Rifles, now living at 1 Tilley Street. This is clearly the same person that lived in North King Street in 1870. This street was also in the Shankill near the back of the Court House on the Crumlin Road.

I doubt very much that the William Waterworth who was bound over to keep the peace was the Staff Sergeant belonging to the Antrim Rifles, as I don't believe a Staff Sergeant would have been a 'young man' and his occupation would surely have been disclosed in court, but he may have been related to him or the other Waterworth's mentioned above.

In July 2023 I purchased a traditional Irish beetle lovingly made from Whitebeam wood by Stephen Ryan of Green Woodwork Ireland. It is a thing of beauty but boy oh boy, it's definitely not something I would want to swallow!

9.
EXAMINING THE HATE CAMPAIGN

I will shortly move on to the next hearing, but before that let's have a look at how the Catholic Nationalist newspaper called *The Daily Examiner* reacted to all this. This paper was notable for mercilessly ridiculing and lampooning those that it considered to be opponents of Home Rule and the Roman Catholic faith.

This vitriol was usually reserved for Protestant MPs, Orangemen, the British establishment and the Rev. Hugh Hanna. A Black man apparently leading their arch enemies prompted this truly appalling opinion piece on the matter which was published on Friday 13 September 1872:

> *"COME on sons of William !" was the inspiriting cry with which, according to the swearing of respectable members of the Belfast constabulary, an Ethiopian, named George Henry Thompson, led on a mob of some 2,000 roughs on the Shankhill Road and adjoining streets on the 18th of last month. How this waif from "Afric's sunny fountains" got himself promoted to the important post of Commander-in-Chief of a mob of the "Sons of William" - always presuming, of course, that the evidence of the policemen is accurate- or how he picked up the phraseology in which he fired the flagging zeal of his tatterdemalion following it is difficult to guess. Yet there he was, black and glossy, like another Othello, braving dangers and encountering perils from paving stones and brick-bats to gain be their recital, on a future occasion, the warm affections of some Desdemona.*
>
> *This coloured person seems to have imbibed with his admiration for the principles which, together with the Constitution of England, the Third William pledged himself to maintain, quite a warlike antipathy to the Fenians; and it was sworn that in the pursuit of these obnoxious individuals he entered houses and proclaimed his intention to annihilate every follower of Stephens* on whom he could lay his dirty clutches. He should, indeed, have been a courageous Fenian who could regard with equanimity a visit from such an angel of light as this political*

*n****r at an hour when graveyards are supposed to yield their dead, and a certain reservation for wicked people of colour, and other folks, is said to lose for a time the superintendence of its master.*

*Such a thing is pleasanter to speculate about than to experience, and, lest it might become too general, we trust we are not doomed to any considerable influx of political n****rs in Belfast - at least black n****rs. It is, doubtless, all very good to suggest to one the truism that Mr. George Henry Thompson is a "man and a brudder," but the increase of such "bruddern" is not desirable at the present moment, if the gentlemen can find no more befitting or profitable employment than leading on mobs even more degraded than themselves. Black men are interesting subjects of study when they appear as keepers of elephants, or as lion-tamers, in menageries, or even as cooks on board American liners; but this interest suffers considerable abatement when we are called upon to regard them as leaders in party politics.*

What the complexion of the mob must have been that followed on the war trail of this amiable specimen of the race that calls us to "deliver their land from error's chain," it was easy to infer from that of their exalted leader, as he stood in the dock like a representation of Innocence modelled in black sugar. They must have been celestial; yes, certainly, celestial is the better word to use, and it can give no offence to polite ears. The "sons of William," who obeyed the command of this child of nature, must have been persons of very elevated sentiment. They numbered two thousand, or more; and it is cheering to find that amongst the admirers of the great King who saved us from accepting brass coin as a legal tender, and snatched us from the terrible fate of having to encase our nether extremities in wooden boxes instead of good leather buskins, there can be found so many ready to admit equality of blood and play the part of white coolies to a coloured potentate like Mr. George Henry Thompson.

We were unable, until our experience of yesterday removed the difficulty, to account for the rather strange story that prevailed in certain parts of the town amongst children and elderly persons of the female sex to the effect that a certain personage, who shall be nameless, was observed in the dead of night at the head of mobs, leading them on in their work of demolition. The identity of this personage was complete, except that the odour which he exuded was more unpleasant than brimstone, and the pedal malformation attributed to him was unobserved or conce led. There was also absent the caudal adornment which those who have seen him declare he carries; but save in these immaterial trifles, there was nothing wanting to establish his personality. We attributed the story purely to an effort of the imagination on the part of some terrified individuals who, in their flight or concealment, fancied themselves pursued or surrounded by the denizens of a region situated in a less variable clime than ours, but it seems now that some grounds really existed for its belief.

*What an exciting sport it must be to this political n****r and his henchmen to go bagging Fenians, and forcing old women to swallow beetles or "curse the Pope" of a starry night in the season "of the year," and how cruel are those "Southern savages,"** the police, for daring to interfere with the legitimate amusements of a coloured gentleman and his retinue of "Sons of William." Alas! poor William! to what base uses they have dragged your name! O! time, what an avenger thou art, and how biting is the irony with which you show to us our littleness! Here is a filthy-looking and repulsive creature sworn to us invoking an "historic name," the more successfully to incite a following of roughs, even more repulsive than himself, to acts of violence and plunder.*

Could anything be more supremely ridiculous - apart of course from its dangerous aspect - than the picture drawn by the two impartial and efficient Sub-Constables Hasley and Doherty of this blackamoor waving his arms, and by voice and gesture calling upon the "Sons of William" to follow him upon his vendetta?

*There is just one thing wanting to complete the sarcasm, and that is a carriage and pair of greys, with outriders and footmen to receive the "cuss" when he escapes from the portals of his prison, and exhibit him in the Ulster Hall at sixpence a head for the platform, and for the body of the house the moderate charge of twopence a skull, as was done in the case of another distinguished victim not long ago- Walk up! If this were done, s**bo could illustrate on some of his friends dressed for the occasion, the modus operandi of compelling an old woman to "swallow a beetle or curse the Pope." An immense success would follow, and as we are ready to make a present of the suggestion to any enterprising individual who may take it up, we may expect to see it acted upon. As a speculation, it must be admitted the last performance was a failure, but that was owing to want of novelty and freshness. There was nothing new in it. It was but a rehearsal of the usual thing about stolen property and card tricks.*

This child of Africa, on the contrary, is quite a sensation, and a short lecture from him upon his induction to the brotherhood of the "sons of William," and his experience in the tented field, would be most entertaining.

Crimea Street was the alleged theatre of the gentlemen's deeds of valour. Crimea Street! What associations! How could the temptation to hunt Fenians and make old women swallow beetles, be resisted in such a locality? The safety *of the Constitution demanded it; "civil and religious liberty" demanded it; and who so fit to put it into execution as this chivalrous n****r and his two thousand braves? For the sake of every interest in our prosperous town, we trust the period will soon arrive when incidents so disgraceful, so humiliating, and so shameful as those revealed in the Police Court yesterday by Sub-Constables Doherty and Hasley will be impossible of occurrence in Belfast.*

* The Fenians.
** The police reinforcements that arrived from the south of Ireland who were mainly Roman Catholics.

I have already given examples of the racial prejudice and stereotyping that the British and Irish press exhibited at this time, but this article is horrifying by any stretch of the imagination, irrespective of when it was written. The author attempts to excuse this by claiming it is simply sarcasm. This is also the first example of them demonising George, and, in their eyes, him becoming the embodiment of what they termed the 'Orange Mobs' that they held responsible for the rioting and destruction of Catholic homes and property. They also say he is an Ethiopian but as we know this was just another racial stereotype at play.

The previous year, on 17 July, the same newspaper had republished this article from the *Catholic Times*:

AN ORANGE N**R**

*THE latest accession to the ranks of Orangeism of which we are cognisant is a true-born son of Africa - a genuine n****r*

*On Wednesday last this "true blue" appeared in Shiel Park, Liverpool, as gaudily bedizened with the July colours as any Orangeman of them all. Than "brother" S**bo none wore his lily more gracefully, or flaunted his colours with an air of greater bravado. He joined the procession in that neighbourhood, and strutted proud as might "Grand Chaplain" Flanagan or "Grand Master" Enniskillen themselves.*

*Unfortunately for his dignity "brother" S**bo, during the day, indulged in rather deep potations - toasting, no doubt, the "glorious memory," and strayed from his party, unconscious the while that in cursing the Pope he might be in close proximity to those who might take exception to his rather strong expressions on that head. Alas for S**bo! this was the thing that exactly happened. After shouting "To hell with the Pope" rather louder* *than usual, he was pounced on by a few women and pommelled - not black, that being his natural colour - but blue and every other colour in the rainbow. His lilies were given to the winds, and his scarfs, upon which he had set great value, torn to ribbons.*

*The result was in the end a free fight; and the last we believe seen of "brother" S**bo was a race for dear life from the grip of a policeman, who was hotly pursuing him. The propagandism of the Orange Society is bearing fruit. We congratulate Brother Johnston, of Ballykilbeg, and the other notorieties for this latest accession to their ranks.*

The Drogheda Argus, in its edition of 22 July 1871, also alludes to a Black man at the Orange procession. In a column entitled *LIVERPOOL NEWS*, the following is included:

A BLACK-A-MOOR

I suppose there are still left amongst your readers some who will recollect a sign which distinguished a house in Dyer-street, kept open for the "Entertainment of Man and Beast," and over whose portals was exhibited a group which represented a poor African, compassionately placed in a tub by two stalwart Irishmen.

The story was that this sable son of Africa had been cast away upon the western shores of Ireland, and being the first of his kind seen there, the simple people who rescued him from a miserable death, believed that his dusky colour was to be attributed to the buffeting he had undergone in reaching the land.

*The first impulse of those peasants was to place the original S**bo in a tub of water and to apply to his sable skin a vigorous application of soap and friction, in the hope that the skin of one whom they claimed as a man and a brother, might become clean as their own. New, I say, this was the tradition of the sign upon which I often gazed with wondering eyes, when wending my way to and from school. But there was affixed a distich more expressive than polite, to the following effect :-*

"Washing and scrubbing from morning till night -
Monam mon dhoul, *will you ever be white?"*

*Although the two sturdy Hibernians could not, by outward application, remove the colour inserted in the cuticle in the case quoted, a striking change was made here a few days ago, in the converting of a black n****r, into a pseudo Orangeman!*

James Westly, a negro, was brought up on Monday before Captain Bourne and J. Brocklebank, County J.P.'s, charged with having stolen a box of cigars from Mr. Kirkup, publican, Fairfield. This worthy admirer of William the Third, tried to emulate the practices of those who followed the Dutchman to Ireland, and being decorated with an Orange scarf, he thought any amount of "looting" was permissible; but the magistrates, moved by Kirkup, could not see the act of kleptomania in that light, and poor Westly has had to go into durance vile for this proof of his adherence to the memory and practices of the men who fought at the Boyne.

(I could not find an account of the court proceedings mentioned above, only being able to find the preceding hearing. A James *Wesley*, 'a man of colour,' was remanded in custody. The allegation being that he had stolen a box of cigars from Mr. Kirkup's hotel, which it was then claimed he was seen in a cart smoking one and distributing others to friends. This was alleged to have taken place on 12 July. No mention of the Orange Order or Orange paraphernalia is mentioned in this account so presumably it was revealed at the next hearing.)

10.
ALWAYS GRINNING AND LOOKING PLEASANT

We now move to 19 September 1872 and George Henry Thompson's next appearance in court. More witnesses have been produced and we have a cameo appearance from Joseph Wilson who was probably the most significant Irish born person of colour living in Belfast at this time. My account of proceedings will deviate a little at times to give brief accounts of him and other people that appeared.

This second hearing was before the Honourable Captain Plunkett, R.M., and once again Mr. McLean, Jnr, prosecuted, and Mr. Steele, Mr. Ward and Mr. Harper defended him.

This time round Sub Constable Doherty said in addition to what he had already sworn previously, that after he had arrested Thompson, he had given him the usual caution and told him he was charged with being one of a riotous mob. Thompson replied that he was guilty. Under cross examination from Mr. Ward he repeated much of what he said previously - that he had seen Thompson in a mob with a stick in his hand; the mob numbered upwards of 2,000 people; he also saw him linked on two men's arms at the front of this mob; he had seen him enter houses where people left soon afterwards; he knew nothing of Thompson's character when he arrested him; and that he hadn't arrested him on 18 August because he only had one policeman with him and did not consider it judicious to do so. He said the reason he did not arrest him until much later was that Thompson had left the town and had been laying low at Ligoniel. In one report he mentions seeing him at different periods from one o'clock till night time on 18 August.

Intringuely, during this questioning from Mr. Ward, he also said, "I am certain it was the prisoner in the mob, and not this gentleman in the solicitors' seat." That person is named in the reports as Mr. Wilson. This can only be referring to the legendary Joseph Wilson (1836-1887), who was of mixed heritage and known in Belfast as 'Black Joe.' He would have been 36 years old in 1872 and was said to have been a well built and sturdy person. He was a rate collector, property investor, rent agent and money lender at this time. Joe made frequent appearances in court. Most were related to his work but not all of them.

He was also a familiar sight in the Shankill area. In the early 1860s he lived at 220 Conway Street. *The Belfast News-Letter* of 19 June 1860 reported that Bartholomew Heyburn, of Millford Street, was convicted for assaulting him. Heyburn was fined 5 shillings and costs. On 1 August 1861, *The Northern Whig* announced the birth of a daughter on 25 July at this address. In May 1862, he purchased numbers 15, 17, 19 and 21 Conlon Street, which were small dwelling houses with gardens, for £72. (In February 1882, Nos 15 and 17 collapsed resulting in the deaths of three young boys from neighbouring streets: Samuel Shaw, aged 10, from 6 Killarney Street, Alexander Gault, aged 8 from Springmount Street, and David Ramsay Geary, aged 9 years and 6 months, from 2 Killarney Street. Joseph Wilson was recorded by the town council as the owner of the properties in 1881 but no entry had been made for 1882 so it was deemed that the council was responsible for them.) Later in 1862, *The Belfast Morning News* carried the sad news that on 5 September, Joseph's brother George, who was named after their father, had passed away at 220 Conway Street aged just 21.

The Belfast and Province of Ulster Directory 1865 lists him as living at 73 Shankill Road, with his profession being a rate collector. In the same year, *The Belfast Morning News* reported that on 2 May, a baby daughter of his called Agnes, had died aged just 1 year and 9 months at this address. *The Belfast Weekly News* of 25 November 1865 in its reporting of proceedings at the Belfast Police Court on Saturday 18 November, included this:

ATTEMPT TO EXTORT MONEY

Joseph Reid, a powerful looking young man, was charged by Joseph Wilson, a tax collector, with assaulting him on the Shankhill Road the night before, and with attempting to extort money from him at same time.

The complainant said - About a quarter-past twelve o'clock last night I was going home, and when at the corner of Hopeton Street, a few doors from my own house, the prisoner came forward to me, caught hold of me by the collar of my coat, and demanded money from me. I released myself from his grip and passed on. On going into my own house the prisoner came to the window, and said that he would mark me, and that he had my house "spotted." I then went for a constable, and had him arrested.

The prisoner said that he remembered nothing about the occurrence, he was so drunk at the time.

The BENCH ordered the prisoner to find bail - himself in £20, and two sureties in £10 each - to keep the peace towards all her Majesty's subjects for the period of twelve months; and, in default of finding that security, to be imprisoned two months in the County Jail.

The Northern Whig reported a racially aggravated assault on Joseph in its edition of 30 May 1867. At the Belfast Police Court on Wednesday 30 May, a case was heard before J. C. O'Donnell, Esquire, Resident Magistrate:

FIGHTING IN THE STREET

John Connolly and Joseph Wilson were charged by Sub-Constable McMahon with having been disorderly and fighting in Hill Street. Mr. Seeds prosecuted. Mr. Harper appeared for Wilson, and Mr. Tittle for Connolly.

*Mr. Harper stated that Mr. Wilson, who has an agency for the collection of taxes in the town, was passing quietly and soberly down Hill Street, when he met two men, one of whom was the prisoner. The second man, who unfortunately was not in custody, shouted as Mr. Wilson was passing, "There goes a bloody n****r." Mr. Wilson went forward to the man and asked him what objection he had to his colour, when the man immediately turned around and gave him a severe blow on the face. Mr. Wilson, seeing no policeman about, struck the man in return. The prisoner, who was in the company with the person referred to, then came forward and took the man's part, and struck Wilson, who then returned the blow and knocked Connolly down. Mr. Mussen, a pawnbroker, was examined, who stated that he saw Mr. Wilson reprimanding a person for calling him a n****r, after which the row commenced.*

After hearing the case, Mr. O'DONNELL said there was no doubt both prisoners violated the law, but Wilson undoubtedly gave the blows under provocation.

The prisoners were each fined 1 shilling and costs.

His appearance at George Henry Thompson's second hearing was presumably as a favour for the defence team. After the chimney sweep shenanigans of the previous hearing this would seem to have been another attempt at some sort of 'fair play' - by bringing the only other notable person of colour living in Belfast to the courtroom. The two were probably of similar physical stature. Were they of a similar age too? Presumably Joseph being there was to place doubts in the minds of the prosecution witnesses as to whether they had the right person. In the newspaper reports only Sub Constable Doherty makes reference to 'Mr. Wilson,' so either the other witnesses were not asked to comment on him, or if they were, it was not recorded by the reporters.

I have only touched on a few fragments of Joseph Wilson's life and trust me, there are far more interesting tales to tell - a whole book could and probably should be written about him. His was an amazing life filled with incredible highs and lows. He did face some racism - not least two racially motivated assaults, one of which I've included - but generally speaking he was clearly accepted in Belfast, and the usual racial stereotypes and slurs are pretty much absent from the numerous newspaper accounts over the years that feature him. He also managed to climb the social ladder before going on the run after failing to deposit some of the poor rate money he had collected in 1874. This caught up with him in 1879 and he served a short prison sentence for embezzlement. Despite this, on his release, he rebuilt his life in Belfast, establishing a popular Oyster and Supper Bar. His death was attended with more controversy when life assurance policies taken out on him by other parties proved to be fraudulent and Joseph Wilson was clearly complicit in this. The subsequent trial of those involved made headlines on both sides of the Atlantic.

There is a very good article about him written by Professor William Hart entitled *Black Joe: The Life of a Black Man in Nineteenth Century Belfast*, which I was able to view online via the ResearchGate website. This account also features in the previously mentioned book *Irish People of Colour: A social history of mixed race Irish in Britain and Ireland between 1700 and 2000* by Conrad Koza Bryan & Chamion Caballero. It tells us that Joe was a Roman Catholic born in Newry to a Black father and a white mother.

Returning to the courtroom, the next part of Sub Constable Doherty's questioning illustrates the racial undertones at play. I quote directly from what the *The Daily Examiner* published on 20 September:

Do you know this man was a prisoner in the hands of the mob?
He was not. He was too pleasant to be a prisoner.

Do you know that "darkies" are always grinning and looking pleasant? (No answer.)
*Did you hear him shout "Sing, darkies, sing." **
No.
Captain Plunkett (Magistrate)- It appears by the evidence of another witness that he shouted "Come on ye sons of William." (Laughter in the courtroom)

* A popular song that was sung at Minstrel shows.

Another new witness then speaks. She is Rose McKelvey from Ross's Place who also gave evidence about the Beetle incident. She stated that on 18 August she lived in Crimea Street. She confirmed that Mrs. Donaghy had also lived in Crimea Street on 18 August and that she had seen her in her house. She saw Thompson go into the house and ask her *daughter* if this was the place where five Fenians lived. Her daughter said yes and he went to go upstairs. Mrs. Donaghy got a grape to put him out. She at length put him out, but he took the grape from her. There were others with him but they stood at the door while he went in. Mr. Steele then cross examined her. She replied that she did not see any other person spoken to except Mrs. Donaghy, that there was a very large mob in the street and when she saw Thompson he was standing in her door. She also said she had not seen any houses wrecked (presumably as in witnessing this taking place) and it was not true that twenty had been wrecked, there were only four of five.

This account, if the newspaper articles have accurately conveyed her words, is a little confusing. At the previous hearing, we learned Margaret lived with her two little daughters and it appeared to be her that had replied to the leader of the intruders. According to Rose, it was a *daughter* who was the one questioned and she replies "yes" to the question about Fenians being in the house.

Margaret Donaghy then appeared. She said on 18 August she lived at 81 Crimea Street and was now living in Inkerman Street. On the evening of 18 August, Thompson and two other men rushed into her kitchen. He asked her if this was 81 Crimea Street, under the lamp. She asked what he wanted. He said Five Fenians. She said she then left the house as she was alarmed.

Captain Plunkett, the magistrate, asked how long Thompson had stayed in the house? She replied she did not know as she had left. In response to a question from Thompson's solicitor, she said "I identify the prisoner as the man who came to my house" and then to Captain Plunkett, said "He had nothing in his hand that I saw". Captain Plunkett, the magistrate presumably wanted to know if he was armed with a stick as the Constables had claimed he had a stick when they saw him in the street or maybe he wished to know if Thompson was holding the grape that Rose McKelvey said he had taken from her.

As you can see, Margaret's evidence has now changed a little from the previous hearing in that she is now sure that it was George Henry Thompson that entered her house with two others. It contradicts Rose McKelvey's evidence as she had just said that Mrs. Donaghy had put him 'out' of the house with a grape and that he had taken the grape from her. Rose also said the two other men had stayed at the door while Thompson went in. It seems again to me that although Margaret is a little more 'on script' with what the prosecution requires, she does not deviate a lot from what she previously said. Their case has not been helped either by the contradictory evidence given by Rose McKelvey which is more in line with what Margaret said at the first hearing.

Sub-Constable Hasley was then re-examined and said that there were four houses wrecked in the street and 21 families forced to leave their homes. He added that there was a large crowd following the accused.

Next up was another new witness and a crucial one for the case. This is Detective Constable Joshua Crosswell. In HWIB, he is incorrectly named as John Cresswell for some reason. There is no John Cresswell in any of the newspaper reports and the typeface is clear. A search of Joshua Crosswell in the newspaper archive and the ancestry website confirms this name as he appears in many other court cases in Belfast from before, during and after this period. He is sometimes called Joshua *Cresswell* in other reports not relating to this incident. He was a Protestant originally from County Leitrim and had served in Sligo and Longford before moving to Belfast, where the first mention of him I can find is in various newspaper reports of Belfast Police Court proceedings from 14 February 1866. An old offender, Rose McConville, was accused of being drunk and disorderly and using party expressions. Crosswell heard her unnecessarily informing the public that she was "a good Papist and a Connaught woman." This induced laughter from the public gallery but didn't save her from being punished with a fine of 40 shillings and costs, or 14 days in prison. He left the Royal Irish Constabulary in 1876, and died on 8 July 1879 aged 45 at Mary's Market, off Townsend Street, Belfast.[1]

Crosswell tells the court that he was near Crimea Street on 18 August. A large crowd was on the Shankill Road. Several people were beaten by a mob and Thompson was in that mob. He came near Townsend Street where stones were "falling like hail." He asked the mob "what were they about?" The mob was throwing stones at a man who rushed into a house. A woman shut the door after him. Thompson ran out of the crowd and knocked at the door. He went up to him and asked if it was his intention to break the door? "He turned round and struck me in the shoulder with his shut fist. He was making to hit me again when Mr. McCullough, the publican, caught hold of the prisoner and threw him off me. When the prisoner first struck me the crowd commenced to "boo," and was very violent."

His answers to questions from Thompson's legal team then follow - presumably querying why Crosswell had not arrested him for this assault or attended the first hearing and given evidence. He replied that he hadn't seen him since 19 August and read about the case in the papers after he was first arrested. He hadn't arrested him at the time as it was not judicious to do so; the Shankill Road was, in his opinion, full of people principally engaged in attacking people they suspected of belonging to the opposite religion.

Once again in these reports we do not have any records of a 'defence' being put forward for Thompson, but from Crosswell's next comments in reply to Mr. Ward, it is safe to deduce what part of it was:

> *"I saw no stones hopping off the prisoner's back. I am not aware that he had to take shelter in Mr. McCullough's public-house. When I caught the prisoner by the back of the neck I did not consider I assaulted him. I only gave him a shove from the door. This was about a quarter to three o'clock. I saw the prisoner kick at the door before I gave him the push. He then assaulted me."*

It would seem that the defence for George Henry Thompson was that it was actually *him* running from the mob and being stoned by them, as opposed to being part of it and indeed leading them (this would tie in to the with the earlier reference to being a prisoner of the mob and the racial stereotype about Black people always grinning and being pleasant.) He attempted to take shelter from this attack in a public house. Crosswell then assaulted him by grabbing his neck and shoving him. This provokes the retaliatory punch in the shoulder by Thompson which was in self-defence.

Anyway, so much for the 'stunning blow to the head' and the 'tossing aside' of both Crosswell *and* Mr. McCullough as told in HWIB! You will also note how Crosswell's evidence changed from him apparently approaching Thompson and asking him a polite question only to receive an unprovoked punch in the shoulder, to one admitting he grabbed him by the neck and shoved him first.

The public house was the *Vulcan Tavern* which sat at the corner of Peter's Hill and Upper Townsend Street - its official address was 87 Peter's Hill and 1 and 3, Upper Townsend Street. The landlord was James McCullough, who died aged 48 on 1 April 1873.[2] His widow Jane went on to run the establishment until 1887 when she retired and sold it by auction. The advertisement for the auction in the *Belfast Evening Telegraph* of 24 August 1887 said the ground floor could host upwards of 300 people and the upper floors, which were reached by two staircases, could be used for accommodation or trade purposes. It added that Mrs. McCullough had been in occupation there for almost 30 years.

The *Vulcan Tavern* was also a place where inquests into sudden deaths in that part of Belfast were held one such was the incredibly sad tale of a young boy called Joseph Kennedy, aged 10, from Hopeton Street, which was reported by *The Belfast Morning News* on Monday 21 November 1870 as follows:

FATAL ACCIDENT-INQUEST

At two o'clock on Saturday, an inquest was held in the Vulcan Tavern, Peter's Hill, before Dr Dill, coroner, and a respectable jury, on the body of a little boy, named Joseph Kennedy, who was killed on the previous evening by being run over at Hopeton Street by a runaway horse and dray. The driver, John Hale, who had been arrested shortly after the occurrence, appeared in custody in the charge of Constable William Mills, of Shankhill Station. Mr. Coates and Mr. Seeds appeared for the prisoner.

Evidence was given by two lads, named William George Guthrie and William Palmer, and by Mary Anne Kennedy, mother of deceased, that shortly after seven o'clock on the previous evening, a horse to which a float was attached, galloped up Shankhill Road, and into Hopeton Street, knocking down and passing over the deceased, a lad of about seven years of age, who was in the act of passing over the crossing. Two girls were saved from being knocked down also by a soldier, who pushed them back as the horse came up. The deceased was lifted up by a man, and carried to Dr Adams', where he remained under treatment until he was brought to his mother's house in a dying state by some policemen from the adjoining barrack. He died the following morning at half past five o'clock, having been unconscious from (when) the accident occurred. There was no person near to the horse when he galloped up to Hopeton Street, but soon after the child was knocked down, the driver, John Hale, who was quite sober, came up and took the horse in charge. He was himself, after a brief interval, arrested by a constable and brought to the Police Office.

The deceased, it appeared, had been sent a message to a drapery house about twenty minutes before the unfortunate occurrence. In reply to Mr. Coates, Constable Mills said he had no evidence to show how the horse ran away. The prisoner volunteered to relate the whole circumstances. He said he was a drayman, in the employment of Mr. Scott, brewer, Cromac Street, and that he had been engaged delivering ale shortly before the affair happened. It was intention to give his horse a drink at the trough on the Shankhill Road, and he got off the float for that purpose, when the animal made a sudden start, and ran away so quickly that he was unable to overtake him until the child was knocked down and the horse had got a considerable distance up Hopeton Street. In July last the same horse ran from Prince's Street to the brewery. On hearing this, the jury declared they were quite satisfied with what had been stated, and found a verdict of accidental death.

At the close of the proceedings, Mr. Coates wished to know from the jury what sum they suggest should be given by Mr. Scott to the mother of the deceased. It was the unanimous desire of the jury that the matter should be allowed to rest in the hands of Mr. Scott himself, believing that he would act handsomely towards the poor woman, who seemed to be deeply afflicted by the sudden calamity.

Upper Townsend Street no longer exists. It ran from Peter's Hill to the Old Lodge Road, with Townsend Street being directly opposite on the other side of Peter's Hill. Today, Shankill Terrace and Upper Townsend Terrace are approximately where it used to be.

Crosswell ends by stating that he saw in court a reporter called Mr. William Henry, who could give evidence as he was on the road that day.

Mr. Henry then plays his first part in this story. It seems he was working for a number of English and Scottish publications reporting on the rioting in Belfast and was probably the only truly impartial witness in the whole affair.

He was on the road for four hours and in the evening of 18 August had seen George Henry Thompson at the head of mobs (and in some reports 'in mobs' as opposed to leading them) on several occasions. However, he said *that the mob seemed to be in command of him rather than the other way round* and in his opinion, were making fun of Thompson. He heard them call him "S**bo" and "Snowball".

Henry went on to corroborate Crosswell's account of the other incident, saying he saw a man that had been beaten and was having stones thrown at him run into a house at Upper Townsend Street. In his opinion, only the actions of Constable Crosswell saved that house from being wrecked. Further cross-examined by Mr. Harper, the journalist interestingly went on to say that he had met Thompson before when he was not part of a mob and that he was "rather attractive" on this occasion. He said he may have mentioned a Black man in one of his newspaper reports but didn't feel that was the cause of Thompson being arrested, adding that there were many more people he witnessed that evening whose behaviour warranted them being arrested too. He also said he could tell the difference between one Black man and another by their faces.

There are a few interesting points in this including the now familiar racial slurs - this time coming from the supporters of George Henry Thompson and proving how terminology used in the press and books was widespread in society. The 'rather attractive' comment means that he was impressed by how George had conducted himself on that peaceful occasion rather than sexual attraction. One wonders where William Henry had met Thompson previously? Had he seen him performing at McCormick's Show? Or perhaps their paths had crossed somewhere else in Belfast or maybe in Ligoniel? The final point of note is that William Henry did not feel mentioning a Black man in his report of the riots had caused the arrest of Thompson. So, I'm deducing that the defence team put this forward as the reason he was arrested. Something along the lines of a Black man had been mentioned in a newspaper report as being involved in the rioting and so the police were simply guessing and felt compelled to arrest him purely because he was the only Black man that they knew of in the area.

I have not been able to find William Henry's reports. He mentions he was working for five newspapers and three of these were the *Liverpool*

Albion, Edinburgh Courant, and *Glasgow Mail.* It's worth taking a brief detour here to reveal more about him.

William Henry was born in Belfast in March 1836 and attended Townsend Street school. When he was a little older he joined the Young Men's Literary Society connected to Townsend Street (Presbyterian) church and took part in their debates,[3] so he was familiar with the Shankill and its environs. He went on to have a long and distinguished career in journalism which included establishing *The Newtownards Chronicle and County Down Observer* in 1873. Featuring a motto of 'Be Just and Fear Not,' the first edition was published on Saturday 19 July and over 150 years later, it is still chronicling the comings and goings of life in the Ards peninsula. He would also serve as a Town Commissioner for Newtownards. On 5 May 1882, he facilitated a visit to the Ulster Hall in Belfast for 100 children from the Newtownards workhouse and 'newsboys' connected with his newspaper. This was for them to see *Hengler's Circus*, whose manager, Mr. Powell, kindly admitted them free of charge.

On 4 October 1888, he was presented with a silver-mounted morocco purse and 200 guineas to mark his 'faithful services during his connection with the Press for forty years.' The money was raised from subscribers that represented all creeds and classes. Contributors included Edward Birney, who gave 10 shillings and was a Justice of the Peace and one of the most prominent Catholic businessmen in Belfast. He owned a factory straddling North Street and Church Street which manufactured, repaired and sold all sorts of footwear. Employing several hundred people, he was widely regarded as the best boot and shoe manufacturer in Ireland. He regularly advertised his business in Henry's publication. The Protestant preacher who Nationalists blamed for the Lady Day riots, the Reverend Hugh Hanna, also donated £1.

The presentation took place at the Strean Hall, Newtownards. Part of his 'thank you' speech detailed his involvement over the years with various publications:

> *…I have had a more varied career as such than most ordinary men, having been at one time or another of my public Life on the staff of the Edinburgh Courant, Caledonian Mercury, Glasgow Daily Bulletin, North British Daily Mail, Glasgow Herald, Glasgow Times, Glasgow Saturday Post, Glasgow Courier, Banner of Ulster, Belfast Times, Belfast News-letter, Northern*

Whig, Morning News, Evening Telegraph, and last though not the least in my professional career, the Belfast Commercial Chronicle, where I commenced upwards of 40 years ago as a compositor under Mr. Drummond Anderson, who was succeeded by his son, the late Mr. John Crossley Anderson, whose remains I followed to the grave only a few days ago. I was also connected as Editor and manager of The Newtownards Independent, and for the last 15 years proprietor of the Newtownards Chronicle and County Down Observer. On all these journals I have spent less or more of my life. I have experience of the working of the Press probably as extensive as that of any man of my age, and I can honestly say that an honourable, upright, and fearless journal is certain to be generously supported and laudably encouraged. (Applause). I need not here state that the Press is a powerful weapon – no doubt worthy of being called one of the estates of the realm – "the Fourth Estate" usually – powerful for good or evil –

"An instrument which falls a soft as snowflakes do upon the clod,
But executes the freeman's will as lightning does the will of God."

Later that month, William Henry appeared at the trial of those accused of taking out fraudulent life assurance policies on Joseph Wilson - Black Joe. He was asked about Wilson's health. He replied that he knew him well and frequently saw him in Belfast and he was in good health the last time they met. Advertisements for Joe's Oyster Bar in Belfast were published in William's newspaper from November 1884 to August 1886. William Henry died on 5 November 1890 aged 54 at his residence in Newtownards.

Returning back to the court proceedings, it's worth quoting the next part of what happened directly from *The Daily Examiner* report of 20 September:

Mr. McLEAN said that closed the case for the Crown.
*Mr. WARD said he did not know what course the Crown intended to take, but if the crown would allow the prisoner to enter into his own recognisances to keep the peace, "s**bo" would not object to do so.*
Mr. McLEAN said the informations were taken with a view of sending the prisoner for trial.
Captain PLUNKETT- Now, you know the course proposed. I intend to send the case to the Assizes.

Mr. HARPER- On the jury he must have six persons of his own nationality.
Captain PLUNKETT- The Attorney-General will attend to that.
Mr. STEELE, for the prisoner, reserved his defence.
The prisoner was returned for trial to the Assizes, bail being refused.

So again, if this is accurate, we even have Thompson's solicitor calling his own client 's**bo.' It shows that even 'educated' people and not just the 'roughs' were using this term, and indicates how normal and accepted such terminology was.

The other telling thing is the request for 'six persons of his own nationality' which the Attorney-General would attend to. This can only mean one of two things: George Henry Thompson was not a native of Ireland, or it was a crude way of asking for six Black people to be on the jury to ensure a fair trial. In 1837, I found a case held at the Belfast Quarter Sessions on Friday 27 October, where an Italian called Guiseppe Corsini was indicted 'for stealing a piece of black silk, containing 12 handkerchiefs.' The account in the *The Belfast News-Letter*, tells us that, 'The following gentlemen, six of whom are foreigners, and six Irishmen, were empanelled to try the case - Owen Murray, Giacomo Forneri, Henry Greer, V. Guerini, John Donnelly, Gaetano Fabbrini, Robert Graham, Modesto Silo, Thomas Bigger, Andrea Silo, Samuel Hart, F. La Moile.' This jury was specifically for this case and as soon as it was dealt with - Corsini was found not guilty - another composed solely of Irishmen was sworn in for the other cases that were heard that day.

The Attorney-General would also make the decision whether the case went to trial so it had not been decided yet.

I now reproduce a brief article from Dublin's leading Catholic Nationalist newspaper, *The Nation*, from 21 September 1872:

Notes.
Was William III a negro? Our debating societies ought to discuss the point. Last week, according to the Belfast Police-Court reports, a full-blooded Ethiopian, "black as the ace of spades," was convicted of leading his Orange brethren in a savage attack on the house of a poor widow whose only garrison of defence consisted of two children under twelve years; the sable brother calling out to his followers, "Come on, Sons of William." If the sons of William are "gentlemen of colour" in the sixth generation, the parent hero must have been a deep black indeed.

Apart from the overt racial stereotyping and lampooning of their Protestant 'enemies' - and already claiming that George had been convicted of a savage attack on Mrs. Donaghy's house when he clearly hadn't - it tells us that Margaret's children were both under twelve years old. The age of Donaghy girls is interesting as in George's trial at the Assizes, which I will come on to soon, we have another Margaret Donaghy, a daughter of the widow, giving evidence and of course Rose McKelvey alluded to her daughter speaking to George in the exchange about looking for Fenians in the house.

11.
ARTISTIC LICENCE

On Saturday 5 October 1872, Belfast's Catholic Nationalist newspaper *The Weekly Examiner* published this from Edward Birney of 21 Church Street, Belfast:

"COME ON, YE SONS OF WILLIAM!"

WHEN courage droops o'er valiant deeds
And hearts for fame grow duller,
If fortune fails when white men leads
Then try the men of colour.

Devouring zeal may chaff a crowd
When beat, yet lead again;
If Abel's offspring shrunk when cow'd,
Let fly the Sons of Cain.

A sable chief from Timbuctoo
Through glory's ardour cheering,
Come on ye Sons of William lo,
De foe are disappearing.

Brave broders of de heavenly dies,
De Orange and Blue complete,
Drive onwards my Apprentice Boys,
Dat never seen de feet.

De Blackguard Fenians live down dare
And pop us when we're drunk,
I'll nether child nor modder spare
As I'm a living skunk.

*Dis coloured person's not de c**n*
To grind behind a trigger;
De bludgeon smash, de ladies swoon,
*And bress de fighting n****r.*

Den on ye Sons of William, on!
Ise general of de forces;
*Grand Master, Tiler, all in one,**
Which de "Black Lodge" endorses.

A fighting soldier for de faith,
King William brought our fadders,
And all that Hughy Hanna saith
When preaching to our modders.

Ise kindred of King William's race
And for de Duch commands,
My Irish brodders now can trace
My birth in nether lands.

Then on ye Sons of William, on !
I'll cleave de doors and winders,
And push de fiery faggot through,
And burn de house to cinders.

I'd die to live an Orangeman true,
And live to die an orange man,
Ise made in 1872,
When scamping at de mountain.

Den, on ye Sons of William, all !
Ye Irish warriors braving,
Pull down de bricks from off de wall;
Pull up de stones de'r paving.

Let drive de pebbles thro' de panes,
And dash de winder shutters,
Take home de beds, den what remains
I'll burn dem in de gutters.

De moon light nights are for de whites,
De'r pale and pass as civil;
*But s**bo fights on stormy nights-*
A roaring, laughing divil.

We'll bivouac behind de bricks,
De bacon flitch we'll carry;
De name to our fourfadder sticks
Dat stole de pork round Derry

Den on ye bacon back, I'll lead;
Nor dam de peeler fearing,
I'll dance de Can-Can when I feed,
And sing de Boyne when beering.

*Den strike de harp we stole last night,***
And break dat crucifixion;
*Hurra for Ballykilbeg's delight,****
I love de contradiction.

And no surrender ! dats de cheese,
For Garryowen and glory,
July de twelfths, and days like these,
*I'll sing to Queen Victory.*****

* Grand Master and Tiler relate to positions held in the Orange Lodge/ Orange Order.
** A harp belonging to Patrick Dunn, which his son performed with, was stolen from his house at 13 Winburne Street - which ran between Hemsworth and Conlig Streets in the Shankill - on 19 August. Patrick's house, which was rented from a Patrick Mullan, was one of a number of properties there that

were wrecked. The perpetrator was alleged to be Hamilton Corry, who was said to have been seen playing it and singing songs to a crowd of people afterwards. He was subsequently arrested by the police and the harp was retrieved, though it was "much injured" by this time. Being a national symbol of Ireland, it appears to have been regarded as a trophy prize for the house wreckers and looters. Patrick put a compensation claim in for £50 for damage to furniture, clothes and other goods and was awarded £13 and 18 shillings. I could find no record of Corry being convicted for the theft. From the early court proceedings it seemed that Patrick Dunn was more interested in compensation for the damage to it rather than Corry being punished, so they may have settled out of court.[1]

*** William Johnston, born in Ballykilbeg, near Downpatrick, was the Member of Parliament for Belfast and a prominent Orangeman at this time. The family home was called Ballykilbeg House. It was mainly down to his efforts that the Party Processions Act had been repealed and he was known as "Johnston of Ballykilbeg."

**** Queen Victoria.

This 'poem' or 'song', in my opinion, can be attributed directly to *The Daily Examiner's* hateful opinion piece published on 13 September. So who was its author? Edward Birney, was, I think, a different one to the esteemed JP and footwear manufacturer / retailer of the same name mentioned in the previous chapter. The proximity of the address to the other suggests that they could have been related though, and ultimately 19-21 Church Street was to become the shop front for the footwear factory belonging to the other Edward Birney. The surname Birney is also often recorded as Birnie, and in this case, Birnie is actually the correct spelling for the author of the 'poem', with Birney being the correct spelling for the JP and footwear magnate.

I managed to find out quite a lot more about the author of 'Come on Ye Sons of William!' and his family which I found fascinating. It is a long story with a number of interesting tangent tales branching off from it - such as the Italian painter whose iconic religious artwork can still be seen in Belfast; more Italians whose descendants who were pretty nifty footballers; some French people and the harp playing Scottish lady who made history when she became the first woman to manage a Gas works in Ireland and probably the first to do so in the world.

Mr. Birnie's full name was Edward Alexander Birnie and he was born around 1812. In *Henderson's Belfast Directory of 1850* there is a listing for Edward Birnie as a grocer and publican at 6 Grattan Street. (Grattan Street is now called Dunbar Street.) However, also in 1850, on Tuesday 28 May, *The Banner of Ulster* newspaper published the following:

BURGLARY IN TOWNSEND STREET

IMPORTANT DISCOVERY.

On Sabbath night last, a most daring burglary was committed on the premises of Mr. Edward Birnie, Townsend Street. Some party or parties succeeded in breaking into the house, and carrying off a cheese, two half-cheeses, several rolls of spiced beef and bacon, a small chest of tea, and a large quantity of other goods. Two parties, each of whom has long borne the name of "thief," have been taken into custody charged with the offence, and a discovery has also been made, which, it is hoped, may throw considerable light upon the numerous robberies perpetrated of late in this town and neighbourhood.

The house of a dealer, named McCullen, residing in Millfield, has undergone a thorough examination, and it is asserted that there has been found, stored in various strange quarters on the premises, a large quantity of goods belonging to parties whose houses were recently robbed. Fourteen large parcels of starch, alleged to have been stolen from the manufactory of Mr. McCullough, several shirts, said to belong to the Ulster Institution for the Deaf and Dumb and the Blind, and a number of the articles taken from the premises of Mr. Birnie, besides various rolls of tobacco, Etc., Etc., are represented as having been found among the heterogenous deposits in McCullen's store.

More might be told, but as the matter will undergo investigation before the magistrates today, it is not desirable to enter into particulars. We trust a clue has, at length, been obtained in this case likely to prove advantageous to the public.

(Another look at the *Henderson's Belfast Directory of 1850* reveals that there is a grocer called John McCullen at 84 Millfield.)

The same newspaper followed this up by covering the court case that followed. Its edition of 5 July gave accounts of what happened at the Belfast Quarter Session held a few days earlier on Tuesday 2 July. Three men were put on trial for the robberies and receiving stolen goods; the victims being Owen Murray, Edward Birnie, Rev. John Martin and W. & J. McCullough.

John McCullen, described as a decently-dressed man who was a grocer and publican, pleaded guilty to receiving stolen goods was extremely lucky to escape with four months' imprisonment. Two 'respectable' persons gave good character references for him. This seems to have swayed the judge not to transport him out of the country for the best part of his life which he had been inclined to do. The lenient sentence surprised those in the public gallery. The account included this description of him:

> *This person, who is a native of Antrim, but had resided for some time in County Derry, appears to have been honest and well-conducted previous to his coming to Belfast, about two years ago; but since that time his spirit-shop was well known to the police as a "night house," and the resort of characters such as those who have now brought him into troubles, through his connexion with them.*

Michael McCann, who had a number of previous convictions, was found guilty and sentenced to be transported for fifteen years. James Lynch was up next, which the newspaper, in an astonishing and totally inappropriate manner to modern eyes, fixated on his physical appearance and reported as follows:

> *James Lynch was indicted for stealing a pair of shoes, the property of Murray aforesaid, and convicted and sentenced to seven years' transportation - principally upon account of the entire failure of prison discipline, on several occasions, in reforming his appropriating tendencies. The outre and peculiarly remarkable conformation of this young culprit's head and face was the subject of general observation and surprise among those in court who could catch a glimpse of him. The head is shaped not unlike an irregular cone or awkwardly formed wedge - the region assigned by phrenologists as the seat of the animal passions occupying a most prominent occipital place - the rest of the head sloping downwards, at a sharp angle, to a forehead so low and narrow that it might almost be covered by the palm of a lady's hand. Two rough and beetling eyebrows overshadow a pair of eyes which twinkle and move from side to side in their sunken orbits as brightly and cunningly as those of a rat. The acute angular declinature of the skull continues down to the chin, which is thin and peaked. Altogether, any one who looked upon the strange*

figure in the dock would be compelled to confess that, if the physical structure of a man's head had anything to do with the development of habitual dishonesty, this youth was born to be a thief. Certainly he has been bred one, and, to the knowledge of the jailers and police, has bettered the lessons taught him. On leaving the dock, he thanked the Barrister for affording him a cheap opportunity of becoming a traveller.

The Belfast and Province of Ulster Directory 1852 has the following entry:
Birnie, Edward, portrait painter; grocer and spirit dealer, 40 Townsend Street.
(6 Grattan Street is listed as vacant so presumably this confirms that Birnie moved to Townsend Street after the *Henderson's Belfast Directory 1850* went to print.)

In April 1856, *The Belfast News-Letter*, carried a number of advertisements for Edward Birnie. This is the one from 12 April:

EDWARD BIRNIE
PHOTOGRAPHIC ARTIST, Etc.,
No. 52, Fountain Street (Corner of Donegall Square North.)
PORTRAITS TAKEN FROM 1s TO 10s 6d each.
Photographs copied in Oil or Water Colours.
Oil Paintings Cleaned and Restored.

This indicates that he was a fairly early practitioner of portrait photography which really started to take off in the 1850s. *The Belfast and Province of Ulster Directory 1858* has two listings and two different spellings of his surname:
Birnie, E., grocer and spirit dealer, 35 Townsend Street
Birney, Edward, photographic artist and portrait painter, 50 Fountain st.

The Belfast Morning News of 12 April 1860 featured this advertisement:

ULSTER PHOTOGRAPHIC GALLERY
IS NOW OPEN, the ULSTER PHOTOGRAPHIC GALLERY, No. 1, CORN MARKET (immediately over the Caledonian Hat and Cap Shop), entrance by First Door in HAMMOND'S COURT, with every accommodation of Waiting-Rooms for Ladies, Children, and Gentleman, Photographic Show-Rooms, Etc., Etc.,

with all the new varieties of PORTRAITS, Single or in Groups, for Frames, Cases, Lockets, Brooches Etc., on Paper or Glass, Plain or Coloured, in Oil or Water Colours, or copied, Life-Size, on Canvas or Paper, in Oil or Crayons.
Miniatures on Ivory; Paintings Cleaned and Restored; Masks taken from Living or Dead Figures.
Landscapes and Portraits taken in the Country in Oil or Photograph, or in any of the surrounding Counties.
BY Signor PICCIONE and BIRNIE, Artists.
N.B. - The Art taught in all its branches.
Open Daily from Eight o'clock Morning to Sunset.
As this is the only Establishment of the kind in Ireland conducted by practical Artists of established skill, the Public may rely on having all Likenesses truthfully and correctly executed.
P.S. - No Likenesses exhibited without permission.

Signor Piccione was almost certainly Felice Mare Piccione, who often used the anglicised Felix as his first name instead of Felice. His surname, like Birnie's, was spelt a variety of ways. An artist, photographer and sculptor, he was born in Italy in about 1803 and died in South Africa in January 1890. I will give a few more details about him as he was responsible for some iconic religious artwork which can still be seen to this day in Belfast and he too lived in the Shankill at one time during the period that he resided in Belfast.

Many newspapers across the UK reported a story in 1836, including the *The Kendal Mercury and Westmorland Advertiser* of 23 April, that mentioned a Signor Felix Piccioni, who they stated was an Italian born in Rome. He lived in Edinburgh and had resided there for five years. It seemed he had purchased a mould and bust of the mother of Lady Brougham at a sale of the effects of a celebrated sculptor called McDonald. Rather than sell these on or make use of them himself, he decided the right thing to do would be to post these with an explanatory letter to Lady Brougham at Brougham Hall in Penrith. However, the Lord of the Manor, not knowing in advance what had arrived and fearing something bad was in the package, refused to open it and returned it to Edinburgh.

The Scotsman or, Edinburgh Political and Literary Journal of 27 January 1838 published this advert:

DRAWING

SIGNOR F. PICCIONI, FROM ROME, begs respectfully to acquaint the Nobility and Gentry of Edinburgh, that he intends opening an Academy teaching the above Art in its various branches, on Monday the 5th February next.
TERMS, 30s. per Quarter.
Hours of attendance from Nine till Eleven Morning, four times a week.
Instructions likewise given in Modelling.
Signor P. takes correct Likenesses in any style, at moderate charges.
29, Haddington Place.

Later that year, on 23 July, Felice Piccioni was married to Jean Renton at Saint Cuthbert's Church, Edinburgh.[2]

The Vindicator, a Belfast newspaper, printed the following in its edition of 10 August 1839:

FINE ARTS

We have been gratified with a sight of some portraits, executed in crayon and colours, by Mr. Piccioni, residing in Corn-market, and were very much delighted with the faithfulness and likenesses, and the beautiful effect produced. Mr. Piccioni's style is very peculiar and rare is the ability with which he works it out.

Such of our friends as wish to have their portraits executed, have an opportunity of having them done so now, skilfully and most moderately.

Interestingly, several later accounts mention that Felix was brought to Belfast by a businessman called Marcus Ward in the 1830s. At this time, Marcus Ward was a bookbinder and stationer, and in 1839, was located at 14 Pottinger's Entry. In July 1841, the store was relocated to 6 Cornmarket and over the years expanded both the services on offer and the range of goods that were sold. I can find no specific record of Felix in Corn Market in 1839, but at this time another Italian, Modesto Silo, who was a carver and gilder, had a store there at No. 21. His brother Andrea/Andrew Silo, worked with him there for a number of years before setting up on his own at 27 Castle Street in 1836. Later Andrea was connected with 37 Ferryquay Street, Londonderry. They may have originally come from the Lombardy region of Italy and some of Andrea's adverts for his store in Derry mention Milan. In 1854, Modesto Silo and Sons relocated to 20 Castle Place, Belfast.

Advertisements for Modesto Silo from 1833 said that in addition to making looking glasses and barometers, he also framed prints and needlework; cleaned and varnished paintings; mounted prints, charts and maps and took masks - presumably of faces using plaster of paris or something similar. So it's feasible that Felix may have operated from Modesto's store as, apart from the Italian connection, it offered services connected with painting and sculpting.

Interestingly, later generations of the Silo family would make a name for themselves in Irish football; another Modesto played for Glentoran in their first season in 1882 and was also captain of the famous club from East Belfast. Later, in April 1888, when playing for the Y.M.C.A., he was also capped for Ireland in a match against England that was played in Belfast. England won 5 - 1. His brother George Silo played with distinction for Cliftonville Olympic. On Saturday 18 March 1893 he scored a goal and set up two others in the Irish Junior Cup Final, when the 'red shirts' from North Belfast defeated Bright Stars Reserves, from Derry, 4-1 in a match played at the Ulsterville ground, Ballynafeigh, Belfast. This triumph prompted a celebratory poem by 'W.J.E.' which was published in the *Ulster Football and Cycling News* of 24 March. Part of it read:

In centre they have got a man
Who is a regular "Posey";
His name is Geordie Silo,
But he's better known as "Rosie."
He keeps his wings together well,
And shoots with deadly aim;
In fact there's lots of Seniors
Who can't equal Silo's game.

George scored Cliftonville's consolation goal in a friendly match away to Liverpool on 4 April which the Belfast Reds lost 3-1. That same year, he moved to Glentoran and played a key role in helping them win their first ever Irish League Championship. The title was clinched on 16 December with George featuring in the side that thrashed Cliftonville 8-0 at the Oval.

Returning to Felix, for part of the 1840s, he appears to have had a strong connection with Cork and possibly lived there for a while. *The Southern Reporter and Cork Commercial Courier* of 1 February 1842 carried this advert:

FINE ARTS

A Splendid Large OIL PAINTING of the ELEVATION ON THE CROSS, Painted by F. PICCIONI, Italian Artist, in the style of the Old Masters - height, 14 feet, breadth, 10 feet 1 inch. From the difficulty of procuring a Room lofty enough in the centre of the City, he is induced to exhibit at Globe Lane, next door to the TEMPERANCE READING ROOM. For the purpose of affording the Clergy and Gentry of Cork and its vicinity an opportunity of judging for themselves, it will be exhibited for a few days.

In order to defray the expenses attendant on the exhibition, the admission will be 6d - Children half price.

Open from 11 till 4 o'Clock each day.

In the 1 April 1876 edition of Dublin's *The Nation*, some interesting characters from Cork were recalled via the reproduction of an article that had originally appeared in the *Cork Examiner*:

Old Cork Celebrities

At Mr. Gilbert's establishment, Patrick-street, there is to be seen a curious old sketch which recalls a period and personages in our local history now fast passing out of living memory. It is a brace of portraits - "Bothered Dan" and "Foxy Norry." More than a generation has passed away since either of them was to be seen about our streets. Dan is the better remembered of the two, and the likeness we have here of him is done to the life.

A sort of half-witted sage, living upon the good nature of a kindly people, he was wont to wander about Cork, decked in the alarming costume of a Highland soldier of the Peninsular War epoch - huge cocked hat, tunic, philibeg, monstrous belts, and a huge star on the breast. For a time he carried a rapier, but in later times this was exchanged for a short truncheon that might have been supposed to represent a marshal's baton. His first appearance in this wonderful costume was on the occasion of (Daniel) O'Connell's last public entry into Cork, when he assumed the leadership of the procession.

His assumption of the military garb attracted him the enraged attention of another public oddity, "Foxy Norry," a virago of amazing and wholly un-feminine forocity (sic), with a shock head of red hair that literally stood on end, while her nether extremities were very insufficiently clad in short and ragged habiliments. This unhappy creature was a source of terror to many respectable citizens, and with good reason, for anyone who, however undeservedly, became the object of her wrath was sure never to forget it as long as he lived. Yet was the poor wretch, as the story went, an object of real pity. Her insanity was said to have been caused by a terrible wrong done her by a brutal soldiery, and hence her detestation of the military uniform. At once she beheld "Bothered Dan" in the Highland garb, her anger was fired, and she made the exhibition which the sketch too truthfully illustrates.

The scene was witnessed by Felix Piccione, an Italian artist who was then eking out a precarious existence by the practice of his art in Cork, and he hurriedly committed it to paper, catching the odd humour of the affair and the strange peculiarities of the characters with complete success. From his picture has been copied the inferior black line portraits of Dan that one sees everywhere, but it was only recently the original came to light when it changed hands at the sale of a private collection. Some controversy arose as to the artist, and when Piccione's name was mentioned nobody thought it would have been possible to have the question settled by an appeal to the painter himself, who was supposed to have long since passed away. By some chance Piccione, now a very old man, was discovered by a gentleman who had seen the picture, and Mr. Gilbert exhibits with it an autograph letter of the artist, putting an end to all doubt on the subject.

He recalls with pleasure the days he spent in the beautiful city, and mentions incidentally, amongst other pictures which he painted, portraits of the late Bishop Murphy, Father Mathew, Dean O'Keeffe, Father McNamara, P.P., Kinsale; Father Macleod, of the North Chapel; Murphy, O'Connor, Etc., and a sketch of Hogan's "Weeping Angel," in Saint Joseph's cemetery. The last thing we need mention about Bothered Dan was that being really bothered one had always to accost him in stentorian tones, and that if properly approached he condescended to confer upon one either the knowledge of some profound political secret, or the freedom of the city. It seems to be one of the odd things about this very realistic and utilitarian age that we have no public oddities at all amongst us now.

The *Irish Weekly and Ulster Examiner* newspaper of 22 December 1894 reflected on the Golden Jubilee of St. Malachy's Roman Catholic church in Alfred Street. The article stated that the foundation stone had been laid by Bishop Dr. Denvir on 3 November 1841, which was appropriately enough the feast day of St. Malachy. He was the first Irish born saint to be formally canonised. The church opened in 1844, with its dedication taking place on Sunday 15 December. The piece went on to describe Felix's incredible contribution:

> *...The three magnificent paintings, which are inserted in the reredos above the high altar, are by many considered by many the most brilliant gems in the interior decorations. That in the centre, which represents the Redeemer on the way to Calvary just outside the city gate, pourtrays (sic) a magnificent and life-like study - almost terrible in its realism. All the figures in the group are of life size, and the artist has abandoned all conventional treatment to produce a scene which almost makes the spectator feel transported back 2,000 years, to become witness of one of the saddest scenes in the awful tragedy of man's redemption. On the Epistle side of the central picture is a representation of St. Malachy in his episcopal robes, and on the Gospel side is a representation of the Assumption.*
>
> *These paintings, which have for years excited the devotion of Belfast Catholics and the approval of every lover of art, were executed by an Italian artist named Piccioni, who was at that time residing in Belfast.*

Also in the 1840's, Felix appears to have spent time in Omagh, County Tyrone. In 1878, one of his sons had sought damages of £1,000 for an incident that occurred in Belfast in which he claimed to have been seriously injured. He was unsuccessful, but that case, was commented on by a journalist in the *Tyrone Constitution* of 29 November 1878 who added:

> *... I refer to this case as the father of the plaintiff, Felix Piccioni, was a great man in Omagh some thirty-five years ago. He was a very good artist, and did capital business while here. He painted an altar-piece for the Fereagh Roman Catholic Chapel, which, I believe, can still be seen.*
>
> *He also painted portraits of members of the principal local families, with whom he was on very intimate terms. He once got into a row while in Omagh, not unlike, some respects necessitated the action above referred to. He painted a portrait, and the living original refused to recognise it as such, and also refused delivery, and sent the painter a written letter in a moment of dire wrath. Piccioni tastefully framed the letter, and hung it at the entrance to his room, having first inscribed over it, "Piccioni's Remuneration."*
>
> *As the next apartment was a public newsroom, the letter attracted a lot of attention, and the writer, a short time afterwards, savagely knocked his fist*

through it. Then a legal war began between the parties, which, however, was settled out of Court.

Fereagh was actually Fireagh - although it was commonly spelled either way at that time - and the church referred to is St. Mary's, Drumragh, which is on the Fireagh Road just outside Omagh. In the days of the Penal Laws, when the Roman Catholic faith was suppressed in Ireland, worshippers defied the authorities and attended Mass in secret and this was usually in outside locations. A rock would serve as the altar and these rocks were, and still are, known as Mass rocks. When the weather was inclement, the service sometimes took place in sheds, barns, or in cabins. The priests who officiated could face transportation to the West Indies colonies if caught. Father Terence McCawell (or McCawill), who succeeded his uncle, Father Thomas McCawell, became Parish Priest of Drumragh in 1721, and used to say Mass at the Mass rock on the nearby Corradina mountain. (This rock is remembered in the poem The Mass Rock in the Glen, written by Omagh man Felix Kearney who was known as the 'Bard of Drumquin.' This was recorded as a song by Irish Republicans and singers Anne and Francie Brolly in 1970.) Father McCawell later built a chapel of sorts at Cavanacaw, and later removed it to Mullaghmore. With the laws being relaxed a little or not being enforced rigorously, in 1764, towards the end of his life, he erected the Roman Catholic church at Fireagh, which was described as a thatched barn without a floor or seats being installed. More renovations were carried out in 1964 and it was rededicated in July of that year. The report of this event, in *The Derry Journal* of 14 July, reveals that a plaque on the church recalls that in 1844 it was reconstructed by Rev. Edward McBride, Parish Priest. This is presumably where Felix played a role - counting back 35 years from 1878 gets us to 1843 which is the correct time frame for the reconstruction of St. Mary's.

The Northern Whig of 3 July 1852 reported:

We have seen a very handsome portrait of the Rev. G. Gibara, the Syrian Ecclesiastic whose peculiar costume and long flowing beard attracted so much attention in Belfast a short time since. It is drawn by Mr. Piccione and lithographed by Marcus Ward, and is being sold for the benefit of Roman Catholics under the Rev. G. Gibara's charge, whose chapel has been destroyed in one of the fierce Anti-Christian tumults that sometimes afflict their country. M. Badier, of Queen-street, has volunteered his gratuitous aid in disposing of the work, and the copies are sold for a very small sum.

The Very Rev. Father Gabriel Gibara, also spelled Jibara, Vicar-General of the diocese of Mount Lebanon, Sidon, arrived in Ireland in 1851 on a fundraising mission. He visited various places including Belfast in November and Armagh in December of that year. In 1852, he is mentioned by *The Southern Reporter and Cork Commercial Courier* of 12 June as being present in Cork. In early July he was in Limerick, where he based himself at 2 Nelson Street[3] and the following month was back in Cork staying at 24 Pine Street.[4]

The 'M. Badier' was Monsieur Charles Badier, sometimes also called Auguste or Augustus Charles Badier. He was from France, and taught French at the Royal Belfast Academical Institution and also at 29 Queen Street at this time. He also appears to have had his own school at Cork in the 1830s where he and his sister taught French and other subjects.

Skipping forward a bit to 1862, the Badier's of Belfast had a very eventful year. On 14 January, Aimée Cécile Josephine Badier, sister of Charles, passed away at 29 Queen Street aged 53. Happier news followed on 1 March when Charles was married to Eliza Ring at St. Anne's Church by the Rev. Dr. Miller. The happiness was short lived though, as on 16 June, after attending a midday service at St. Malachy's Roman Catholic church, Charles collapsed on the way home. A passing doctor tried to help him and a horse drawn carriage that was passing by stopped, and he was loaded onto it and ferried back to his residence in Queen Street where two doctors attended to him. Despite the medical assistance, he failed to recover and died there at around 5pm. His remains were interred at the Friar's Bush cemetery on 18 June. The contents of his residence were auctioned off on 3 July and this included around 162 engravings of Father Gibara - I wonder if these dated back to 1852 or were more recent ones?

1852 was also the year when Jean and Felix Piccione had their second child in Belfast - Francesco/Francisco Antonio who was known as Francis. (He too would go on to be a photographer and also play a prominent role in the Belfast Young Men's Catholic Association. On 10 November 1872, Francis married Maggie Coyle at St. Mary's church in Belfast. They named one of their children Felix.)

The Coleraine Chronicle and Antrim and Londonderry Advertiser of 16 April 1853 reported on a Testimonial and Supper held at the Shakespeare Hotel in Belfast to honour Mr. R. E. Hunter, who it said was a reporter noted for his literary and dramatic talent. The event concluded with the presentation of a full length portrait of Hunter in the character of *Hamlet*, who he apparently gave a masterly impression of. The artist came in for praise:

> *...The likeness - executed by that talented artist Signor F. M. Piccione - was considered remarkably striking.*

In 1862, Felix Piccione made a number of financial contributions to the Butchers' and Subscribers Soup Kitchen, 72 Hercules Street.[5] *The Northern Whig* of 20 June 1862 carried a notice from the managers of the soup kitchen which included an acknowledgement of one of his donations, and stated that on the previous day they had supplied broth, bread and beef to upwards of 950 of the "necessitous poor".

In *The Belfast and Province of Ulster Directory 1863-1864*, "Piccione, Felix, Artist" is recorded as living at 3 Hobson's Row. This was 'off Bowers-hill, Shankhill-road.' According to the same directory he was still there in 1865. Hobson's Row was later renamed as, or absorbed into, Aberdeen Street - this probably took place around 1868. In 1870, it tells us he was residing at 7 Aberdeen Street, which ran from the Shankill Road to Luke Street. Whether he and his family were living there during the riots of August 1872 I cannot say. There is an account in *The Belfast News-Letter, Morning Edition*, of 21 August which includes:

> *...About one o'clock, a band of young men and girls went down Aberdeen Street, and about half-way towards the bottom they commenced to smash the house of a Catholic resident. The man, who was in the house at the time, came to the door to see who threw the stones, and as the mob continued to pelt, he retaliated by throwing stones in return. Just as the affair became critical, a sub-constable came running down the street, and succeeded, to some extent, in restoring order. In a little time the street was cleared by a party of constables, under the sub-inspector in charge of the district.*

Aberdeen Street and Luke Street are two more of the Shankill's old streets that have disappeared and can only be found on vintage maps of Belfast.

In the present day, a section of Argyle street which runs from the Shankill Road to the Argyle Business Park is approximately where part of Aberdeen Street was. To be specific, its junction with the Shankill Road is where the poignant memorial to the victims of the Bayardo Bar atrocity stands.

Erected by the Bayardo Somme Association, it remembers the five Protestants who were murdered by the Provisional I.R.A. in a brutal sectarian gun and bomb attack on the evening of Wednesday 13 August 1975. They were William John Gracey (63) and his brother-in-law Samuel Andrew Gunning (55), who were shot dead on the street outside the bar as the slaughter began. They both lived in Aberdeen Street. The terrorists then turned their attention to the pub itself and left a bomb with a very short fuse inside the hallway. It was nearing closing time and some fifty to sixty people had been enjoying a drink and a sing-song. A woman customer saw smoke coming from the black and white duffle bag that contained the bomb and shouted a warning. However, just seconds later, as people frantically tried to escape and take cover, the device exploded and brought the roof and walls crashing down on top of them. Amid the debris, Joanne McDowell (29), the mother of four children, and Hugh Alexander Harris (21), known as Hughie to his friends and the father of a young child, lay dead. Linda Boyle (17), was critically injured and died in hospital a week later. Forty four other people were injured and a lot of damage was done to surrounding properties and vehicles parked nearby.

Less than two months earlier, on 18 June, another attack on the pub had been thwarted when a customer bravely picked up a cylinder bomb that had been left in the doorway and threw it into the middle of the road. It exploded leaving a crater 18 inches wide and a number of people were injured by flying glass from windows that had been blown out of nearby properties. The manager of the bar during this troubled period was, by pure coincidence, also called George Thompson.

The Weekly Examiner and Ulster Weekly News, of 17 May 1884 mentions Felix and we learn that he is now living in South Africa. From there he is still supporting a charity in Belfast and it confirms his close attachment to St. Malachy's church:

ST. VINCENT DE PAUL SOCIETY

The numerous friends and acquaintances of Mr. Felix Piccione, artist, who was for many years conspicuous as an active and energetic member of St. Malachy's Conference of the St. Vincent de Paul Society, will be glad to learn that he has favoured an intimate friend of his in Belfast with a very interesting and truly characteristic letter, together with a liberal donation for the funds of the Conference to which he belonged before he left here for Natal, South Africa.

He and his family would make a great subject for a book - there is so much more that can be told about them and their time in Scotland, Ireland and South Africa. Another of Jean and Felix Piccioni's sons was called Giacomo (James.) He was a successful horse trader in Belfast who moved to South Africa around 1879. It appears his father and other family members followed him which explains why Felix died there. In 1892 James purchased the Greenfield Farm in Kwa-Zulu Natal. The farm played a key role in supporting the British during the second Boer War - with horses being supplied to the army, soldiers being billeted there and part of it acting as a prison. The farm was noted for horse breeding and a quick internet search will reveal much more about it.

Rewinding a little and returning to Edward Birnie, the listing in *The Belfast and Province of Ulster Directory 1863-1864* states:
Birnie, E., grocer and spirit-dealer, painter and photographic artist, Hercules-place, and 35 Townsend-street.

The Belfast Weekly News of Saturday 28 February 1863 tells us of a court appearance by Edward Birnie:

BELFAST POLICE COURT

THURSDAY.
[Before EDWARD ORME, Esq., R.M., and W.T.B. LYONS, Esq., J.P.]
TWO OF A TRADE
James W. Ingram was charged with having assaulted Edward Birnie.
The parties had been in partnership as photographic artists at Hercules Place, and disputed about the "property."
The case was dismissed, as the evidence was not satisfactory.

The Belfast News-Letter of 21 October 1865 reported that fifty three applications were on the licence sheet at the Belfast Quarter Sessions held on the previous day. In this book I have recorded the spellings of licence and license exactly as they appeared in the newspapers hence why they differ from time to time. These applications included the following:

SPIRIT LICENCES

Edward Birnie, 19, Church Street, Belfast, transfer from 35, Townsend Street, granted.

Shortly after opening this new venture, Birnie found himself unwittingly embroiled in the mysterious case of Robert Jeffrey. Aged about 35 and married with six children, Jeffrey was a Carter who had travelled to Belfast on the evening of Wednesday 13 December 1865 from Ballywalter on the County Down coast. He arrived with his horse and cart at Alexander Clotworthy's Stabling Yard, 89 Ann Street, between eight and nine o'clock in the morning of 14 December. Clotworthy said he came and went throughout the day, loading the cart with goods he had purchased for his customers around and about Ballywalter. He left the stabling yard between seven and eight o'clock in the evening - leaving the cart behind. Clotworthy did not witness this personally but heard he had left in the company of Patrick McCann, who acted as a porter for Jeffrey when he was in Belfast and knew him well. McCann said this was to buy some Besoms (brooms) which Jeffrey had forgotten to get for one of his customers. On their way to do this, they met two women at the corner of Church Street, who seemed to know Jeffrey and asked him how the people were in Ballywalter (or in some reports, Ballyhalbert). McCann said he did not know these women. The four of them then went to Birnie's pub where Jeffrey brought several glasses of whiskey for them. At around eight o'clock they all left the pub together. McCann said he went to a nearby gateway; when he returned Jeffrey and the ladies had gone. He could not find them despite looking in nearby streets and pubs. This was the last time Robert Jeffrey was seen alive.

The Belfast Morning News of 5 January 1866 reported that on 3 January the magistrates at the Police Court had held an investigation into the mysterious disappearance of Jeffrey, who at that stage had been missing for several weeks. His relatives accompanied by the Rev. David Magill from Ballywalter Presbyterian church were in Belfast looking for him. Patrick McCann was briefly detained in custody but discharged on 11 January. The article said that it was strongly suspected that Jeffrey had met with foul play somewhere. *The Northern Whig*, also on 5 January, covered this story and was more explicit in expressing what it suspected had happened:

> *The disappearance of a man under such circumstances must be regarded as not only unusual, but alarming. It is well known to the public that of late bodies have been found in the dock, and that the only verdicts at the inquests were "found drowned," no explanation of how the people got into the water having been obtained. It is feared that Jeffrey has met his death in this way violently.*

Robert Jeffrey's dead body was recovered from the River Lagan on Tuesday 16 January 1866. and the inquest did indeed give a verdict of 'found drowned' exactly as *The Northern Whig* predicted. Edward Birnie gave evidence stating that the party had been drinking in his pub, but as he had only been open for six weeks he had no familiarity with Jeffrey or the two women. Jeffrey paid for the drinks and they left together at about eight o'clock. He knew Patrick McCann from before moving to the street and confirmed that he had returned to the pub looking for Jeffrey.

The two mystery women were never found. At the Inquest, which was held at the General Hospital in Frederick Street by Robert Foster Dill, Esq., M.D., Borough Coroner, on 17 January, it was strongly suggested that they were from Caxton Street, which was located between Academy Street and Edward Street, approximately where The MAC is located in present day Belfast.

McCann had taken James Jeffrey, brother of Robert, to a house in Caxton Street when he came to Belfast to look for his missing sibling. Back home, James said he had heard three or four times that his brother and McCann were frequenting this house. When they arrived, they had a conversation with two women there. One asked McCann, "Is that man (Jeffrey) got yet?" and he replied "No, this is his brother." James also said that one of the women said McCann and his brother were regular visitors to her house with money and without money, and lifting a child, she said "There is a boy he would rather have than his own, and many a time he nursed it on his knee."

When McCann was quizzed about this and his seemingly intimate knowledge of Caxton Street, he denied it all; saying he had never visited it previously and only gone there with James Jeffrey to search for Robert at his request.

A policeman was then sent to Caxton Street to fetch the woman who allegedly said this. She was Mary Ann Douglas, who duly arrived at the hospital and gave her take on what had happened. She agreed that McCann and James Jeffrey had called at her house but denied saying what James Jeffrey had claimed, though she did say that about six months previously Patrick McCann and Robert Jeffrey had visited her house. It seems that neither she nor the other woman were suspected of being the two mystery women, and Patrick McCann was not suspected of being involved either in the disappearance of his friend, but it was clear that people were keeping quiet and not letting on all they knew.

A man named Andrew Stewart spotted the dead body floating up the river with the tide under the Queen's Bridge on 16 January. He reported this to Sub Constable Patrick McKenna who was on duty on the bridge. They got a boat and together retrieved it. McKenna said there was nothing in the pockets but some matches in the vest pocket.

Dr. David Nevin Moore, House Surgeon at the General Hospital, stated that the death appeared to have been caused by drowning. There were no marks of violence on his body. There was a slight contusion on his head, but in his opinion it must have been inflicted after death.

The Northern Whig published another article about the case on 19 January which asked: WAS ROBERT JEFFREY DROWNED OR MURDERED? It went on to state that Caxton Street was 'one of the most disreputable and dangerous places in Belfast' and that 'The denizens of that infamous locality are all known to and by one another; the curiosity of these wretched women regarding one another and those who visit them is notorious.'

The author certainly seemed to think that the offer of a reward would entice someone to spill the beans about the two mystery women and concluded with:

The probability is that the unfortunate man was robbed and murdered in one of those infamous dens, and his body conveyed to the docks and cast into the river. This is not the first case of "Found drowned" in the harbour or river that

> *has given rise to such a suspicion; and it is incumbent on the authorities to have this affair most strictly followed up, and the truth, if possible, ascertained. The open verdict of "Found drowned" will not satisfy the public sense of justice, the grounds for suspecting that a foul crime has been perpetrated in some of the dens of this town being so grave.*

Later that year, a number of Belfast based newspapers published favourable articles about the annual public examination of the Belfast Model National School located in Divis Street. This was a cross-community school for children of all faiths that would nowadays be known in Northern Ireland as an integrated school. From the account published in *The Banner of Ulster* on 22 December, we learn that a Lavinia Birnie was listed among the pupils in the Girls Junior Division. They were examined in the subjects of Grammar and Geography. Lavinia was among those who obtained a Premium award.

In 1868 we hear of Alexander D. Birnie, who was also an artist and photographer. *The Northern Whig* of 10 October 1868 carried this advert:

ALEXANDER D. BIRNIE,
ARTIST AND PHOTOGRAPHER.
IS NOW PRODUCING THE FINEST PHOTOGRAPHIC PORTRAITS
from Carte de Visites, up to life-size, Plain and Coloured, at the very cheapest rates.
Carte de Visites, 6s per doz.; 4s per half doz.
First-class Pictures Guaranteed.
Picture Frames at half the usual price.
27, DONEGALL STREET
(Opposite the Brown Linen Hall).

This was Alexander Denis Birnie, son of Edward, who was clearly following in his father's footsteps. A baptismal record for St Patrick's church Belfast from 31 January 1847 includes a Denis Alexander Burney, son of Edward Burney and Eliza McIver or McIvor. Despite the forenames being in a different order and another variation of the surname, this would appear to be Alexander and also gives a name for his mother and Edward's wife. Eliza in this instance was short for Elizabeth. I could find no further information on Elizabeth, but a daughter was named after her as we shall see shortly.

The Belfast Morning News of 29 December 1869 in its *Births, Marriages and Deaths* column reported a Christmas day tragedy:

DEATHS

December 25, at Church Street, Belfast, Sarah, daughter of Mr. E. Birnie, aged 11 years.

The Belfast Morning News of Wednesday 6 April 1870, published a notice from a William Johnston, who announced that on and after Monday 11 April, he would be starting a car from Mr. E. Birnie's, 19 Church Street (Third door from North Street), for Ligoniel. It would leave four times a day from Mr. Birnie's at 10am, 12 noon, 4pm and 9.30pm. Journeys from Ligoniel to Mr. Birnie's were scheduled at 9am, 11am, 2pm and 6.30pm. Anyone calling with Mr. Birnie could avail themselves of a card with the times. As mentioned previously, a car of this period was actually a horse drawn cab, taxi or carriage. In this case, it was essentially what we would know as a bus service and could probably seat up to 12 people.

This service appears to have been set up to rival an existing one. Robert Montgomery of Ballysillan published an advert in the same newspaper on Wednesday 27 April. He thanked his customers for their long standing support and reminded readers that he still continued to run cars every weekday as usual. These left from the Post Office in Ligoniel, and in Belfast, from Mr. Grainger's, Ligoniel Tavern, Church Street. The Ligoniel Tavern was located at 17 Church Street so must have been almost next door to Edward Birnie's establishment.

As an aside one wonders if George Henry Thompson ever used either service when he worked in Ligoniel for Mr. Martin? Edward Birnie could well have encountered him if he did, which perhaps added more ire to his poem/song.

In Chapter 2, I mentioned the Lord Chancellor of Ireland, Thomas O'Hagan, giving a speech before prizes were distributed at the *Belfast and North of Ireland Workmen's Exhibition* at the Ulster Hall in May 1870. Ahead of this, both Edward and Alexander Birnie were praised for their contributions to it by *The Belfast Morning News* in its edition of Wednesday 25 May:

> *As this was originally conceived as a Workmen's Exhibition, we are delighted to find a number of the working men engaged in the higher style of art, and*

producing works not only creditable to themselves, but calculated to sustain the proud position which the Exhibition occupies in every respect as a complete success. Among these we might mention some by Mr. Edward Birnie. One of them, "Napoleon at Fontainebleau," has the quiet pose of the original, which evidently belongs to the French school. "The Flight from Egypt," by Mr. A. D. Birnie, is also very meritorious. Copied as it is from an engraving, it has not the force, doubtless, of the original picture, but still it shows a tendency in the right direction. "The Gleaner," by Mr. Edward Birnie, is a picture of considerable promise, and is very much admired.

The Belfast News-Letter, Monday Morning, 30 May 1870 reported that Edward Birnie's painting of Napoleon had earned him one of the three second class medals that were awarded in the Oil Paintings category. The others went to Miss Mathilda Stoker, Queen's Institute Dublin, for Springtime near Miltown, County Dublin and Mr. G. Roberts, for his painting of the Albert Memorial Clock Tower - the now famous Belfast landmark which had been completed the previous year.

In the applications for spirit licenses at the Belfast Quarter Sessions held in the summer of 1874, we learn from the 10 July edition of *The Witness*, which was published in Belfast and cost one penny, of another transfer:

Alexander D. Birnie, 21, Church Street, transfer from Edward Birnie - granted.

This did not stop Alexander Birnie from continuing as an artist and he became noted for his portraits of eminent figures from the Roman Catholic church. This was published in the *Ulster Examiner and Northern Star* of 8 April 1875:

THE BAZAAR

MAY BE SEEN TODAY, AT MR. GREER'S, DONEGALL PLACE,
A LIFE-SIZE LIKENESS OF THE MOST REV. DR. DORRIAN,
PAINTED IN OIL, BY MR. A. D. BIRNIE,
DONEGALL STREET.

The above beautiful picture will be Balloted for at the coming Bazaar in the Ulster Hall in the Last Week of April.
Tickets: Sixpence each.

May be had at Mr. GREER'S, and at Messrs. O'NEILL & MALLON'S, York Street.

Adjacent to this advert was another:

ST. PATRICK'S NEW CHURCH
(DONEGALL STREET).
LAYING THE FOUNDATION-STONE.
HIS LORDSHIP THE MOST REV. DR. DORRIAN will lay the FOUNDATION-STONE of the above Church on SUNDAY, 18TH APRIL (The Third after Easter)
FATHER BURKE WILL PREACH.

Patrick Dorrian was born in 1814. He was ordained as a Priest in 1837 and was Bishop of Down and Connor from 1865 until his death on 3 November 1885.[6] *The Nation*, the fiercely Nationalist publication based in Dublin, in its edition of 7 November, reflected on his passing. Its front page article began with 'Catholicism and patriotism in Ireland have this week lost one of their ablest and bravest champions.'

This appeared in *The Weekly Examiner and Ulster Observer* on 20 February 1876:

THE CATHOLIC BAZAAR - PORTRAIT OF FATHER BURKE
There is at present on view in the establishment of Messrs. O'Neill & Mallon, booksellers, Queen's Buildings, York Street, a magnificent oil painting of the illustrious Dominican, the Very Rev. Thos. N. Burke, O.P. This beautiful portrait, which has been executed by our talented townsman, Mr. A. D. Birnie, in a manner that reflects much credit on the eminent artistic skill which produced it, will be ballotted for at the bazaar to be held on Easter week in aid of the New Catholic Hall, and will, no doubt, form one of the most interesting objects of attraction which the public will have an opportunity of inspecting at the bazaar.

Born in Galway, Thomas Nicholas Burke (1830-1883) was a noted preacher, lecturer and staunch Irish Nationalist - a key influencer if you like. A book called *Faith and Fatherland* containing lectures that he gave in

America was first published in 1872, and advertised as essential reading for Irish people in the leading Catholic Nationalist newspapers in Dublin (*The Nation*) and Belfast (*The Daily Examiner*). The transcripts of these lectures had already been widely published in various Irish newspapers. Father Burke gave a lecture at St. Stephen's church, New York, on 30 April 1872. In it he touched on the emancipation of slaves in the United States. He argued that this had taken place too soon and that Black people should essentially have been converted to the Roman Catholic faith first to prepare them for their freedom. One part of this lecture, the whole of which appeared in *The Daily Examiner* of 28 and 29 May 1872, read:

> *What religious freedom have you given them? Have you touched their hearts with grace? You have given them, indeed, forms of religion, which you boast are suited to them, because you allow these over-grown, simple children to bellow and cry out what seems to be the word of praise and of faith. Ah, my friends, it is not this corporeal exercise that will purify their hearts, strengthen their souls, subdue their passions, and make them, first of all, respect themselves and then respect their fellow-citizens of the land. You have emancipated them, but you have not freed them.*
>
> *They shall be free only in the day when these poor darkened intelligences shall have been led into the full light of God's knowledge, and when the strong animal passions of a race that from whatever cause it be, seems to have more of the animal than many other races of mankind; when their strong passions are subdued, their hearts purified, their souls cleansed, graces received to be prized and to be retained; then, and only then, will you have emancipated the negro.*

In its edition of Saturday 5 August 1876, *The Weekly Examiner and Ulster Observer* published this advert for A. D. Birnie:

FLAGS AND BANNERS PAINTED TO ORDER
PORTRAITS of the EMINENT PATRIOTS
O'Connell, Grattan, Curran, Etc., or any other Designs, at very Moderate Prices, by
A. D. BIRNIE, ARTIST and PORTRAIT PAINTER,
68, DONEGALL STREET, BELFAST.
Estimates and Designs on Application.

The Weekly Examiner and Ulster Observer of 13 July 1878 included an event that had taken place the previous year:

MARRIAGES

CAHILL - BIRNIE - October 24, 1877, in St. Patrick's Catholic Church, Belfast, by the Rev. James Hamill, Adm., assisted by the Rev. Father O'Hara, William Geoffrey Cahill, Strokestown, County Roscommon, to Lavinia Genevieve, youngest daughter of Edward Alexander Birnie, Esq., Artist, Belfast.

I will hazard an educated guess that this is the same Lavinia Birnie who attended the Belfast National Model school in 1866. At the time of the marriage, William Geoffrey Cahill was serving in the Royal Irish Constabulary and was stationed in Belfast at the Landscape Terrace Barracks off the Crumlin Road. He resigned his position, and the couple emigrated to Australia. They took a ship called the Highflyer which sailed from London on 2 August 1878, and were among 100 other Irish emigrants that arrived four months later at Maryborough, Queensland, on 2 December. The record for this states both their ages as 23.[7]

William rapidly made a name for himself down under. He did a number of significant jobs in the legal profession and also served in some senior military roles before becoming the Police Commissioner for Queensland in 1905.[8] In 1912 he was made a Companion of the Order of St. Michael and St. George by King George V.[9]

William Geoffrey Cahill's exploits in Australia are well documented on the internet and he has an entry in the prestigious *Australian Dictionary of Biography*. This tells us he died in 1931, was predeceased by his wife, and that they had no children. The entry mistakenly says that Lavinia's surname was Bernie - yet another variation of Birnie. Predictably enough this is repeated in other online accounts.[10] In all these easily accessible online accounts, she is sadly just a footnote with nothing told of her life on the other side of the world. For the record, Lavinia Cahill nee Birnie, died on 24 April 1928 and is buried in the Catholic Cemetery, Nudgee, Queensland next to her husband.

The Belfast and Province of Ulster Directory 1880 contains the following information:

Birnie, A. D., artist and portrait painter, 68 Donegall St; res., 21 Church st
Birnie, Edward A., spirit dealer, 21 Church st

The Ulster Echo of 5 November 1883 reported the following in its coverage of the Annual Licensing Sessions:
Mary Ann Birnie, Church Street, transfer from Alexander D Birnie.

Alexander Birnie followed in the footsteps of his sister Lavinia and emigrated to Australia, where he married Mary Jane Jackson in November 1895. In 1902 they had a daughter who was named Levinia Elizabeth. Alexander died in 1929.

The Ulster Echo of 19 November 1886 reported that Edward Alexander Birnie - artist, photographer, publican and author of a very questionable poem/song - passed away on Thursday 18 November at 21 Church Street aged 74.

In the *Belfast Evening Telegraph* of 24 May 1887, this advert appeared:

FOR SALE
ON Exhibition, at the Ulster Frameworks, Royal Avenue, superior Oil Painting of Queen (life size), by late Edward Birnie; £10.
(The Bank of England Inflation calculator suggests that in August 2025, that would be around £1,146).

In 1889, Mary Ann Birnie succeeded in transferring the spirit license from 21 Church Street to 12 Gresham Street. We learn of this from *The Belfast News-Letter* of 1 May 1889:

BELFAST RECORDER'S COURT
APPLICATIONS FOR SPIRIT LICENSES.

(Municipal Buildings - 30 April 1889)
In re MARY A. BIRNIE.
This was an application by Mary A. Birnie for a license for the premises 12, Gresham Street.
Mr. Shean appeared for the applicant.
Mr. G. L. MOORE opposed, on the ground of too many houses in the locality.
Mr. SHEAN explained that the premises 21, Church Street, from which the applicant asked a transfer, had been licensed for twenty-six years. The license was procured by the father of the present applicant, and her brother and herself had occupied them ever since. A short time ago the landlord of the premises served a notice

to quit calling upon the applicant to give them up, and they now applied for a license for the house No 12, Gresham Street, instead of the other. The license which she held at present would be handed over to the Court, and, as the landlord did not oppose, he (Mr. Shean) thought there should be no objection. The applicant was trying to earn a living for herself and sister, and when Mr. Moore knew the circumstances, he (Mr. Shean) was sure he would not persist in his opposition.
Mr. MOORE said that after the explanation of Mr. Shean he would withdraw the opposition on behalf of Mr. Wilkinson.
The application was accordingly granted.

This account confirms that Mary Ann and Alexander were both children of Edward Birnie.

In the *The Irish News and Belfast Morning News* of Wednesday 18 July 1900, the passing of Mary Ann Birnie is reported:

DEATHS

BIRNIE - July 17, at 12 Gresham Street, Mary Ann Birnie, eldest daughter of the late Edward Birnie, artist - R.I.P. [The remains of my beloved sister will be removed from the above address on to-morrow (Thursday), at two o'clock, for interment in Milltown Cemetery. Australian Papers please copy.]
ELIZABETH BIRNIE

Mary Ann was around 50 years old at the time of her death.

The Belfast News-Letter of 21 August 1900 published a *STATUTORY NOTICE TO CREDITORS* relating to Mary Ann Birnie. In it we learn that her sister, Elizabeth Birnie, also of 12 Gresham Street, is the Administratrix for any claims or demands.

The Irish News and Belfast Morning News of 20 September 1900 reported that the license for 12 Gresham Street had been transferred to Elizabeth Birnie the previous day.

Elizabeth married Joseph McGrath on 2 November 1901 at St. Mary's Roman Catholic church, Belfast. Joseph was a widower. His profession was recorded as 'foreman' and he was residing at 5 Violet Street, Belfast. His father's name was Daniel McGrath who the marriage certificate states was a farmer.

On Monday 20 January 1902, at around half past nine in the morning, Belfast suffered a devastating tragedy when a supporting wall of the five storey Smithfield Flax Spinning and Weaving Mill, located in Pipe Lane by Smithfield Market, collapsed. This in turn caused the almost simultaneous collapse of most of the top floor, which itself then cascaded through the floors below, sending a tidal wave of heavy machinery and masonry on top of all in its path. Several hundred people were working in the mill at the time. Despite the best efforts of those that survived, passers by, Roman Catholic clergymen, the police, ambulance and fire brigade - who all pulled people from the rubble - a total of 14 people died. Most were killed instantly with a few dying a short time later from their injuries in Belfast's hospitals. They were all women and young girls. Some were Protestants and some were Roman Catholics, and many of the victims resided in the Shankill area:

> *Ellen Scott aged 14, of 4 Letitia Street, doffer; Alice Cunningham (20), 17 Jude Street, reeler; Mary Ann Burns (18), 34 California Street, spinner; Mary Williamson (22), 69 Sultan Street, spinner; Mary Ellen Burke (19), 39 Arnon Street, spinner; Mary Alice Kerr (20), 79 Union Street, spinner; Annie Jane Hunter (16), 8 Sackville Street, doffer; Martha Williamson (18), Mitchell Street, spinner; Martha McAuley (13), 49 Wall Street, doffer; Alice McDonald (18), 4 Lorton Street, preparer; Ellen Corr (40), 14 Artillery Street, drawer; Ellen Jane Scott (14), 49 Eighth Street; Mary Jane Duff (60), 23 Wilson Street, reeler; Elizabeth (Lizzie) Campbell, (22), 117 Bristol Street, reeler.*

Lizzie Campbell was one of those who died in hospital. She passed away in the Royal on 28 January having never regained consciousness. Lizzie had worked at the mill for seven years. On the day of the disaster, she was engaged in the reeling room on the top floor with Alice Cunningham and Mary Jane Duff. She earned around 10 shillings a week in pay. Her remains were removed from her home and interred in the family burial ground at Comber, County Down, on 30 January. Her father William, who was a stonecutter, was later awarded compensation of 3 shillings a week for a period of 3 years.

A relief fund was set up by the Lord Mayor that quickly raised over £3,000. This received donations from all classes and religious creeds, as did a similar fund set up by the *Belfast Evening Telegraph.* At the inquest, one of the jury members was Joseph McGrath, husband of Elizabeth.

12 Gresham Street was a short distance from the disaster scene - one wall of the mill faced Gresham Street. One of the saddest tasks of the jury members was to accompany the coroner and view the bodies of the deceased at their homes or homes of their relatives. The coroner noted the cross-community rescue efforts and particularly praised the 'corner boys' who rushed to the scene to help.[11]

In 1905, the license for the public house at 12 Gresham Street was transferred from Elizabeth Birnie to Joseph McGrath with no objection from the police.

The Irish News and Belfast Morning News of Wednesday 15 April 1908 reported that the licence for 6 and 8 Upper Library Street was transferred from John Brennan to Joseph McGrath. In October of that year, Joseph applied for, and was awarded, compensation of £5 and 3 shillings for damage to glass at this address.

Later in 1908, Joseph McGrath was accused of being drunk on his own licensed premises at 12 Gresham Street on 3 September. The case revolved around a dog. Hyman/Hymon Rosenbloom or Rosenblum, of 20 Gresham Street, accused McGrath of taking his dog from the street, abusing it, and then refusing to give it back until he proved ownership of it. Rosenbloom said McGrath then assaulted him and put him out of the pub. Rosenbloom spoke to Constable Ferman about this and the policeman visited the pub to investigate. Ferman believed that McGrath was drunk but confirmed that McGrath had said the dog would be returned if its ownership was confirmed. In response, Joseph denied being drunk, saying he had only had a few drinks after returning from a trip to London that day. Elizabeth, his wife, backed him up, and said that the dog and its owner had been causing trouble in the pub prior to Joseph arriving home, and that she had asked Rosenbloom to leave several times. She had been pushed by him in response. Rosenbloom was cross-summonsed for this. The case was first heard in September and adjourned until October when the summons against Rosenbloom was dismissed and Joseph McGrath was fined 5 shillings and 12 shillings 6 pence in costs. McGrath's solicitor asked for the fine to be increased to 21 shillings to enable Joseph to appeal against this. That appeal was heard in January 1909 and the original fine was upheld. Joseph's main concern appears to have been having a conviction to his name which could be held against him when it came to licensing matters for his public houses.[12]

The death of Elizabeth McGrath was reported in *The Irish Weekly and Ulster Examiner* of 29 October 1910:

> ***McGRATH*** - *Tuesday, 25 October, at 6 and 8 Upper Library Street. Elizabeth McGrath, beloved wife of Joseph McGrath, 6 and 8 Upper Library Street, and 12 Gresham Street, and daughter of the late Edward Birnie, artist, late of Church Street, Belfast.*

With the death of Elizabeth, the Birnie connection seems to have come to an end, but there was an amusing twist in the tale in 1923, albeit from sad circumstances. Before we get to that, I will briefly look at what happened to Joseph McGrath following the death of Elizabeth.

On 12 August 1914, in Belfast, he married Ina G Richmond. Ina G Richmond's full name was Christina Galbraith Richmond. She was from Scotland, and followed her brother John Richmond to Ireland around 1899, where he had been appointed manager of the Kilkenny Gas Works. Her initial plan had been to be his housekeeper, but instead, she worked alongside him and learned the job inside out. Both were also shareholders in the company.

The siblings shared a love of music and drama. John played the flute, piccolo and clarinet, and Ina played the harp and liked to sing. They played together and separately at many events in the 'Marble City' and at many venues straddling the religious divide - John was definitely a Presbyterian and had an affiliation with the Protestant Hall during his time there. Not long after they had arrived, Ina performed at the Soldier's Parlour which was attached to the Methodist Church in William Street. Her performance drew praise in *The Kilkenny Moderator and Leinster Advertiser* of 29 March:

> *Miss Richmond, sister of the new Manager Kilkenny Gas Works, afforded the audience a regular treat in vocalism. She possesses a voice of beautiful quality and good range, and displayed great natural ability combined with much culture in her treatment of the two items she contributed. These were "Ora Pro Nobis," which was admirably interpreted, and "The Better Land," which we have rarely, if ever, heard sung more tastefully.*

The Soldier's Parlour was refurbished later that year and renamed as The Military Hall. Many of the soldiers who used it in 1899 were sent to South Africa to fight in the second Boer War - the 3rd Battalion of the King's Royal Rifles left Kilkenny in early November.

On 21 February 1908, both Richmonds' were part of the orchestra that accompanied the famous Irish tenor John Francis McCormack when he performed at the new Roman Catholic Church of St John the Evangelist - also known as the O'Loughlin Memorial Church. Ina played the harp and her brother the flute.

That same year, Ina was appointed as the Manager of the Magherafelt Gas Lighting Company. At her leaving function in Kilkenny, on 7 April, which was reported in *The Kilkenny Moderator and Leinster Advertiser* of 11 April, she was presented with a number of gifts and sang 'The Irish Emigrant' while playing the harp. A number of speeches were made praising her and wishing her well. Her brother gave a long one, part of which included:

> *His sister was going to take up a position that was unique, as she was the only woman who had ever gained a position of this kind. If they looked around them they would see that the women were filling positions, which some little time ago no one would dream of, and which were looked upon as a certain place for men. No person ever dreamed of women filling positions as they do at present. There was the women's suffrage politically, but he was not going to go into anything political, but he believed that a great number of their claims were right and just.*
>
> *In a great many of the positions which women had taken up they had proved themselves equal to men at all times. Even in their own country they were taking up those positions. In the county Roscommon there was a lady practising as a veterinary surgeon, and she did her work well, and was in great demand in the district she belonged to. She was considered an eminent authority in her own sphere. There was also a lady in Galway, who was in the position of borough or county surveyor, and they also had women pleading cases in court, taking the place and the positions which were formerly held by men. Well, his sister was just after breaking the ice in a new direction (applause), that of manageress of a gas works.*

Her appointment to manage the gas works in the County Londonderry town made headlines across the UK and beyond, and some of the stories included a photograph of her. She is believed to have been the first woman in history to have been appointed to do this job. It was a hands-on job rather than sitting behind a desk and supervising others.

Her love of music continued and she helped to establish the Magherafelt Orchestra. On 20 November 1912, Ina sang two songs - 'Red, White and Blue' and 'Believe me of all those endearing charms' to the accompaniment of the harp at a public meeting of the Magherafelt Branch of the South Derry Women's Unionist Association held at the Town Hall. The meeting was to oppose Home Rule for Ireland.

After her marriage to Joseph in 1914 she left the job and the newlyweds lived at Craigfernie, Downshire Road, Holywood. They had one daughter, Josephine Richmond McGrath - who was born in July 1915 and was known as Joy. Joseph continued to own both the pubs in Belfast. On 20 January 1922, *The Belfast News-Letter* reported the following:

BELFAST MAN'S FALSE MOUSTACHE

Michael Keaney, a young man, residing at Eliza Street, appeared at the Belfast Custody Court yesterday on a charge of having assaulted Joseph McGrath, 12 Gresham Street, and, further, with having had in his possession a loaded revolver and a false moustache. District-Inspector Nixon prosecuted. For the defence, Mr. John Graham stated that the prisoner, who formerly lived in York Street, had provided himself with a revolver for the purposes of self-defence. Regarding the false moustache, Mr. Graham, replying to the magistrate, stated that prisoner had had it for a considerable time. Accused was sentenced to ten weeks' imprisonment.

An earlier report of the incident, which saw Keaney refused bail and remanded in custody, stated that Joseph was hospitalised as a result of this assault.

Joseph McGrath died on 4 June 1926 and was buried in Milltown Cemetery. *The Northern Herald Incorporating the North Down Herald and County Down Independent* paid tribute to him in its edition of 12 June:

With Regret

Mr. Joseph McGrath, one of the really respected residents of Holywood, passed away there - at Craigfernie - last weekend, that is on Friday. Deceased was well known and his genial disposition endeared him to many friends.

Joy was just ten years old at the time. As a young girl she was a talented dancer and as she got older, she combined this with acting and became known as one of the leading amateur actors in Northern Ireland. In June 1940, Joy McGrath married Ferguson Grainger at the Church of Saints Philip and James, Holywood. Both were members of the Holywood Players, a local amateur dramatic troupe. Her uncle John Richmond gave her away. The couple soon relocated to Muckamore and went on to make a lasting impression there - establishing the Ferguson Grainger business empire and playing a big part in the local cricket and tennis clubs. They were also instrumental in creating the Muckamore Branch of the Antrim Division of the Unionist Party in 1947.

Joy's pioneering mother, Christina Galbraith McGrath died on 8 March 1956 in her 80th year. Her funeral took place in Whitburn, West Lothian, Scotland.

In 1958, Joy was pictured in the *The Belfast Telegraph* playing the harp for members of the Antrim Division Young Unionist Association at Ashville, the family home, prior to a rally at the Protestant Hall in the town. I wonder what she was playing for them and whether she knew that her mum had done something similar back in November 1912?

And now, to conclude this chapter which has veered off in many different directions, we return to Joseph McGrath when he was very much alive and the story of a compensation claim he had lodged with the authorities. This related to paintings by Edward and Alexander Birnie and other damage to his pub *McGrath's* at 6 - 8 Upper Library Street. This was situated on a sectarian fault line - where Nationalist Carrick Hill met the Old Lodge Road and Peter's Hill, with Brown's Square not too far away. All of these were mainly Loyalist areas, or roads that led to them. In the fierce conflict of 1920-1922 which marked the creation of Northern Ireland and the Irish Free State, it was inevitable that the pub would be targeted and in June of 1922 it was. There are photographs of it in contemporary newspapers showing boarded up windows and soldiers at a barricade strung across the road nearby to control access to and from Upper Library Street.

The proceedings in court were reported by the *Northern Whig and Belfast Post* of Saturday 26 May 1923:

"PRICELESS PICTURES"

PUBLICAN CLAIMS TO POSSESS ORIGINALS

Amusing Belfast Case.

A Belfast publican, claiming to be the possessor of a large number of priceless original oil paintings – Gainsborough, Reubens, Turner, Van Dyck, Kneller – appeared before Mr. John Leech, K.C. (Deputy-Recorder), at the Claims Court yesterday, in the person of Joseph McGrath, who sought £1,000 for damages to household goods and £1,500 for damage to premises when his public-house, 6 and 8, Upper Library Street (Carrick Hill) was burned on the 2nd June, 1922.

Mr. John McGonigal, K. C., for the applicant (instructed by Messers. E. & L. Kennedy), said the largest part of the claim was for oil paintings. The applicant's first wife was the sister of a well-known Belfast painter, Edward Alexander Birney, who had collected a great number of pictures, which came into the applicant's possession. These, along with some painted by Edward Alexander Birney, were valued at £4,610.

His Honour remarked that the claim had been considerably increased. It originally had only been for £1,000, with the other claim for £1,500.

Mr. McGonigal said he noticed that amongst the paintings was a Gainsborough, a Sir Joshua Reynolds, and a Turner.

Mr. Beattie – Up in Carrick Hill! (Laughter.)

Mr. McGonigal said that Edward Alexander Birney had painted, amongst other prominent people, Mr. Augustus Doran, Mr. W. J. Ashcroft, proprietor of a local theatre.

Mr. Beattie – Otherwise "The Solid Man."

*Mr. McGonigal – Also the late Mr. John Rea, solicitor; Master McGra', the well-known Lurgan hound.**

His Honour – Was Master McGrath any relation to Mr. McGrath? (Laughter)

Mr. McGonigall – He had also King William III just before crossing the Boyne, the Earl of Belfast, and Oliver Cromwell.

Mr. Beattie – Who always insisted on having the wart on the side of his nose painted in. (Laughter.)

HAD THE PICTURES STORED

His Honour- Had the applicant a picture gallery in his public-house? – No, he had them stored.

Mr. Beattie – An immense capital locked up in Carrick Hill.

The applicant said that on the day his premises were burned two policemen were shot close by.

Mr. McGonigal – And you had all the pictures mentioned in the list.

The applicant – Oh, this is not a tenth. There were between five and six hundred.

He produced cards which, he said, had been rescued from the destroyed paintings. Amongst these was "J. P. Corry, Esq.," by Edward Alexander Birney; a card of a portrait, also by Birney, of the right Rev. Dr. Knox. There were also a Rubens and a Rembrandt.

He was sure that the pictures were originals, amongst them being the original of "The Last Supper," by De Vinci. (sic)

Mr. Beattie – Do you not know that the original picture of "The Last Supper" is painted on the walls of a monastery in Italy? It is such a big picture that a hole is cut in the Wall for the monks to pass through. And yet you say that it was up in Carrick Hill. (Laughter.) And you say that Turner painted pictures like "The Naughty Boy" and "The Bloodhound?" - Yes. Turner's were priced at £100 a piece.

"You should have sent those to Christy's (sic) in London," said counsel, "and got £10,000."

"I agree with you there," replied the witness, amidst loud laughter.

Counsel picked up a card of Reynolds' valued at £400 pounds.

"It was worth far more," said the applicant. The picture was entitled "The Cup Tosser."

He was questioned as to how he arrived at the value of the paintings, and it was elicited that they were valued by Mr. Hall, of Botanic Avenue, "a picture expert."

Counsel- Did he see the pictures? - No.

There was a "Duchess of Devonshire" valued at £40. "Surely he was dreaming," said counsel.

Witness- He was not.

Counsel- Was she bareheaded or not? - I don't know.

KNOWN OUTSIDE BELFAST

Don't you know there is not a picture of importance that experts have not traced? Well, here is a good one- £30 for "Dan Leno," by Birney. Sure Birney was never known outside Belfast?

Witness- Oh, yes, he was.

Counsel- Well, where did he exhibit?- He sent some to London, and got them back again too. (Laughter.)

Counsel- I should think so.

Witness- Well, he has them in the City Hall now.

What are the paintings in the City Hall?

- I'm not going to tell you.

His Honour said that according to the particulars there seemed to be two Birneys, A.D. and E.

Further paintings were "Waiting for the Countess," by Landseer, for which £100 was claimed, a Sir Godfrey Kueller ("The Earl of Mar"), and a Van Dyck.

"But are these not copies?" asked counsel.

Witness- Sure all pictures are copies. (Laughter.)

His Honour- It seems ridiculous that these pictures could be originals.

Mr. Beattie- "The Last Supper" shows that. The thing is monstrous.

His Honour- If it had been known that Mr. McGrath had these pictures all the buyers in the world would have swarmed round his shop. However, it is most unfortunate that all these valuable pictures have been lost to the world.

Mr. Beattie pointed out that the tabs were those found on cheap shop pictures.

The applicant still asserted that the paintings were original.

His Honour- It is evident he believes that they were.

The case was adjourned for a short time, after which Mr. McGonigal informed his Honour that the case had been settled at £350 in the £1,500 claim, the other being withdrawn by consent.

* Master McGrath was a legendary greyhound that won the Waterloo Cup three times in 1868, 1869 and 1871. After his third and final win in February 1871, he was taken to Windsor Castle to meet Queen Victoria who is said to have patted him. He was owned by Lord Lurgan and died on 24 December 1871 at Brownlow House, Lurgan, County Armagh. His triumph in 1869 was immortalised in this song:

MASTER McGRATH

Eighteen-sixty-nine was the date of the year,
The Waterloo sportsmen and more did appear,
For to gain the prize, and to bear it awa',
With the Champion of England, against Master McGrath.

On the 12th of December, that day of renown,
McGrath and his keeper they left Lurgan town;

A gale on the Channel it soon drove them o'er -
On the 13th they landed on fair England's shore.

And when they arrived in big London town,
The great English sportsmen they all gathered round;
And some of the gentlemen gave a "ha-ha,"
Saying is that the great dog you call Master McGrath?

Then one of the gentlemen standing around,
Said what about you or your Irish greyhound,
For you or your greyhound we don't give a straw -
And we'll humble the pride of your Master McGrath!

Lord Lurgan came forward, and said "Gentlemen,
If there's any amongst you has money to spend,
For your nobles of England I don't give a straw,
Here's 5,000 to 1 upon Master McGrath!"

Then McGrath he looked up, and he wagged his big tail,
Informing his lordship - I know what you mean!
But, noble Brownlow, don't fear them, ava,
"For I'll tarnish their laurels," said Master McGrath!

Then Rose stood uncovered - the great English pride,
The master and keeper they stood by her side,
The hare was let off, and the crowd did hurrah,
There's the pride of all England against Master McGrath.

As Rose and the Master, they both ran along,
Now I wonder, said Rose, what took you from home;
You should have stopped there in your Irish demesne,
And not come to gain laurels on Albion's plain.

Well, I know, said Master McGrath, we have wild heathen bogs,
But you will find in old Ireland there's good men and dogs;
Lead on, bould Britannia, give none of your jaw -
Snuff that up your nostrils, said Master McGrath.

Then the hare she led on, with a beautiful view,
And swift as the wind o'er the green field she flew;
But he jumped on her back, and held up his paw -
"Three cheers for ould Ireland," said Master McGrath.

- Ireland's Saturday Night. 11 March 1916.

12.
BORN IN THE USA?

On 7 October 1872, the second list of claims for compensation arising from alleged losses caused by the riots made to Belfast Town Council was published. Margaret Donegan is on this, seeking £5 for damage to furniture and articles at 81 Crimea Street. Also putting a claim in for this address - and numbers 83 and 99 - is a George McIldowie. This is for £12 and 10 shillings. He has claimed for damage to the houses themselves. Presumably he was the owner or agent for them and therefore Margaret's landlord. You can see her surname is spelled Donegan here and not Donaghy. There are also separate and substantial claims from a Martin Keegan and a Susan Taylor for damage to furniture and stock at 143 Crimea Street. The 'Date of alleged injury' for all of these claims is 20 August. This seems to be the date that furniture was burned in the street, or was settled on as the date it was incinerated for legal purposes.

On 28 October at the Belfast Quarter Sessions, Mr. McLean, Crown Prosecutor, said he had been instructed by the Attorney-General to apply to his Worship to have George Henry Thompson sent on to the Assizes for trial, charged with riot. The application was granted. The Assizes dealt with the most serious criminal matters and happened twice a year.

We now move to 8 November 1872 where some crucial information about Thompson's nationality is seemingly revealed. There are two accounts that I found of this and *The Daily Examiner* report was the most detailed:

ADMISSION TO BAIL

George Henry Thompson, a coloured man, who had been in custody since the 17th September, awaiting his trial for taking part in the recent riots on the Shankhill Road, was admitted by Mr. O'DONNELL to bail on his own recognisances in the sum of £10 to appear at the next Assizes. The considerations which are said to have influenced the Bench in making the admission to bail were, that the prisoner was a foreigner, being a native of America, and consequently able to procure no bail, and that a wife and child were depending on him for support.

Is this where we finally solve the question of where he was originally from? It clearly states he is a native of America and the Resident Magistrate, Mr. O'Donnell, must have been satisfied that this was true. It is hard to know exactly what background checks took place to confirm his nationality, but presumably his accent and speech must have been the main corroborating factors, and maybe he had some documents referencing America. There is no mention of Dr. James Rea, the American Consul in Belfast, or any Consulate staff being present in the courtroom. In cases involving American citizens, the Consul sometimes attended. Which is not to say that no contact had been made with the Consulate as it could have been and just not mentioned in court.

The alternative suggestion, as we have seen from the account of his performances at McCormick's Show, was that he was from Jamaica.

Also the newspaper account says that he has a wife and child depending on him for support. Again, the court must have accepted this was true. Was the court told he had a wife and child in America depending on him? Or was his wife and child living in Belfast? Presumably this would have been relatively easy to verify and the local police, who were pretty clued up on what was going on in the town, may have investigated this and passed their findings on. They could even have been living elsewhere in the UK, but assuming this wife and child were indeed living in Belfast, this takes up back to Chapter 1 and Walker's Lane. My gut feeling is that the very last tale is the key that unlocks the reason why George Henry Thompson is in Belfast. Let's revisit what it said:

A BLACK FROM NEW YORK

Belfast Police Court - Monday 29 October, 1866:

Henry Thompson, a black, from New York; Benjamin Hunter, and Mary Jane Brown were charged by Constable Drought under the following circumstances :- The constable stated that he heard a great noise proceeding out of a house in Walker's Lane, and when he went to the place he found the prisoners acting in a very disorderly manner. The black was choking the female prisoner, who was struggling with him, and Hunter was also acting in a very violent manner, and he charged the woman and the black with attempting to strip and rob him in the house. When he (the constable) went forward to arrest the black man, the woman then turned round and tried to rescue the black from custody. Drought stated that every time the black man is in the town he takes up in this house in Walker's Lane, and helps the woman to rob people who go into the house. On Saturday night two people had been robbed of their watches in this house.

Hunter was discharged, and Thompson and Brown were each sent to jail for one month at hard labour.

I can't prove it, but I believe Henry Thompson and George Thompson / George Henry Thompson were the same person. I suspect, initially, he was a sailor or seaman who regularly crossed the Atlantic on vessels that docked at British and Irish ports. Many Black men from America, the Caribbean and South America worked on ships. Most worked on deck, while others were cooks and stewards. After long and often arduous journeys, on reaching their destination, some seamen (of all races) would have sought out places where they could drink copiously and enjoy the pleasures of the flesh.

I did find one other account of a Black sailor, this time from 1863, who was called George Thompson. This involved an incident that took place between nine and ten o'clock at the Bute Castle public house in Frederica Street, Cardiff, Wales, on the night of Tuesday 17 November of that year.

After being remanded a number of times, he appeared at the Cardiff Winter Assizes on Tuesday 22 December. The accounts that appear in several Welsh newspapers of his first two hearings and then his trial at the Assizes are very confusing to make an accurate story of, but it seems that a group of six to eight Black sailors were drinking at the pub that night. A dispute arose between Thompson, who in one account was described as a young sailor, but in another is stated to be 26 years old, and another sailor called William Dixon, or possibly the dispute was with another among the party called James Hammond. This seems to have been over a girl named Ellen Williams who was drinking with them. One report said she was a sex worker. To cut a long story short, a pistol was discharged and Hammond was hit in the hand. Ellen said that George Thompson had fired it and he was arrested by a P.C. Williams, either at a brothel or a lodging house nearby. He was under the influence of drink but apparently admitted to firing it but did not intend to shoot anybody. When P.C. Williams asked him to hand over the pistol he said some of the other men had taken it away. At his actual trial at the Assizes, both Dixon and Hammond claimed they did not see who fired the pistol and no one else in the pub did apart from Ellen Williams. The judge found the evidence very 'confused,' including that which was given by a medical doctor. He said only Ellen Williams had given a credible account - assuming she had told the truth. He decided that Thompson had fired the gun but probably did not realise it was loaded, and a jury found him guilty of unlawful wounding. He was sentenced to two months' imprisonment with hard labour. From the accounts of Frederica Street during this period that I looked up in old newspapers, it would have given Walker's Lane a run for its money in terms of criminality and vice.

In 1866, Henry Thompson - if Constable Drought is to be believed - was a regular visitor to Belfast and had clearly formed a strong bond with a sex worker at a brothel in Walker's Lane. Why he was helping her rob other visitors to the brothel is anyone's guess. Perhaps as a young man or perhaps not, on his first visit to the town, other members of the crew that the ship he was on had taken him to Walker's Lane. He might have enjoyed what he found there. Perhaps an attempt had been made to rob him? Perhaps he got the better of his assailant(s) and some sort of alliance had formed after this? Maybe Mary Jane Brown offered her services for free if he helped her relieve other clients of their property and maybe he took a cut of the proceeds? Easy money to supplement his seafaring income.

If Henry Thompson was frequenting brothels when in Belfast it isn't beyond the realms of possibility that he may have fathered a child or children. After sailing off into the sunset, would he have known this? On returning to Belfast in or around 1872 had he discovered he had a child and decided to stick around, do the right thing and try to support his family? It is also possible that the mother of the child said she was married to him when in fact this was not the case. I don't really think the authorities would have done any serious checks to verify this.

An example of this, by possibly the same woman in the account from 1866, was reported in the *Belfast Evening Telegraph* of 12 August 1875. To summarise, Mary Jane Brown was charged with being drunk disorderly in a street off Walker's Lane in August 1875. Police evidence stated she was shouting and abusing a man. She defended this by telling the magistrate that the man was her husband and would not behave himself. She was then asked if she was married to him and replied "well no, but I live with him." This was met with laughter in the courtroom and she was sent to jail for a month.

If his wife/partner and child were from, and living in Belfast, this may have also convinced Mr. O'Donnell that George would not flee from Ireland, which could easily have been done.

Another factor in this situation could have been that the County Antrim jail, which is presumably where he was held, was already overcrowded before an influx of prisoners arrived following the Lady Day riots. Excess prisoners were being placed in other jails, including the County Down jail, but the County Antrim jail had to pay for them (food and prison expenses) and were losing out on profits from work that they did.[1]

You may be thinking that three different names have been used by Thompson - Henry, George and then George Henry - so how does this theory make sense? Well, this was common practice for petty criminals back then - along with the use of aliases. There were no centralised records kept at this time, just local ones. Convictions in Belfast were recorded in what was known as the 'Black Book' - and although there may have been some sharing at a regional level, generally people with convictions would not be known elsewhere unless they had achieved notoriety in newspapers or books. Exactly what details were kept I could not say, but presumably name, age, address and sentence handed down were included. In February 1872, when George Thompson appeared in court for fighting in Townsend Street, if he was indeed the same person as Henry Thompson who had been imprisoned in 1866, he would have been aware that there was a record of this. So it seems likely to me that either his wife/partner or perhaps his colleagues at McCormick's Show have probably advised him to use a different name to try and avoid any linkage to that offence which could be used against him at that appearance. Or he himself already knew to do this. As things turned out he was discharged but presumably this was entered in the Black Book. Then for the court appearances relating to the riots he becomes George Henry Thompson. Again, I think this is a calculated move to try and hide any connection with the incident in Townsend Street. It appears to have worked, as in the newspaper accounts there is no mention of the fight that occurred there involving him. This is something we will see more of later.

Many of the prisoners in custody for riot related offences were bailed in the early part of September when things had calmed down on the streets. Others were bailed in October. For the charge of riot, bail was normal. If George had been charged with house wrecking or noticing to quit as well, it may well have been a different story with no guarantee of the granting of bail.

Of course, not everyone was happy that George had been bailed. A long letter was published in *The Daily Examiner* on 13 November entitled: MAGISTERIAL LAW AND CATHOLICS. It was a diatribe against what the writer said was bias against Catholics from both magistrates and the police during the riots and sentencing compared to Protestants. As for George, after inferring that a police officer had deliberately been removed from the area where house wrecking took place on Sunday 18 August, the author wrote:

> *"A man of colour, who was brought up and charged with being a ringleader of riotous mobs, and urging them on as "brave sons of William," has, after a few months' incarceration, been admitted to bail on his own recognisances, to appear when called on. This gentleman in black was not brought to justice by the "efficient, brave, gallant officer" referred to; and one of our most impartial "Cawtholic"* magistrates has thought fit to allow this riotous n****r out on his own "recognisances!" It may not be out of place to ask, how many Catholic prisoners have our worthy R.M.s and borough J.P.s admitted to bail on their own recognisances since the riots? Mr. O'Donnell can probably give the answer."*

* Cawtholic was a derogatory term used by some Nationalists to describe Catholics that supported or were part of the establishment / pro-British.

On 30 December, *The Daily Examiner* published another of its trademark sardonic rants, this time implying that the residents of the Shankill Road were totally out of control. It claimed that two Protestants had been mistaken for Catholics and savagely beaten. This was proof that no one was safe from the 'Orange ruffians' that resided there, and implied you were risking your life just by walking in the area:

> *...There is indeed, no estimating the risk and danger which foot passengers incur in the endeavour to explore this* terra incognita, *this stronghold of Orange ruffianism, this hotbed of brutal and unalloyed savagery. The uncivilised Redskin who, lurking in the primitive woods of his native wilds, seizes his opportunity to dash with tomahawk and scalping-knife upon the*

> *unsuspecting settler, or swoop down upon the band of immigrants with his fierce and terror-striking war-whoop, may have some touch of nature in him; but in the debased and cowardly rowdy who makes his haunt on the reservation running from Peter's Hill to the Shankhill Burying-ground there is nothing but a spirit of the most diabolical scoundrelism.*

It goes on to include another reference to George Henry Thompson:

> … *On a celebrated occasion, a Belfast attorney advanced the remarkable statement that from personal appearance alone he was able to discover a man's theological convictions. The "Sons of William," who followed the sable descendant of Cain in his forays against the Papists during the August riots, have just illustrated that the Belfast's attorney's theory, however unerring in his individual case, leads to grievous mistakes when attempts are made to give it general application. This may, of course, arise from a lack of discriminating power in clumsy practitioners, or from over zeal in distinguishing themselves on the part of those heroes who won laurels in the cohorts of the fighting n****r; but let it arise as it may, we have the broad fact before us that it is open to serious miscalculation.*

The reference to Cain relates to a story in the Book of Genesis in the Old Testament of the Bible. Cain murdered his brother Abel and a 'mark' or curse was placed on him as punishment. As with the above, some interpreted this in racial terms, claiming that Cain was 'punished' by being made into a Black man. Sable is a colour - dark brown or black.

13.
COMPENSATION

On Wednesday 19 February 1873, Margaret Donaghy (again called Donegan) appeared before the *Police and Law Committee* at Belfast Summons Court in regard to her compensation claim. *The Belfast Weekly News* on 22 February, published this account of what transpired:

In regard MARGARET DONEGAN

The claim in this case was for £5 for injury to furniture and wearing apparel in 81, Crimea Street on the 20th of August.

Mr. Barry Martin Smith appeared for the claimant.

The claimant was examined, and detailed the articles which were destroyed. (Other reports state that beds, mattresses, bed clothes, furniture consisting of two clocks, chests etc. and everything in the kitchen were destroyed. Also the door and window cases were torn down.) The mob hunted her for her life like a criminal. (Laughter.)

Mr. SMITH- Had you to scale any walls in your flight?

Claimant- Yes; I had to climb over seven walls. (Laughter.) And my little girl fainted in my arms. The noise, and the roars, and bawls of the mob would have frightened the wits out of anybody. (Laughter.)

Mr. SMITH- Like so many lions in the forest. (Laughter.)

Claimant- They tore down the door and window cases, and acted in a most furious manner.

Mr. SMITH- You have not recovered your strength yet?

Claimant- I never made a shilling since. I got such a shock that I could not thread a needle. (Laughter.)

Mr. SMITH- I hope the Committee will take that into account.

The CHAIRMAN- Injury to the nerves. (Laughter.)

The COMMITTEE allowed £2 13s

(Around £270 in August 2025.)

So at least Margaret got something but sadly not the full amount. I suspect she, and many others who had put claims in, had been primed to really exaggerate their stories in the hope of getting the full amount from this committee. This clearly made it an entertaining occasion at times for the public gallery as the laughter indicates.

At a hearing on a different day, George McIldowie, who claimed £12 10s for injury to houses 81 (where Margaret lived), 83 and 99 Crimea Street was awarded £6 11s 6d.

For 143 Crimea Street, Susan Taylor who claimed £80 accepted an award of £26 10s and Martin Keegan, who claimed £37 4s 6d was awarded £12 10s. She kept a grocery and provisions store and Mr. Keegan had lodged there.

Susan deposed that there was a quantity of tea, sugar, bacon, rice, soap, flour, oatmeal, confectionery etc. which was destroyed. Her furniture, bedding and other articles were stolen. She calculated her loss at £60 and had offered to take £27 10s rather than come into court, in consequence of bad health. Some of the things were taken to the street and burned. Four tons of coal was taken away. She said there was 20 lbs of tea in the house. Her claim included £5 for a velvet jacket and £9 for two nearly new silk dresses. When she returned after the wrecking, some of the shop fittings remained but "even the very bannisters of the house" were carried away.

In Martin's case, he said that he was a hunting-groom on a yearly salary of £25. He deposed that among other things destroyed were five suits of clothes, a leather portmanteau (a large travelling bag), and a trunk. There was £11 in the portmanteau.

Susan appeared as a witness for him and said that when the mob attacked her house, she ran away to get a float and managed to get some furniture and Martin's portmanteau and trunk on it. However, the mob pulled the things off the float and made a bonfire of them which burned for two days. She didn't see the portmanteau burned.

James Wallace, the owner of the Brick Works at Dover Street which was the scene of the first major attack on the Lady Day procession was awarded £57 2s 6d for damage to bricks and brick covers. The online 'inflation calculator' on the Bank of England's website suggests that £57 equated to around £5,405 in August 2025.

A cursory read of other claims seems to indicate that successful ones usually received around half of what was claimed, or slightly less.

14.
IS THE TRIAL READY FOR ME?

On Saturday 22 March 1873, the day of reckoning arrived for George Henry Thompson. This is when he appeared at the Antrim Assizes. The following is a composite of several newspaper reports with a few corrections to mis-reported dates:

Before Mr. Justice LAWSON

George Henry Thompson, a man of colour, was indicted for a riot and unlawful assembly on the Shankhill Road on the 18th August, and also assaulting Sub-Constable Crosswell. The prisoner having surrendered and been arraigned.

The DEPUTY-CLERK of the CROWN (Mr. McCormick) said- Are you guilty or not?
Prisoner- I don't mind at all. (Laughter.)
Mr. McCORMICK- Are you ready for your trial?
Prisoner- Is the trial ready for me? (Laughter.)
His Lordship- Silence in court.
A plea of not guilty was entered.
A jury was then sworn, composed as follows:-
Robert Usher, sen., George Daly, William Eaton, Daniel Fall, John Galbraith, James Hagan, Hugh O'Boyle, William John Palmer, William Saunderson, Robert Usher, Isaac Walker, and James Aitcheson.

Sub-Constable Andrew Doherty deposed, in answer to Mr. HENDERSON, that he was on duty on the Shankhill Road on the 18th August. A little before three o'clock he saw a disorderly mob there. The prisoner was in the mob. He had a large stick, which he waved over his head, shouting and cheering. He went into Crimea Street and entered several houses, and afterwards witness saw the parties leaving. There were about five or six houses wrecked in that street on that day. There were about 2,000 in the mob, and witness was afraid to arrest the prisoner at the time, so he arrested him on the 11th September.

The prisoner said he had no questions to ask the witness.

Sub-Constable Gilbert Hasley deposed that on the day in question he saw the prisoner being carried on the shoulders of some people in a mob of 2,000, some of whom were armed with sticks. The prisoner waved his hand over his head and shouted, "Come on ye sons of William." (Laughter.) The conduct of the mob was calculated to excite terror and alarm.

Sub-Constable Crosswell deposed that he saw stones thrown by the same mob, and a number of men brutally beaten. He saw the prisoner in the mob and in front of it, when a man was being pursued by it. The man ran into a house next to McCullough's public-house. Witness held up his hands and asked what the crowd meant. They desisted for a moment. The prisoner came forward from the crowd and kicked at the door of the house into which the man escaped, and witness tried to prevent him, when he turned round and struck him on the shoulder with his fist, and the crowd commenced to boo.

*William Henry deposed that he was on the Shankhill Road on the 18th August. He saw the prisoner in a riotous and disorderly mob there. The mob for some time appeared more active than he, and seemed to lead him on. He saw the man who was pursued by the mob, and saw the prisoner knock at and attempt to burst open the door of the house in which the man took refuge. The crowd was making a cat's-paw of him, calling him "s**bo" and "Snowball." He saw Sub-Constable Crosswell interfere to protect the house, which, but for the interference, would have been wrecked.*

Margaret Donegan deposed that she resided in 81, Crimea Street, and that on the 18th August the prisoner and some others came into the house, and said they were looking for five Fenians. (Laughter.)

Margaret Donegan, mother of the last witness, corroborated her daughter's evidence. She told him that she had nothing to make Fenians of but a few little girls. He went out and came in again, and attempted to go upstairs, when she took a grape to prevent them. One of his companions took it from her, and made to strike her, but the prisoner prevented him, and said he would never strike a woman. She had to leave her house on that night, and her furniture was burned on the next day.

This closed the case for the prosecution.

Mr. McCORMICK- Have you any witnesses?

Prisoner- I have, but they are not here.

Mr. McCORMICK- Do you wish to say anything to the jury?

Prisoner- I never was in the woman's house at all. She does not know whether it was a black man or a sweep. (Laughter.)

HIS LORDSHIP then charged the jury, who returned a verdict of guilty on all counts.
Sentence deferred.

This reveals that he no longer had legal representation and that none of his witnesses turned up, so he was left to stand alone and fend for himself on that fateful day. Why was this? There could be many reasons for the lack of legal representation, such as a lack of finances to pay for solicitors, but it is extremely sad that his witnesses failed to attend and support him. Their testimony probably wouldn't have changed the outcome, but it could possibly have made a difference.

For the first time in this story we actually hear some words from him. The initial "Is the trial ready for me?" suggests he was going to put on a performance; the courtroom was a stage of sorts after all. However, this did not transpire as he failed to cross-examine the prosecution witnesses and his only other contribution of note was to distance himself from the allegation that he had entered Margaret's home and calling into question whether she knew the difference between a chimney sweep and a Black man. Of course, he wasn't a solicitor, but it is surprising that he didn't really put up any defence to his accusers. He had clearly recognised the incursion into Margaret's home was a serious allegation however he had not formally been charged with housewrecking or noticing her to quit. Perhaps he miscalculated here and thought he had been charged with these offences which is what led to him challenging her statement?

Another theory for his lack of engagement with proceedings after his initial bravado could be that he was simply resigned to his fate, and probably knew a spell in prison awaited him.

The other thing that stands out a mile from the trial is Margaret saying that George intervened to prevent one of his companions from striking her with the grape. This hardly sounds like the actions "of a man demented" which is how HWIB described him when he was in Margaret's house. There was also no reason for Margaret to say this if it wasn't true. I suspect that despite everything, she must have had a little bit of sympathy for him.

On Friday 4 April 1873 he learned what his sentence would be from Mr. Justice James Anthony Lawson. *The Northern Whig* of 5 April reported it as follows:

ASSIZE INTELLIGENCE - ANTRIM CROWN COURT

Before the Rt. Hon. Justice LAWSON.

YESTERDAY morning, at a few minutes past ten o'clock, his lordship took his seat on the Bench, and proceeded with THE RULING OF THE BOOKS.

THE RIOT CASES
THE COLOURED "SON OF WILLIAM."
HIS LORDSHIP -

George Henry Thompson, you have been found guilty of a most serious riot, or series of riots. It appears you headed a tumultuous mob of people on the Shankhill Road, which threatened violence to various inhabitants, and ordered them to leave their houses.

You were put forward as the head and ringleader of this crowd. Now, I may inform you that if you had been found guilty of an offence which would have enabled me to pass upon you a sentence of penal servitude, I would most assuredly have done so; for in every case in which persons have been found guilty before me of the shocking offence of driving people by force out of their dwellings, I make it a rule - a general rule - to pass as heavy a sentence as I can.

As you have not been found guilty of that particular offence, I pass upon you the heaviest sentence the law enables me to pass, and I hope it will be an example to others, and deter them from being ringleaders in these riots. You are to be imprisoned for two years, and kept to hard labour.

Presumably he made his way along the now famous underground tunnel that connected the courthouse to the prison across the road to begin his sentence.

In England, *The Leeds Mercury* of 5 April mentioned George in its reporting of the sentencing of the rioters:

THE BELFAST RIOTS
(SPECIAL TELEGRAM.)

BELFAST, Friday, - At the County Antrim assizes this morning Mr. Justice Lawson pronounced sentence on the prisoners convicted of offences connected with the recent Belfast riots. The heaviest sentence was that of ten years' penal servitude each on two men convicted of forming part of a riotous mob which attacked the house of a publican named Kerr. Shots were fired from the mob, and the prisoners were arrested in the act of breaking a window, one with a stick the other with a cleaver, and they threatened the lives of several persons who interfered. Robert Eddes, for violently intimidating a family to leave their house, was sentenced to penal servitude for seven years. James Keatley, a publican, found guilty of heading an unlawful assembly, was sentenced to two years' imprisonment. A similar sentence was passed on a man of colour, named Thompson, convicted of heading a riotous mob. In addition to these sentences four persons were ordered to be imprisoned for two months, ten for three months, one (a woman) for four months, ten for twelve months, and four for eighteen months' imprisonment, with hard labour in all the cases. His Lordship said the Government were determined to put a stop to what seemed to be a habit in Belfast on such occasions, namely, taking the law into their own hands; and he hoped the sentences he had passed would deter others from the commission of similar offences.

The Mail of London also mentioned him in its report of the sentences handed out that was published on 7 April.

While Thompson going to prison seemingly marked the end of his story in Belfast, it will come as no surprise that it was absolutely not the end of his story for the *Examiner* stable of newspapers. Articles were published that alleged bias against Catholic prisoners in both the sentencing process and terms of imprisonment. One of these appeared before Thompson and others had been sentenced so was treated as contempt of court.

George's sentencing being deferred for a few days following his conviction and then the punishment he eventually received was the 'proof' for its argument. It compared the sentences given to two Catholics who had been convicted of evicting Protestants from their homes and were instantly given seven years with penal servitude, to that which Thompson received, conveniently ignoring the fact that he had *not* been convicted for house wrecking or evicting Catholics. Justice Lawson made it clear he felt that he *had* been involved in this activity but no victims had come forward to confirm this. In my opinion, the prosecution clearly expected and wanted Margaret Donaghy/Donegan to be their star witness and prove this, but she didn't play ball. This time the vitriol was largely directed at Justice Lawson, with George described as 'the brutal African' and 'black anarch' who led 'the most merciless mob in the world' as they forced out 'hundreds' of Catholic families from the Shankill.[1]

The author of the article was never revealed so it was Daniel MacAleese, the registered proprietor of the newspaper, who faced the wrath of the judicial system. He was fined £250 (£23,707 in August 2025) and sentenced to four months in jail for contempt of court. He definitely *did* enter that imposing Belfast landmark via the tunnel. The judge refused his request to be allowed to cross over the road and enter through the front gate.

The fine was quickly paid off from funds raised by his outraged supporters, who viewed the whole thing as an attack on the freedom of the press and 'proof' of more bias against Belfast's Catholics. They were not alone in believing it was an attack on the freedom of the press and the story was widely reported across the UK. At subsequent meetings in his support, we find George's name being raised and the story being embellished yet further. At a meeting in Coatbridge, Scotland, on Thursday 1 May, a speech by a Mr. John Ferguson included the following:

> *...That judge was Judge Lawson. (Hisses.) He must have been taking lessons from Keogh on the way as to how Ireland should be pacified. Well, in Belfast there was brought before him an extraordinary character who had turned people out of their houses, who had called himself a son of William, and headed a body of 2,000 men as a kind of bodyguard. This gentleman was called William Henry Thompson, a gentleman of colour - a darkey. Well, the poor man was taken up, and I suppose a man of colour is as good an Orangeman as any other man. (Laughter.) This worthy character, who was charged with hunting Papists in broad daylight from street to street, breaking into houses, and knocking down policemen with a club, was found guilty, and ordered to stand aside. Two other men had been found guilty of turning people out of their houses in another part of the town to make room for Catholics that had been disturbed out of a riotous neighbourhood. There were people in the streets who, having been driven away from their houses, were left without house or home; and these two prisoners, actuated by a species of moral justice, if there was no legal justice connected with it, took occasion to make room for the people who had been driven out of their homes. These two prisoners were found guilty and sent to penal servitude for seven years, while a man, who had been convicted of hunting Papists and knocking down policemen with a club, was sentenced to two years' imprisonment; and when the other two prisoners got seven years for doing what was certainly illegal; but which, under the circumstances, might be open to some extenuation...*[2]

As well as the obligatory racism, Ferguson has changed Georges' name, ignores the fact that he was not convicted of house wrecking and makes a false claim that he knocked down policemen with a club.

Daniel MacAleese ended his days serving as the Member of Parliament for North Monaghan. Paying tribute to him after his death on

1 December 1900, Father Crickard, at a meeting of the Belfast Catholic Association drew applause when he said:

> *He was gifted by Providence with great talents, which he used in defence and promotion of the two causes that were dear to the true Catholic's and the true Irishmen's heart - the cause of Faith and the cause of Fatherland.*[3]

The Daily Examiner was of course not shy in pronouncing judgement on George's final appearance in court. It does contain that publications customary offensive language but the mockery of this article is squarely directed at the Protestants of the Shankill - the 'Sons of William':

> *HISTORY teems with examples showing to us the fluctuating and volatile character of public respect for great men. Not less in remote times than in those modern days in which we participate do we find the worship of the populace fickle and unstable, showing the extreme of ingratitude, and making manifest the truth that he leans on a shadow who hopes long to secure the applause and support of the crowd. We shall not weary our readers by citing instances to establish the accuracy of these observations beyond a slight reference to the case of George Henry Thompson, convicted of riotous behaviour in Belfast in the latter days of August last.*
>
> *Mr. Thompson is a man of colour, and if he be not a Sir Knight of the Black Preceptory* he should be, as he could advance indisputable claims to enrolment in that distinguished body of chivalrous gentlemen. When the excitement of August was at its height, and the work of demolition and carnage had attained a magnitude exceeding that occasioned, as we have been authoritatively informed, consequent on the capture of many a conquered city, George Henry Thompson acted a conspicuous and, it would seem, a courageous part. He espoused the cause of William the Third and liberty, and inscribing on his banner the celebrated quotation from the mouth of the Dutchman- "The Protestant religion and the Constitution I will defend"- he took the field at the head of two thousand braves.*
>
> *George Henry did not put on his paint and feathers, and go out upon the war trail without meaning business. Captain Jack, with his handful of Modoc warriors in their stronghold of the Lava Beds,** is not more in earnest in the blood-letting line than was the Ethiopian Orangeman with his two thousand faithful followers in the lanes and alleys abutting on the Shankhill Road. He braved every danger, and, like another Hercules, with a ponderous club he smote the lion of Popery, driving it from its haunts on the Shankhill to the more congenial quarter of the Falls.*

This dark gentleman was for a time the idol of his followers. In their raids he encouraged them by stirring references to the sacrifices made in the cause of civil and religious liberty by their forefathers. He addressed them paternally as "My sons of William," and in return was hailed with cheers, and greeted as a second deliverer, wanting only a grey steed to complete the resemblance to the immortal hero of the Boyne. In an evil moment Mr. Thompson, elated no doubt by his great success, led his two thousand gutter-warriors to the assault of a house in which a hunted Papist had found temporary shelter. He sought to unearth the quarry, but an officer of police interposed, and marred his laudable intention. Protestantism was in danger; the Constitution was threatened, and George Henry, realising the weighty interests at stake, smote the constable, and made a vigorous effort to carry the house by storm.

The sequel finds the Black Knight in the criminal dock, without a friend, without a sympathiser, deserted by the "Sons of William," and standing up a living monument of the ingratitude of the mob. He was repudiated by the solicitor for the Orangemen, and their counsel beat a retreat out of court the moment the poor African put his wooly head about the outworks of the dock. Answer ye "heroes" of the Shankhill Road, and say how is this? Why is your leader, your chief, your second William, deserted in the hour of his need, and abandoned without a word of defence, a word in extenuation, to whatever fate justice may have in store for him? Where are the two thousand braves who looked into the whites of his eyes and greeted him with loud huzzas in the hour of his triumph? Alas! no one is forthcoming of all those for whom he braved danger and forfeited his personal liberty in defending religious freedom and keeping intact the Constitution. So has it ever been, and so we fear shall it ever be.

This poor Ethiopian Orangeman, or Sir Knight of the Black Preceptory, or whatever other title he may be known by in the brotherhood, presents in his case but the invariable lesson taught by history, He was a true and zealous commander-in-chief when the services of such a one were invaluable. In the hour of his triumph he was borne upon the shoulders of the Sons of William, and the members of his band vied in plying him with big pints of porter and forcing upon him other characteristic tokens of their admiration and esteem. Now he is friendless, with no one to speak a word on his behalf, the memory of his anti-Popery exploits forgotten by his friends, and not even a chaplain of the Orange Brotherhood to give him a character.

Mr. Thompson may well take a leaf from the book of Diogenes and turn cynic. The two thousand braves for whom he dared so much brought no succour *to him in his hour of trial, and now lies in his cell awaiting sentence for valorous deeds performed in the interests of Orangeism, the Constitution, and civil and religious liberty. Happy Constitution! happy civil and religious liberty! that in the hour of trial can always reckon upon the strong arms and willing hearts of fighting n****rs like George Henry Thompson.*

* The Royal Black Institution (Preceptory) is one of the Protestant Loyal Orders. Members are known as Sir Knights.
** Captain Jack was an Indigenous American called Kintpuash who was chief of the Modoc tribe of California and Oregon. In 1872 & 1873 the Modoc War took place between the Modoc tribe and white American settlers after the Modoc tribe had been forced off their land and moved to a reservation elsewhere.

Racism aside, it perhaps does make some valid points about the lack of legal representation and witnesses apparently not showing up to give evidence.

Looking at all the evidence presented at the two hearings and trial, one wonders if he was a willing actor in the theatre of mayhem that engulfed Belfast or was he coerced unwillingly onto that violent stage? Did he choose to lead the mob or did the mob choose him to lead them as the witness William Henry suggested in court? We have seen that George clearly had a connection with the Shankill area and if his wife/partner was from the Protestant tradition, he may have identified with them. In which case he might have decided to lead them of his own accord on 18 August 1872, and drink probably played a big part in that.

Equally, he may have just been making his way through the Shankill on his way to Millfield and got caught up in the excitement and unusual circumstances that prevailed. Through the fight at Townsend Street, his acting at McCormick's Show, his job at nearby Ligoniel and possibly living in Millfield, he would have been known to many of those out on the streets, and others would have been aware of him even if they did not know him personally. As a lone Black man, who may have had a physically imposing stature, he would have stood out even more. He could have been talking to acquaintances and sharing a drink with those who were assembled, when one or more of the mob decided that he was going to lead them. These calls would have been rapidly taken up by the rest of the mob and included racial terms that were commonly used at that time. One thing is for sure, if this was the case then he would have had little choice *but* to lead them. No matter how strong he was or how good he was at fighting, politely declining the request of a mob of 2,000 people, many of whom were drunk and had the battle fever on, was simply not an option. And lead them he did in a very theatrical style to boot.

In terms of actual violent behaviour it was fairly minimal - kicking and banging on the door next to the Vulcan Tavern in Upper Townsend Street; punching Constable Crosswell in the shoulder in response to Crosswell grabbing him and lining up a second punch before Mr. McCullough intervened to stop him. At Margaret's house he was one of three men who entered without permission and clearly scared her and her young daughters. However, in her own words, he made no threats of violence to her, he did not order her to quit and ultimately intervened to stop one of the other men from striking her with the grape.

As a comparison, it is worth looking at the case of James Keatley, a white Protestant who was the landlord of the Townsend Street Tavern, 50 Townsend Street. He was also charged with leading a riotous mob and other offences. Police evidence told of him being carried on shoulders, arms and sticks being waved about etc. In his defence there were similar claims to those made in George's second hearing, that the mob had adopted him as their leader against his will, and once in that position, he had no choice but to go along with them. He said he was waving his arms in an attempt to get the mob to release him rather than encourage them. In terms of a defence, it was probably quite fanciful, but his solicitors did make this salient point though:

> *Their worships had cognisance of the fierceness of Belfast mobs both in their magisterial and judicial capacity, and they know that those mobs would turn on a friend as readily as a foe.*[4]

Mr. Keatley's witnesses *did* turn up to support him. To the evident surprise of Judge Lawson, he was cleared by the jury of riot and other offences but found guilty of unlawful assembly and received a two year prison sentence. Lawson stated that he would have added hard labour to the punishment if he had been convicted of the other offences.[5]

When Rev. Hugh Hanna appeared on the Shankill Road during this unsettled period to try and calm the situation down, reports say that as soon as he left his car (horse drawn cab) he was immediately lifted up onto the shoulders of those nearest to him. It does seem to have been a common occurrence with those being carried having little choice in the matter.[6]

Margaret Donaghy - or Donegan - was a brave woman who along with her daughters went through an utterly terrifying and appalling sequence of events. Living in Crimea Street, she was also a Shankill Road woman at this time. What became of her after all this I do not know, but hopefully she and her family had a peaceful life.

As for the racism in the newspapers, it wasn't quite over yet. On 26 July 1873, the *Drogheda Argus* published this, which was reproduced from another paper called *The Nation*. The 'song', to the tune of the minstrel song 'Camptown Races,' was written by Timothy D. Sullivan.

"DE SONS OB WILLIAM"

Amongst the crowd of Orange rioters last year in Belfast one of the most conspicuous individuals was a negro, who distinguished himself by his efforts to rally and inspirit the Orangemen, and lead them on to frequent charges against the "Papists." "Come on, Sons of William," he was often heard to say, before sallying forward to action. Very likely, though the words have not been reported, he had much to say also about the "glorious deeds of 'our ancestors' at Aughrim, Derry, and the Boyne."

He certainly had just as much right as nine-tenths of the Orange Brotherhood to use such language; and probably he knew as much as a majority of them about the real history and character of the events referred to. In the accounts of the demonstrations on last Saturday we do not read of the appearance of this sable admirer of the "glorious, pious, and immortal memory," but we have reason to believe he turned up at one of the festive gatherings which closed the day's proceedings, on which occasion he delighted the company by the performance of the following lyrical effusion :-

De sons ob William sing dis song-
Doo-dah! doo-dah!
De sons ob William mighty strong,
Doo-dah, doo-dah, dah!
We's gwine to booze all night,
We's gwine to booze all day,
We must uphold our ancient right,
An' dat's just what I say.

King William was a fine ole boss,
Doo-dah! doo-dah!
We lubs himself, and lubs his hoss-
Doo-dah, doo-dah, dah!
We'll toast dem bof all night,
We'll toast dem bof all day,
Till William's sons hab got all tight,
For dat's our good ole way!

Our brave forefaders won de Boyne,
Doo-dah! doo-dah!
To sing dere praises all should join-
Doo-dah, doo-dah, dah!
We's gwine to speech all night,
We's gwine to speech all day;
We've Broder Johnston here all right,
Will anybody bring John Rea?

I can't endure dat Pope at all,
Doo-dah! doo-dah!
Because his sense is berry small,
Doo-dah, doo-dah, dah!
We'll cuss him well all night,
We'll cuss him well all day;
For we're de babes ob hebenly light,
And dere we leads de way!

Why should we all wear wooden shoes?
Doo-dah! doo-dah!
Or ledder ones if don't choose?
Doo-dah, doo-dah, dah!
We asks de same all night,
We asks de same all day-
We must uphold our ancient right,
An' dat's just what I say!
- Nation.

In December 1875, just in time for Christmas, T. D. Sullivan's collection of Irish Verses called *Green Leaves* went on sale priced at one shilling.[7] 'De Sons Ob William' was included. As stated in Chapter 2, Sullivan is most famous for writing the Irish Nationalist anthem 'God Save Ireland.' He and his brother Alexander were the driving force behind the fiercely Catholic Nationalist newspaper *The Nation.* He also served as the Lord Mayor of Dublin and as a Member of Parliament for various Irish constituencies. Like Daniel MacAleese, he also served time in prison.

15.
WHITSUNTIDE IN COTTONOPOLIS

After George Henry Thompson was imprisoned the trail in the newspaper archive goes cold; I can find no further direct mentions of him other than in the meetings in support of Daniel MacAleese and the claim made by W. B., the author of the letter from Australia in 1933, about his appearances at the Penny Theatre. This said that he had died shortly after his release from the 'clink.'

However, on 28 May 1874, *The Ulster Echo*, which at that time was a brand new evening newspaper based in Belfast, published this in what was its 3rd ever edition:

A "N**R" IN TROUBLE**

AT the Salford Borough Police Court, yesterday, before Sir J.J. Mantell, George Alex. Thompson, a negro from Jamaica, was charged with gambling with a box and dice on the Manchester racecourse on the previous day.

Detective-Sergeant Kirk having stated the case, prisoner said that he usually played with knives and rings, but a man gave him a box and dice to take care of, promising to give him a share of anything he made by them. He had lived in Manchester 19 years, and had never been brought up in a police court before.

Sir J.J. Mantell- I see there is only one case of gambling at the races yesterday?

Detective Kirk- Yes, sir, because we swept them off the course before the racing commenced.

Prisoner was sent to jail for seven days. The prisoner, if we mistake not, took a prominent part in the riots on the Shankhill Road in 1872.

The following day, 29 May, *The Ulster Examiner and Northern Star* published the same story, changing the headline and the final paragraph slightly. They republished the same story in their Saturday edition, *The Weekly Examiner and Ulster Observer* on 6 June. Their headline was

A "SHANKHILL WARRIOR" IN TROUBLE and the last paragraph read:

> *The prisoner, it is believed, is the coloured man, who in the August riots of 1872, used the rallying cry "Come on, ye Sons of William!"*

As we have seen, this publication was obsessed with Thompson so it is not surprising that they were interested in the story; the only surprise was that *The Ulster Echo* had beaten them to the punch.

The story was quickly picked up by the *Newtownards Chronicle*, which, on 30 May, repeated, word for word, what the *The Ulster Echo* had printed. The significance of this being that this was the newspaper published by William Henry, who was the gentleman that exhibited a large degree of sympathy toward George at his trial in Belfast, and as we saw from his presentation to mark 40 years in the newspaper industry, was very well connected and respected in that field. This would suggest that the newspaper was sure of its facts and presumably had verified them. The headline, with its use of the 'N-word,' seems to indicate that any previous sympathy for George had now gone.

Someone at one of the Manchester newspapers that covered the court case must have telegraphed the details to the *Ulster Echo* and maybe all of the Belfast papers. Or perhaps a member of the public did so. There were large Irish populations in Manchester and Salford, with both the Orange and Green traditions well represented. The Orange lodges of Manchester, Salford and the surrounding areas held a procession on Saturday 11 July from Manchester city centre to Pomona Gardens. Some 2,000 men and women from 32 lodges took part accompanied by marching bands. On Monday 17 August there was a very large attendance at a meeting of the Salford branch of the Irish Home Rule Confederation of Great Britain which was held at the Temperance Hall in Ford Street.

Other than these three newspapers, all based in or near Belfast, I could find no other Irish publications carrying this story. I find it quite telling that two of them had vested interests in the story of George Henry Thompson and his escapades in August 1872.

Of course, the glaring things that would seem to indicate that this person was in fact *not* the same person else are the different name, the claim that this person had lived in Manchester for 19 years and was a

Jamaican - all of which would appear to contradict what we knew about George in Belfast. Also the fact that this conviction was received just over a year after George was sentenced to two years with hard labour in Belfast would suggest that if it was the same person, then he did not serve the full sentence handed down to him by Justice O'Donnell in Belfast and was released after a year or less.

To find out more I decided to check the Manchester based newspapers via the British Newspaper Archive. The first result, from *The Manchester Courier and Lancashire General Advertiser* of 28 May 1874 was almost identical to what the two Irish papers printed, the only minor difference being that they printed J.I. Mantell - which was correct - instead of J.J. Mantell. Then I found this account in *The Manchester Evening News* of Wednesday 27 May:

THIS AFTERNOON'S POLICE
SALFORD BOROUGH COURT
(Before Sir J. I. MANTELL.)
GAMBLING ON THE RACECOURSE.

George Alexander Thompson, a Jamaica black, of Charter Street, Manchester, was charged with gambling on the racecourse. Detective-sergeant Kirk said that at about half-past one o'clock on the previous day he found the prisoner gambling on the Manchester racecourse with the box and dice produced.
Sir John said he saw that this was the only case of gambling at the races.

Detective-sergeant Kirk said the police sent all the gamblers off the course before the races commenced, but the prisoner "tried it on" afterwards. The prisoner said he once lived in Manchester 19 years, ***but had been out of it for three years.*** *(my emphasis). He had a wife and three children now staying in Charter-street, and he would not be guilty of a similar offence if discharged this time. The Prisoner was sent to gaol seven days.*

The significant parts here are George Alexander Thompson stating he had been out of Manchester for three years and also had a wife and three children now staying in Charter Street. The three years could easily be the time spent in Belfast and the claim to have a wife and three children is remarkably similar to what was said by George Henry Thompson at his bail hearing in November 1872 back in Belfast, where we were told there was a wife and (one) child relying on his support. Sadly we were not told where they lived but presumably the authorities in Belfast must have been satisfied that they did exist. It is possible they lived in Manchester or somewhere else in England rather than Belfast, although personally I doubt this. It is also possible that he had wives or partners in different places. No centralised records were kept for marriages. Another possibility was that the wife and child/children claims were not true, but this would have been a risky strategy to adopt if the courts *did* decide to call his bluff and check them out. The offence of gambling at the racecourse was relatively trivial in the wider scheme of things and George Alexander Thompson is making a great play of his connection with Manchester and his family. Was this really necessary for such a case? Something must have worried him to do this.

So if this was the same person then why the change of name? As alluded to previously, this was actually par for the course for habitual offenders in those days - and as we shall see, this person does become a prolific offender. At a meeting in Coventry with the acclaimed author Adam Wood, an expert on crime and punishment in the UK during Victorian times, he confirmed that subtle name changes and/or the use of aliases were common tactics employed when appearing in the dock in a new town or city. George Henry Thompson had been made infamous in Ireland and beyond through his association with the riots of August 1872, and also the case of Daniel MacAleese. So, with this appearance in Salford, a subtle change of name, a claim to have lived in Manchester for 19 years, having no previous convictions and also being from Jamaica rather than America would be consistent with him trying to throw the magistrate off the scent to any previous conviction in Belfast which may have resulted in a heavier sentence. Alternatively, the Jamaican reference could have been a lazy inference made by the reporters at court rather than from anything said by George Alexander Thompson himself - an assumption that because he was a Black man then he must be from Jamaica.

We saw in Belfast that at his first appearance in court in February 1872 for street fighting, his name was given as George Thompson. When he appeared in connection with the riots he was called George Henry Thompson. I mentioned a case from 1866 which I cannot be sure is him, but if it was, then the name given then was Henry Thompson - this would indicate two definite and possibly three subtle name changes in Belfast alone.

Was he released early from prison in Ireland? This is entirely plausible. Then as now, sentences for lesser offences were rarely served in full. Significantly, efforts were being made by the well-to-do people of Belfast - including clergymen of all denominations - to secure an amnesty for those imprisoned for offences committed in the riots of August 1872. In February 1874, a Memorial (petition) had been sent to the Lord Lieutenant of Ireland urging him to consider this. It said there were still about twenty one men in jail, fourteen Protestants and seven Roman Catholics, and while acknowledging the bad behaviour that saw them imprisoned, pointed out that all the major Catholic and Protestant processions of 1873 passed off without incident. They suggested that as Belfast was now a peaceful place again the prisoners could safely be released. This effort was led by Thomas McClure MP, who was soon to be created a Baronet. The response was negative but it was suggested that the incoming Lord Lieutenant, James Hamilton, the Duke of Abercorn, might consider it. At the same time there was also major pressure on the UK Government to grant an amnesty to Fenian prisoners. And while those imprisoned in relation to the riots were not 'political prisoners', they were not far removed from this label due to the sectarian nature of the disturbances. Also, as previously mentioned, the County Jail was overcrowded and this could have been a factor too.

I could not find any reports of prisoners being released but that is not to say it didn't happen. George and others could have been quietly released without any fuss. The chances are that if he *was* released, it would have been in early April 1874, or possibly February if the two months he served on remand were taken into account. This would mean he spent a year in jail in total. If he was the same person as this George Alexander Thompson, then he left Belfast straight away and made his way to Manchester. He would clearly have been a marked man in Belfast where the threat of violent retribution being meted out to him by Nationalists was very likely.

The Manchester Races - known as the Summer Meeting - took place during the Whitsun Week holiday. This holiday was a huge celebration in and around Manchester, which like Belfast, was a rapidly expanding city.

The 1871 census put the population at 357,979 and that of Salford at 102,449, giving a combined total of 460,428.[1] On Whit Monday, the streets of 'Cottonopolis', as the Northern powerhouse was nicknamed at this time, were thronged with thousands of celebrating revellers. The race meeting began on Tuesday.

An alternative view of Manchester's celebrations was published in Belfast by *The Weekly Examiner and Ulster Observer* on Saturday June 6 1874:

WHIT-WEEK IN MANCHESTER

TO THE EDITOR

SIR, - This being the first Whit-week I have ever been in Manchester, I cannot let it pass over without making a few remarks, not on the week, but on the inhabitants of this "Cotton City," who look on this week with pleasure, and seem to say, "Today let joy be unconfined." Foundries, smiths' shops, engineers' shops, and ironworks of every description are at a standstill, for on the streets you can observe thousands of the hardy sons of toil attired in the best they can afford, trudging through the principal thoroughfares, and their clumsy gait gives you to understand at once that few of them are Irish. Factories are also stopped, for on the streets, lanes, and entries you can see numbers of pale-faced, repulsive-looking, half-drunken women, whose very presence forcibly informs you that they first saw the light in some of the dark and disreputable dens, of which there are far too many in this city. If a person who, having seen the fair, virtuous, and pure-minded girls of Erin, would then turn and look at the girls of this country, he would see a contrast that would make him stare indeed. Business men have closed their shops, and clerks have thrown down their pens and quitted their desks, for you may observe numbers of fancy cabs bearing off their living freights to Belle Vue and other parks, where the pleasure-seekers enjoy themselves by indulging freely in rum and beer, and partaking of pies and other eatables that would disorder the stomach of any person except the glutton himself - John Bull. The hum and noise of the very noisy throng meet your ear at every street corner and make a person long to return to "the peaceful spot, the quiet cot, beside old Divis Mountain."

The Union Jack floats from every public building in the city, but this is not remarkable when we know that it waves over you at home. During the week many disgusting scenes I have witnessed - scenes that, thank God, are nowhere to be seen in Ireland. Men here are not abashed, nor are women ashamed, to utter shocking blasphemy and foul language on the public streets. Domestic broils are the order of the day amongst the lower orders of the people here. What would be said of a man in Belfast if, after leaving the beer shop, he came home and committed a murderous assault on his heart-broken wife and weeping little ones? Yet such brutal conduct is looked on as pleasing pastime by enlightened (?) Englishmen. You will not be inclined to credit it, but I assure your readers that it is a fact that women here go to the beer shops, quaff off their glasses, and parade the streets half drunk, forgetful of every womanly virtue and quality. Licentious passions burn fiercely here, for the people imagine that if "they lead a life of pleasure it is no matter how or where."

And no stringent measures are adopted by the Executive to prevent this state of affairs; but we know well that if Rory of the Mountain gives a caution to some West British landlord, then Coercion Acts are soon framed for you on the other side of the Channel. Even our enlightened journalists here do not raise their voices to allay crime - on the contrary, they rather encourage it by giving publicity to the worst trash in their journals. They publish often things you dare not. We know that if an Irish editor tells his countrymen that they should not be serfs in the land where their fathers were freemen, "ere the emerald gem of the western world was placed in the crown of a stranger," he is thereupon "warned" that if he dares to assert the truth his property will be confiscated and himself imprisoned. I am firmly convinced that the youth of this country would not grow up so utterly devoid of grace and so forgetful of the duty they owe towards God, were it not for the immoral prints they read and which some people are in the habit of terming "polite literature." The writers of this so-called literature endeavour to make acts of crime appear as deeds of heroism, and this has an evil tendency on youthful and untutored minds. There is one thing, at all events, certain- viz, that if a nation's righteousness is her only strength, then, beyond all doubt, England is the weakest country in Europe. The Irish element here is pretty strong, and our countrymen and women are sober, respectable, and industrious, and are not unmindful of the land they left in chains and sorrow. They have taken little part in the public amusements here this week, for, like myself, they do not feel at home in Saxon society - in fact, it is seldom the Irish green and Saxon red blend in friendship together. But there are some low, ignorant Irish here who would, if they could, deny the old place; and it would amuse you to hear them try to change their dialect. But I never look on parties of this stamp as Irish. They are but mongrels from Ireland, who, to gain favour at the hands of "big wigs," would deny God as soon as country. But the Celt is ever true, and prays and works for the welfare of the land of his nativity-

The Irish heart, the Irish mind,
May travel earth, o'er ocean roam;
But ah! the Irish soul can find
No joy but in an Irish home.

In conclusion, I only wish our people here to spurn English literature. No Irish man or woman should lift an English print in their hands.

- I remain, dear sir, yours faithfully, J.D.
Salford, May 29, 1874.

George Alexander Thompson was arrested at the racecourse on Tuesday 26 May. Morning mist had cleared from the Irwell Valley and a beautiful afternoon greeted the punters at Salford. The races that day were the Trial Handicap Stakes, which was won by *Mendip*; The Maiden Plate, which *Clarion* won by three lengths from *Serbad*; The Copeland Stakes, where *Thirkleby* beat the favourite *John Peel*; The prestigious De Trafford Cup - which was a mile in distance and offered the most prize money of at least 200 sovereigns - was won by *Tyro*, who beat *Owton* by a length; The Pendleton Stakes, for horses aged 2 years and upwards was won by the favourite *Margarite*, who was sold for 100 guineas after the race to a Mr. Philips, and last but not least, The Philips Handicap Plate, with a prize of at least 100 sovereigns to the winner. This was run over five furlongs, straight, and won easily by the favourite *York*, with *Instantly* coming in second some four lengths behind.[2]

We learned from the court report in the *Manchester Evening News* that George Alexander Thompson said he lived in Charter Street with his wife and three children. Later that year, in October and November, the same newspaper published an astonishing series of articles entitled 'Criminal Manchester' which gave a remarkable insight into the murky underworld that existed in the city. An unnamed correspondent, with a guide from the criminal fraternity called 'Mac', explored what he said were the four principal areas that housed the criminal population - namely Charter Street, part of Deansgate, Ancoats and Gaythorne. The articles, which were so popular that the newspaper quickly published them in book form in time for Christmas of that year, included a vivid account of a visit to Charter Street. The exploration of several boarding houses, known as cribs or dens, formed part of this tour. Printed on 23 October 1874, the tale included the following:

> *At 'Fat Billy's," not far distant, the accommodation was somewhat similar, though the chambers generally, being smaller and more numerous, the wooden partitions were differently arranged. In contrast with the whitewash of the walls and ceilings, the doors had all been coated with coal-tar, and the smell of this pervaded the whole house. Its antiseptic qualities are of course well known, and the idea of thus applying them is worthy of encouragement. The floors and beds were scrupulously clean, even though many of the lodgers were far from appreciating the blessings of cleanliness. In the largest room of all were some half dozen beds and here a curious scene was being enacted. A young negro, with face as black as the tarred doors, was sitting on the side of his couch, holding his face between his hands, and swearing in the most horrible broken-English, for he was enduring the scourge of toothache with about as much fortitude as a child exhibits when first becoming acquainted with molar teeth. To add to his discomfort, he was made the butt of his companions, who were exercising their wit upon him with merciless severity. The remedies that were suggested to "darkie" were as astonishing as unique, and he could scarcely refrain from grinning himself at some of the expressions. It was a sight to be remembered, for a more powerful picture it would have been hard to have designed. The low-browed room looked weird and desolate in the half-light, and the figures of the inmates, in every possible attitude and in every variety of motion, showed forth strangely in the gloom. Restless, and with no signs of possible sleep, here was one sitting straight upright in bed; and there, half-dozing, was another reclining with cheek resting upon his uplifted arm; others lay at full length, with their hands locked beneath their heads - a favourite position with your outcast, who has often thus to supply the want of a pillow when shelterless. Some few were lying passively, with eyes closed, heedless of the tumult, and only showing by their uneasy movements that they were not slumbering. And in the midst of all the white figures that shifted and swayed in the uncertain twilight, with ghostly shadows lurking in dark corners and dancing on the walls, there reared itself the dark image of the poor Man of Colour, as if the unholy Genius of the spot had come to mount guard over his subjects. We watched the "fun" until it appeared as if the n****r would never get to rest at all, and thinking I would see if he could stand a practical joke, I pulled out a small penknife and proposed to "cut his*

> *gums." This latest advanced cure was received with roars of delight by the rough spirits in bed, but Darkie cried off when I showed him the steel, and suggested that I should put my finger in "and feel." I had too much respect for my own flesh and blood to tempt the unfortunate "contraband" to cannibalism, and so left him in his pain to solace himself as best he could.*

One can only wonder who the Black man was that the undercover reporter had met at Fat Billy's and what became of him. I don't think it was George Alexander Thompson but who knows? It's clear that Charter Street was not a place for the faint hearted though.

16.
MOSSLEY WAKES

In 1874, the small mill town of Mossley lay some 9 miles east of Manchester and was close to Stalybridge and Ashton-under-Lyne. Back then, it had a summer holiday festival known as *The Wakes.* These were originally religious in character, but with the industrialisation of England, these wakes became more of a works holiday with less emphasis on the religious aspects. In late July, Mossley put its best foot forward and hosted that year's celebrations. A slightly cynical account of proceedings was given in *The Reporter*, a newspaper published in Stalybridge, on August 1, 1874:

MOSSLEY WAKES

The annual holiday in celebration of "the wakes" has come and gone, and some people are improved in health and strength, whilst others are poorer both in body and pocket. There are two classes more especially to be found in connection with such festivals - those who appropriate the holiday to sightseeing and healthy recreation, and those who devote the whole of their savings to a general drinking spree, and imbibe all sorts of adulterated rubbish, without giving the slightest attention to the rules of nature.

Both parties have distinguished themselves in connection with Mossley Wakes - the former will remember the holiday with pleasure and satisfaction; the latter will have cause to regret their gluttonish and guzzling career. As at other wakes in the neighbourhood, a number of stalls, shows, hobby horses, steam bicycles, and other grim-cracks arrived on the ground for the amusement of those who keep the wakes in the old fashion, but more especially for the entertainment of the juvenile portion of the population.

Prominent amongst the few shows that considered the wakes worthy of their presence was "the world-renowned Miss Anderson's Temple of Magic." Professor Anderson was a clever fellow in his way, and no doubt made himself celebrated as "the Wizard of the North." He has left relations who follow out the "profession" of conjuring in some of the largest halls in the provinces. What relationship can be claimed by the "world-renowned" character at Mossley, it would be difficult to tell. The "lady" did not give a display of her talent "free gratis for nothing," but her chief man appeared in front of the show, and after "swallowing" about a pound of cotton wool, he pulled from his mouth as much silk ribbons as would set up a small milliner's shop - a "feat" which astonished some people. Then there was Williams's exhibition of moving figures, representing disasters at sea and the exploits of a lifeboat crew; and in company with it Mr. Crawford, formerly an operative rope maker, had set up his show of models, which have been much admired. These were the only "intellectual exhibitions" on the ground. They were surrounded by stalls for the sale of articles of various descriptions, and at a short distance off the young men fired away to their heart's content down four rifle tubes belonging to the Cottamses and the Williamses. Then there were a couple of "national portrait galleries," and these, with the attractions already mentioned, formed the whole of the "fun of the fair" ground. The publicans did a "roaring trade." Most of them had provided "musical" attractions. "Little Dick, the great comic," established himself at the Stamford Arms. Mr. James Nield, of the Crown Inn, announced to visitors that he had engaged a serio-comic dancer, a negro melodist dancer, a stump orator, an Irish comedian, and above all Mr. J. Friedenhamer, the celebrated accordeonist, from Manchester; the whole being accompanied by Mr. J. A. Clegg on the pianoforte. Mr. J. Green made his "first appearance" in Mossley at the Fleece Inn, as a "great comic and motto vocalist." He was accompanied by other "stars," who quite astonished the natives. It was announced that Mr. William Young, "the comic" - not the comet as some people would have it - would appear at the George Hotel, and at the same house a public "soiree" was held, Mr. Ormrod's band playing for dancing.

On Monday night the public-houses were besieged with people anxious for a drink, but a large percentage of them were unable to get served, and many of them found more accommodation in Lower Mossley - outside the pale of the fair.

On Monday and Tuesday evening the rush cart was revived. The demonstration was amusing to many spectators, but it had an opposite tendency to what was understood in ancient times, as the bearing of rushes through the streets for the decoration of the church on a festival day. There was no churchism in connection with the Mossley rush cart - the main object was to secure as many coppers as possible for the benefit of those who had undertaken the display. It was a gaily dressed cart, drawn by four horses, having youths, fantastically decorated, on their backs. In front of the horses about a dozen men performed the antics peculiar to Morris dancers, and the whole was accompanied by a drum and fife band. They started each evening from Mrs. Seel's, the Shears Inn, and the collectors received liberal sums of money as they proceeded along the routes assigned to the "processionists." In addition to the above attractions there was a miscellaneous concert as the Mechanics' Institution, the "stars," including Mr. William Rooney, the "celebrated Lancashire tenor," and a couple of individuals who made up a "screaming burlesque and negro entertainment." Mr. John Hayes was the pianist.

On Saturday and Sunday a flower show was held in the band room at Brookbottom, under the auspices of the Mossley Brass Band, the members of which played selections of sacred and operatic music at intervals. These formed the features of the wakes so far as home "pleasures" were concerned, and it must be confessed that there was a fair combination of "show, song, and luxury" to "lift off from man this burthen of mankind."

On Monday the amalgamated trip to Liverpool was a great success, and on Tuesday the trip to Scarborough, under the same management, was well patronised. On Wednesday there was a general rush by road and rail to Belle Vue Gardens to witness the representation of the Battle of Waterloo, and this "outing" terminated the wakes of 1874. It must not, however, be forgotten, that a great number of the residents availed themselves of the opportunity to visit the sea-side for a few days. The Isle of Man, Southport, and Blackpool received their proportions of Mossleyites, and we hear that such excursionists received much benefit from the change of air and scene.

It is here that we have our next account of George Alexander Thompson - or rather William Alexander Thompson - and it is from the same issue of *The Reporter*:

S**BO AT THE WAKES

William Alexander Thompson, a negro, was charged at the Ashton County Sessions on Wednesday, with having, on the 28th of July, at Mossley, been found playing, in a certain open public place, to wit the Market or fair ground, with a certain instrument of gaming at a pretended game of chance. Prisoner pleaded not guilty.

Sergeant Fowler said that at half-past seven last night he was on duty at Mossley, and saw a great crowd of people assembled on the Market ground with the prisoner in the centre and the board produced on top of a tea box. There was a penny put down on one of the cocks painted on the board, and the prisoner wanted the people to stake their pence on such and such cocks. He went forward to get hold of the prisoner, but the prisoner made a dart under the people's legs and ran off. He (witness) then took possession of the board and afterwards apprehended the prisoner. If a person put a penny down on the board there were four chances to one against him, for there were eight cocks, and he only got a penny to his own if he won.

The prisoner prefacing his remarks with the observation that he understood he was in a Christian country, said the board did not belong to himself. The officer had stated the case different from what it was.

(To the officer): Didn't you see me standing up when you came up to me?

The Sergeant: I saw you standing up asking the people to put their pennies down.

Prisoner: Well, if I was standing up and the thing on the ground I could not be attending to it.

The sergeant added that on being searched 6s. was found on the prisoner and of that amount 2s. was in penny pieces.

Prisoner: Well, a person might have a hundred pounds on him and have it all in coppers and silver. If I was standing up how could I be gambling with the thing on the ground?

The Sergeant: He was shouting at the top of his voice, calling attention to his board.

Prisoner: Please, sar, I come to races and fares as well, and dere are many people dat know me in the town dat I am in here. I go to public-houses and sing Irish comic songs and dance with clogs. I also sells brooches, earrings, and so forth. Jack Cooper, Bill Long, and other very respectable people know me. I went into a public-house, and after I had finished a song a young man asked me to drink. I had got 18d. in copper; you see, sar, day were very "stand" company. I said I did not care to drink these strong liquors, but if he would order a ginger beer I would try it. He would not do this and was spitting in my face for refusing to drink de beer, and I shoved him away from me. I den went out of his company and walked towards the fair ground, and I was standing looking at the people playing on de fair ground. A man had another board and was selling three balls for a penny, and if you get one ball true you had a cigar. And there was knives and rings as well. Two men and women are master ob dat affair.

Mr. Hadwen (presiding magistrate) Why did you run away?

Prisoner: I thought he was going to take me up for shoving de fellow down. I am 19 years in England, sar, and hab neber ben up before.

Sergeant Ashton said people had come to him complaining about the prisoner cheating people, and he put Fowler on to look after him.

The prisoner: I was only de servant as I hab a soul to be saved.

(To the audience): Hab any ob you seen me in de town singing comic songs? (Laughter.)

Mr. Hadwen: Listen to me, you are sentenced to 14 days' imprisonment, with hard labour.

Prisoner: Well, I have a wife confined last Friday night. If you fine me I will pay it.

Mr. Ludlum: They cannot fine you; stand down.

*S**bo was then removed, but he was again put into the box at a later stage, and Mr. Ludlum applied that the expenses of his commitment and conveyance to gaol might be stopped out of the money found upon him.*

Mr. Coulthart: Have we power to do that?

The Clerk: You have.

Mr. Ludlam: It rests entirely with the magistrates. We are directed in all cases to apply.

Mr. Hadwen: How many children have you?

Prisoner: Three; my wife was confined last Friday. She is in Manchester. I do not tell a story. I hab my return ticket in my pocket.

Four shillings were ordered to be stopped from the prisoner's money.

This is clearly the same person as George Alexander Thompson. He says he has been in England 19 years and has three children which is identical to what was said at the court appearance in Salford. His wife is confined in Manchester, which, if true, presumably means she was recovering from giving birth. The reference to singing Irish comic songs in public houses is very interesting to say the least. Of course, with large Irish communities in England at this time, these could have been learned from them, or he could have heard others performing them in pubs and just copied them, but if I am correct in believing him to be the same person as George Henry Thompson, then the chances are these were learned in Belfast. Maybe it was this person who Mr. James Nield of the Crown Inn at Mossley had hired as a 'negro melodist dancer' to perform at his public house during the wakes? Singing and dancing certainly fits with what George Henry Thompson was doing at McCormick's Show in Belfast.

The account also shows he is very much living at the margins of society. The style of speech attributed to him seems to flit between standard English and the stereotyped Black English we saw so much of previously. If William *was* flitting between the two, perhaps he was going into 'character' and hamming it up to play to preconceptions of Black people held by white people at that time? William also stated he has never been up before in court. It may have been true for this location and using this name, but certainly wasn't true for elsewhere. This is also where a subtle change of name comes in handy due to the lack of shared criminal records and to confuse anyone who may have recognised his name in the reporting of the previous recent case at Manchester racecourse. If this person was indeed George Henry Thompson, then was the change of name to William also a nod to his escapades in Belfast? Or could it have been a nod to another famous William

Thompson of that time - the former champion bare knuckle fighter from Nottingham known as Bendigo?

On the same page of this newspaper was another report in a column entitled *SPARKS FROM THE ANVIL* which criticised the behaviour of locals and visitors to the Wakes in Mossley. Part of it read:

> … *A public-house was also "favoured" with the company of a n****r who had evidently drunk ardent spirits, not until his hair curled, because that is natural to him, but until his brains were topsy-turvy. He had been fighting with the "champion of the village," and he boasted he had conquered him. Such a conclusion to the conflict could not be concealed, consequently, with arms extended like windmill sails, he proceeded to the railway station, to curse, and swear, and reel about to the great annoyance of a number of respectable passengers. He declared himself prepared to fight anyone in Mossley, and there is no doubt in his own opinion he could beat "Akeybo." He would be a fit match for him, and if he "licked" him he might match himself with a still blacker man than himself, for it is said Akeybo beat the devil.*

The newspaper does not link this account to the court report of William Alexander Thompson, so one can only ponder if they are referring to him or another Black man that attended the Wakes? As for Akeybo I have no idea what legend or myth that is related to.

17.
RINGLEADER

So what more information could be found about George Alexander Thompson who had now become William Alexander Thompson?

Another plunge into the British Newspaper Archive revealed that he goes on to appear in numerous court cases for similar offences, mainly at racecourses across the north of England. He is sometimes referred to as a ringleader of cardsharpers from Manchester. Cardsharpers were experts at cheating at card games, often using sleight of hand or doctored cards to help them. Accomplices would play the part of 'dupes', pretending to win on games to lure punters in and to also act as lookouts for the police. It wasn't uncommon for them to have fake money - counterfeit coins and what were termed 'flash' notes. Illegal gambling on various games was rampant at racecourses, in railway train carriages, popular markets and also at fairs during this period - in fact anywhere where crowds gathered. By the 1870s, the railway network pretty much covered the whole of England and made travelling to events where people congregated in large numbers easy. People also walked a lot further in those days too. Interestingly, I can find no accounts of a George Alexander Thompson or William Alexander Thompson in court reports for this activity prior to 27 May 1874.

Here are a selection of newspaper reports about Mr. Thompson's subsequent exploits to show how prolific his court appearances were and which clearly demonstrate what a precarious life he led in Victorian England.

THE SHEFFIELD DAILY TELEGRAPH, TUESDAY 22 JUNE 1875:

DONCASTER BOROUGH POLICE, MONDAY.

Wm. Alexander Thompson, a black man, was charged with illegal gaming by playing the three-card trick. The case having been proved, defendant stated that as it was a pound to a penny against him he would speak the truth. He then related how, seeing a friend win £30 by the same game, and being told if he was apprehended he would always have more than would pay the fine, he was induced to try his hand. He also very readily communicated the information that it was always 2 to 1 against the public winning, and should the man with the cards happen to have two or three colleagues it was 100 to 1 against any man picking out the right card. Defendant was fined £1 and 13s. costs.

THE LEEDS TIMES, SATURDAY 16 OCTOBER 1875:

BRADFORD: A TRIO OF SHARPERS.

At the Borough Court, on Tuesday:

Wm. Alexander Thompson, an enterprising gentleman of colour, who stated that he came from Birmingham, was charged with a similar offence. He was seen gambling with a marble and a board, and offering to bet two to one on the result. He took a lot of money. When apprehended three cards were found upon him. He offered the officer who took him into custody 8s. to let him go. Prisoner stated that the game was fair, and had been patronised by the "nobilities." He played for nuts and not for money, and he would be obliged to the magistrates if they would let him go. The Chief-Constable said that the nuts were merely used by the prisoner as a blind. Thompson was sentenced to two months' imprisonment.

THE LIVERPOOL WEEKLY COURIER, SATURDAY 31 MARCH 1877:

PICKPOCKETS AND SHARPERS AT THE RACES

At the Basnett-street Police Court on Saturday (24 March), before Messrs. Thomas Brocklebank and H. B. Gilmour, about thirty persons of the lower class of the betting and sporting fraternity were brought up in custody charged with sharping and other offences at the Aintree races.

… Wm. Alexander Thompson, a man of colour, was charged with playing at the three-card trick at the racecourse on Friday. Thomas Smith, a labourer, of Liverpool, said that the prisoner and three others were by the roadside, prisoner having three cards, one of which was the queen of clubs and the two others dummies. Witness bet a sovereign that he would pick up the queen of clubs, and then he saw prisoner shuffle the cards so that witness picked up a "dummy."

Witness wanted his sovereign back, but the only coin the prisoner had was a bad sovereign, which witness got out of his mouth.

Prisoner: A man like him would swear anything. He would swear black was white, and white was no colour. (Laughter.) Dis fellow dropped a sovereign on de floor, and de five of us was havin' a scramblin for de sovereign. (A laugh.) I work in ironworks, I'm a puddler, and know nothing about cards. Sentenced to two months' hard labour.

This was the day that the *Grand National* took place - Friday 23 March. Sixteen horses ran and *Austerlitz* won, with *Congress* in 2nd and *The Liberator* in 3rd.

THE PRESTON CHRONICLE AND LANCASHIRE ADVERTISER, SATURDAY 12 APRIL 1879:

PRESTON QUARTER SESSIONS.

SECOND COURT, WEDNESDAY.- Before C. R. Jacson, D. Irvin, and other magistrates.

ALLEGED THEFT BY A NEGRO.

William Alexander Thompson, 25, a negro, pleaded not guilty to breaking and entering the dwelling-house of Adolphus Henry Shroeder, Paradise-street, Preston, and stealing therefrom one coat, one waistcoat, and two pairs of trousers. Mr. Hulton prosecuted.The prisoner urged that the property was given to him by a man whom he met in the street. A verdict of not guilty was returned, and the prisoner was discharged with a severe reprimand.

Interestingly, another document exists for this incident. The record from HM Prison, Preston, corroborates the age and also gives Thompson's profession as a Tailor. It also mentions a previous conviction from Manchester on 14 June 1878. I have been unable to find any newspaper reports about this though.

THE STOCKTON EXAMINER, SATURDAY 23 AUGUST 1879:

Thursday (21st) Before E Henderson and Thos. Mellanby, Esqs.

CARD SHARPERS

Wm. Thompson, a coloured man and the ringleader of a gang of sharpers, was charged with playing the "three card trick." He was sent to Durham Gaol to undergo two months' hard labour without the option of a fine.

THE COURIER (LIVERPOOL), SATURDAY 8 NOVEMBER 1879:

GAMBLING AND THEFT AT THE RACES

Mr. H. A. Bright and Mr. F. Hollins sat at the Basnett-street Police Court yesterday, to dispose of a number of prisoners who had been arrested during the races at Aintree on Wednesday and Thursday. William Alexander Thompson, of Manchester; Joseph Bristow, Liverpool; Wm. Hughes, Liverpool; and Robert Bolton, Liverpool, were fined 20s. and costs for gambling.

And then the trail goes fairly cold. In the 1880s I have some reports which could be the same person and one from the early 1890s:

THE GRAVESEND JOURNAL, DARTFORD OBSERVER AND COUNTY INTELLIGENCER, SATURDAY 17 SEPTEMBER 1881:

Friday, Sept. 16. Before Mark Martin, Esq. (Mayor), G. Taylor, and G. Spain, Esq.

William Thompson, a man of colour, charged by P.C. Vellensworth with being drunk and disorderly in the market-place on the previous night, was fined 2s 6d, or four days'.

THE MORNING POST, WEDNESDAY 11 JANUARY 1882:

POLICE INTELLIGENCE

LAMBETH

William Thompson, 33, a man of colour, living in the Mint, Southwark, and described as a "fire eater," was charged with being drunk, disorderly, and using obscene language in the Walworth- road.

Police-constable 232 P said the prisoner was in the habit of going about the streets "eating fire."

Mr. Chance wanted to know what that meant.

The witness replied that the prisoner, after getting persons around him, would put lighted matches into his mouth.

Mr. Chance asked how many matches, or if it was a boxful. (Laughter.)

Witness said single matches; after going through a performance he collected money from the crowd. Last night, as there was an obstruction, he told the prisoner to go away, when he refused, became very violent, and used bad language. So violent did his conduct become that he had to be taken to the station. He had before been charged at Southwark Police-court.

Mr. Chance said if the prisoner went on in such a way he would be severely punished. If he liked to "eat fire," as he termed it, he must do it without causing a disturbance in the street. He ordered him to pay a fine of 5s., or five days.

If this is the same person then there is a discrepancy with his age from 1879 when he was recorded as being 25. In 1882 he would have been 28 if his age was recorded accurately in 1879. Having said this, William may well have given different ages just as he gave different names to deliberately confuse the authorities. Alternatively, the authorities could have simply ascribed an estimated age to him themselves.

THE SHIELDS DAILY NEWS (SOUTH SHIELDS) MONDAY 3 JULY 1882:

LOCAL INTELLIGENCE

CARD-SHARPING AT GOSFORTH

Wm. Thompson, described as a person without a place of abode, was charged at the Moot Hall Police Court, on Saturday, with having played the three card trick at Gosforth on the 29th ult. (29 June)

The Chairman (Mr. J. P. Mulcaster) said that he never saw so many card-sharpers at any race course as there were at Gosforth Races; there was a perfect street of them. The magistrates were determined to put the practice down.

The sentence of the Court was that accused should be imprisoned for fourteen days.

(There is no mention of this Wm. Thompson being Black in this report.)

DERBYSHIRE ADVERTISER AND JOURNAL, FRIDAY 7 SEPTEMBER 1883:

CLAY CROSS. POLICE COURT.

Monday. Before C. BINNS, Esq.

Wm. Thompson, who said that he was a native of Africa, was charged by police-constable Dooley with being drunk and quarrelsome in Market-street, on Saturday night.

Committed to prison for seven days, in default of paying a fine of 2s. 6d. and costs.

THE YORKSHIRE HERALD, TUESDAY 22 SEPTEMBER 1891:

THEFT FROM A LODGING HOUSE

A coloured man, named William Thompson, was charged at Middlesbrough yesterday with stealing a purse, containing two florins, two eardrops, and two rings, the property of Jane Farmer. The prisoner, who lodged at the house of the parents of the prosecutrix, entered her bedroom during the night, and took the purse from a pocket that was hanging on the bed-post. Prisoner pleaded, in mitigation, that he was drunk at the time and got into the wrong room. P.C. Dobson deposed to arresting him, when he was quite sober. He was sentenced to six weeks' hard labour.

After the last report from 1891 I can't find anything else that is definitely William Alexander Thompson / William Thompson. With some of the above reports I can't be 100% sure that it is the same person as there may have been other Black men called William Thompson or in some cases a white man of that name.

So what became of him? Well I can't be certain but did come across this intriguing article from a Sheffield newspaper called *The Weekly Telegraph* dated Saturday 29 April 1899:

A Racecourse Tragedy.

Numerous tales are told relating to incidents on the racecourse, but these are more or less concerning the horses, trainers, or jockeys. A police-officer, (who is now an inspector in a Lancashire town) once had a very exciting experience on one of our race courses.

He and several other officers were told off to watch a party of cardsharpers, who had been a regular pest. The ringleader was a tall, well-made black man. One afternoon the officers made a determined attempt to arrest them, the inspector making a dash for the black. That individual, however, took to his heels and ran down an adjacent field, opposite which a row of bookmakers were standing. The "bookies," seeing the policeman in chase, at once began shouting "2 to 1 on the Bobby! 2 to 1 on the bobby!" The policeman had "run from scent to view," when his quarry jumped into a ploughed field. Pursuer and pursued had not gone much further before a cheer went up from the crowd as they saw the blacky fall and lie quite still. The officer ran to seize his man, but he was too late. Over-exertion had done for the "darkie," who was dead as a door-nail.

Despite my best efforts I couldn't find anything in the British Newspaper Archive to corroborate this story - surely it would have made the papers when it happened and an inquest held into the death? I did find a remarkably similar story but the victim was not William Alexander Thompson. He was at the same meeting though, and was convicted for gambling offences. It was at Aintree on the day that the Grand National took place - Friday 23 March 1877. This particular death was widely reported:

THE BRADFORD DAILY TELEGRAPH, MONDAY 26 MARCH 1877:

SUDDEN DEATH ON A RACECOURSE - On Friday afternoon, after the running of Grand National Steeplechase at Aintree, the police were pursuing three card-sharpers over a ploughed field, when one of the fugitives dropped down and expired immediately.

And from *The Liverpool Daily Post* of Tuesday 27 March 1877 we have this:

THE SUDDEN DEATH AT AINTREE

INQUEST YESTERDAY

Yesterday morning, the county coroner (Mr. Driffield) held an inquest at the Railway Inn, Fazakerley, on the body of James Crook, hawker, who died under circumstances already briefly reported.

Sergeant Robinson stated that on Friday last he and Police-constable McBeth were on duty at Aintree Racecourse, where they saw the deceased and several other men playing the three-card trick. They succeeded, with the aid of other constables, in capturing six of the gang, but the deceased and three companions escaped. Subsequently, however, they were discovered in a field behind the Railway Inn, Fazakerley. They gave chase, and after running some distance Crook fell down, and died before medical aid could be procured.

James Eldon, who was in custody, said he had known the deceased for five or six years. The deceased was a hawker and lived at Dukinfield, Cheshire. They met at the Grand National, and he (witness) was subsequently captured in a field by a policeman; and he afterwards learned that the deceased, who had run with him, had dropped down dead. Crook seemed to be in robust health, and ran very well.*

*Joseph Holcroft,** who said he was a shoemaker, living at Manchester, stated that he first saw the deceased running across the fields. He did not know him before. They were both running to catch a train, and they saw an officer whom they took to be a gentleman farmer. The deceased fell down without being touched by anybody.*

Elizabeth Crook said she was the wife of the deceased. He was forty-four years of age, and she had been married to him twenty-four years. He left home on Monday last, and told her that he would go to Liverpool in the course of the week. He had always been a healthy man, although he drank immoderately when he could get it.

The Coroner, at this point, said he and the police had expected that the friends of the deceased would have stated that the deceased had been in ill-health, or had been subject to heart disease, or something. Therefore, a post-mortem examination had not been ordered. If, however, the jury was satisfied that death must have occurred from natural causes, together with the excitement the man had undergone in trying to escape from the police – and if they did not care to know the precise failure internally – they could come to a decision without the aid of a medical man. If they were not satisfied, he would adjourn the inquest and order a post-mortem examination.

Several jurymen said they thought the evidence was quite sufficient. "He had died from heart disease or something sudden, and it was quite clear that no violence had been used."

A verdict was returned to the effect that the man had "died from some internal disease during excitement brought on by being chased by the police."

* James Eldon, also spelled Elton in reports, and ** Joseph Holcroft, whose surname was also given as Foxcroft and Foxgrove in earlier reports, were with James Crook when the police, who were in plain clothes, began their pursuit. After the inquest, they were both sentenced to three months' imprisonment with the money that was found on them being confiscated to pay for their upkeep in jail.

Maybe just maybe the story altered over the years? There is mention of a ploughed field and a sudden death after a chase by the police. The policeman is now an inspector in Lancashire, so maybe Sergeant Robinson was promoted in due course?

However, if we assume it is a *true* story, then the chances are it *had* to be William Alexander Thompson. Most of his cardsharping / gambling exploits took place in the North of England and he was most definitely regarded as a ringleader in this activity. Chances were he was also a tall and physically imposing man. Could there have been more Black men doing the same thing at that time? If there were, I did not find any reports of them during this time period and in the locations associated with William Alexander Thompson.

If he did meet his end in a ploughed field running away from the police, is it possible the usual formalities of an inquest were dispensed with because he was a Black man on the wrong side of the law? Did no one come forward to identify him? Does he lie in an unmarked grave in a churchyard somewhere near a racecourse?

18.
THE SON OF THE SON OF WILLIAM?

In late 1876, there are newspaper reports of Black man called William Bennett from Matlock Street, Shankill Road, reportedly cursing the Pope and in some accounts, shouting "Come on ye sons of William!" He was fined for his troubles. There are even suggestions that, despite the different surname, he is the son of George Henry Thompson. One account which claims this gives his age as 10, which would take us back to 1866. If true, that would tie in with the account of Henry Thompson from New York who was convicted that year for fighting in Walker's Lane at a brothel. A Rachel or Rachael Thompson is next in the dock (in most reports) saying she is a "son of William." Thompson is of course the same surname as George's. William Bennett's court case and hers don't appear to be linked in any of the reports though.

I reproduce the articles below so you can try and decide for yourselves if there really was a father / son connection or it was just a case of very creative writing from the authors of those claims, linking the cases purely because both involved Black men from the Shankill area of Belfast and the 1872 case involving George being referenced in court.

For me, they amply demonstrate the difficulty of putting together an accurate telling of the tale when there are so many variances in the reporting of the same event - one even inaccurately states that George received seven years in prison for his part in the 1872 riots. Also the report saying William Bennett was just ten years old seems quite fanciful. I am sure every report would have noted a boy of ten being in the dock and not just one if this truly was the case, but who knows?

Belfast Evening Telegraph, Wednesday 27 December 1876:

THIS DAY'S POLICE

CUSTODY COURT

Before J C O'Donnell Esq., R.M. and Samuel McCausland Esq., J.P.

PARTY EXPRESSIONS

A coloured man named William Bennett was charged with shouting, "Come on, ye sons of William," and with cursing the Pope. The offence was proved, and defendant fined 40 shillings and costs, or, in default, one calendar month imprisonment.

Rachel Thompson was next placed in the dock and charged with declaring herself a son of William, of Dr. Drew, and Dr. Cook. She was also drunk and disorderly at the Albert Crescent Barracks. The Bench, owing to an appeal made on prisoners behalf by her sister, imposed the moderate fine of five shillings and costs.

Susannah Smith was charged with drunkenness, and shouting "Hell roast the Pope and Joe Biggar." After being arrested in Malvern Street the prisoner persisted in making use of the expressions until she was brought to the office. The Bench fined her 40 shillings and costs.

The Ulster Echo, Wednesday 27 December 1876:

BELFAST POLICE NEWS

CUSTODY COURT

Before J.C. O'Donnell, Esq., R.M. and Samuel McCausland Esq., J.P.

SONS OF WILLIAM

WILLIAM BENNETT, a negro of about 10 years and son of a noted coloured gentleman of the same name, who got seven years for participation in the riots of 1872, and who was described as leading his forces through the perturbed districts of the town with the war cry of "Come on ye sons of William," was placed in the dock for cursing the Pope. Mr. Harper said it struck him that the first coloured man who was charged with a political offence got so much that the second one should get off all together. Mr. O'Donnell said he could not follow the precedent set in the case referred to, and would impose a fine of 40 shillings and costs.

The next case, though not necessarily having any affinity with the former one, had some indirect coincident circumstances. The prisoner accused was Rachael Thompson, and the offence charged was declaring herself a "Son of William, Drs. Cooke and Drew," and numerous other defunct celebrities. Her political fervency exceeded her discretion, and she selected the Albert Crescent Barracks wherein she might assert her claims to a noble ancestry. An energetic constable in that office, however, not believing in the principle of the "lion being bearded in his own den," arrested her. The prisoner's sister appealed for leniency, and declared her inability to pay a fine, but on the Bench imposing a penalty of 5 shillings and costs, she produced a large quantity of silver and gold.

Ulster Examiner and Northern Star, Thursday 28 December 1876:

BELFAST POLICE COURTS - YESTERDAY

CUSTODY COURT

Before Mr. O'DONNELL, R.M., and Mr. McCAUSLAND, J.P.

PARTY EXPRESSIONS

Wm. Bennett, of Matlock Street, * *about seventeen years of age, and of colour, was charged with drunkenness and disorderly conduct, and also with using party expressions by cursing the Pope. The prisoner admitted the charge.*

Mr. HARPER observed that the last man of colour who was charged with conduct of this description got so well punished that it occurred to him the next man of colour should get off without any punishment.

Mr. O'DONNELL said he could not concur in taking that as a precedent for no punishment now.

Fined 40s and costs, or one month in jail.

* I could not find anyone with the surname of Bennett living in Matlock Street in the *Belfast and Province of Ulster Directory 1877*. There are two William Thompsons listed; one a leather-cutter at No. 11 and the other a carpenter at No. 42.

The Northern Whig, Thursday 28 December 1876:

BELFAST POLICE COURTS - YESTERDAY.

FIRST COURT.

Before Mr. J. C. O'Donnell R.M.; and Mr. S. McCausland J.P.

PARTY EXPRESSIONS

Fanny Smith was charged by Sub-Constable Adam McCaffrey with having been drunk and disorderly in Malvern Street, off the Shankhill Road. The Prisoner was cursing the Pope and Joe Biggar. (Laughter.) Fined in 40 shillings and costs.

Wm. Bennett, a man of colour, was brought up in custody, charged with having been drunk and disorderly in the public street, and making use of party expressions by cursing the Pope. Mr. Harper said he was present at the Assizes in Belfast when Judge Lawson passed a sentence on a man of colour for shouting " Come on ye sons of William," that he thought ought to have been a warning to people of his complexion. A fine of 40 shillings and costs was imposed.

Robert Miller was charged by Sub-Constable Flanagan with having been drunk and disorderly in Great Patrick Street. After being arrested he cursed the Pope. A similar penalty was inflicted.

Rachael Thompson was brought up in custody of Sub-Constable McCaull, charged with having been drunk and disorderly in the public street. the prisoner shouted that she was a true blue, and one of the sons of King William. The case was treated as one of drunkenness, and a fine of 5 shillings and costs was imposed.

(Also) The Northern Whig, Thursday 28 December 1876:

We are not yet done with party expressions. This Christmas they appear to have been very much on the lips of some zealous Protestants, male and female, black and white. People in other parts of the United Kingdom cannot understand what it is which induces enthusiastic persons in Belfast, generally of the very poorest classes, to relieve their minds by cursing a King WILLIAM or the POPE.

Yesterday Mr. O'Donnell had in succession before him three of these cases. It will be remembered that during the riots of 1872 a black man was distinguished by his ardent Protestant zeal. He led to the attack on a public-house not far from High Street a band of zealots almost as determined as himself. His cry was, "Come on, sons of WILLIAM! The black man was captured by the police, and sentenced by Mr. Justice Lawson to a long term of penal servitude.

The boy is the father of the man, as the man is the father of the boy. The black man left a son six years of age. That boy is now ten, and was yesterday placed in the dock for cursing the POPE with juvenile precocity. A solicitor urged that as the father had received such a heavy sentence the son ought to be let off altogether. Mr. O'Donnell, as was to be expected, did not see the force of this plea. On the boy, who had so well profited by the paternal example, the RESIDENT MAGISTRATE inflicted the usual fine 40 shillings and costs.

A lady, too, with the name of RACHEL THOMPSON, was accused of publicly calling herself a "Son of WILLIAM", and also of two other distinguished Protestant celebrities who had assuredly very little in common with the PRINCE OF ORANGE, Dr. COOKE and Dr. DREW. She declared that she could not pay a fine; but, on being sentenced to find five shillings and costs, she produced a considerable sum in silver and gold.

Another lady, even more resolute, was accused of anathematising the honourable Member for Cavan and the POPE in the same breath. She wished them to be roasted; she wished them to be sent together to the infernal regions. She persisted in giving loud utterances to these not very charitable aspirations while she was being taken to the Police Office, and even when she found herself within its walls. She too was fined 40 shillings and costs.

*What is the world outside Belfast to think of such exhibitions? People who do not know us are utterly unable to enter into this sectarian spirit, which seems at once to be so ludicrous and lamentable. The clergy of all denominations have yet a very great work to do. Even all Dr. PORTER'S sympathies as a Christian missionary and as Dr. COOKE'S son-in-law ought not to be with the Turks. There is a great field for missionary and truly apostolic work at home. The people sentenced yesterday called themselves Christians and Protestants, and think that they are following in the footsteps of Dr. COOKE and Dr. DREW.**

*Dr. Henry Cooke (1788-1868) and Dr. Thomas Drew (1800-1870) were evangelical Protestant clergymen. Cooke was a Presbyterian and Drew belonged to the Church of Ireland. As well as being a staunch Orangeman, Rev. Dr. Drew was a notable opponent of slavery and played an important role in Belfast's abolitionist movement. It's worth going on another slight tangent to take a brief look at his anti-slavery stance.

The Vindicator of Saturday 7 November 1840 carried this notice:

IMPORTANT

Anti-Slavery Meeting.

AT a PUBLIC MEETING of the BELFAST AUXILIARY to the BRITISH and FOREIGN ANTI-SLAVERY SOCIETY held on Thursday Evening, October 29, 1840, in the Presbyterian Church, Rosemary-street (in connexion with the General Assembly),

The Rev. THOMAS DREW in the Chair:

The following Resolutions were unanimously adopted:-

Moved by the Rev. Dr. EDGAR, and seconded by Rev. WM. GIBSON -

1. That the warmest sympathy and most hearty congratulations of this Meeting are hereby tendered to that noble and self-devoted band of Emancipators in the United States of America, who, with a zeal and power reflecting honour on the human name, are labouring to free their coloured brethren from a degrading Slavery, sanctioned by the American Government, and, to the disgrace of Religion, patronised by American

Churches; and that they be encouraged to persevere in their noble efforts by the success which has already crowned the labours of British Emancipators, as well as by the plain assurance of the word of God, that liberty shall yet be triumphant.

Moved by the Rev. JOSIAS WILSON, and seconded by JAMES STANDFIELD, Esq. -
2. That, while we applaud the Christian enterprise and admire the national greatness of the Americans, we look with shame and abhorrence on her legalised system of Slavery, and are constrained to express our opinion, that the British Churches should refuse the right hand of Christian fellowship to such members of Churches of America as shall continue to be participators in the sin of Slavery.

Moved by the Rev. Dr. BRYCE, and seconded by Dr. SCOTT -
3. That, having heard with deep regret, that certain Irishmen in the United States, Cuba and the Brazils, are Slave-owners, and that others of our countrymen in America are hostile to the abolition of Slavery, this meeting express, with the strongest feelings, their abhorrence of such conduct, and hold it up before the Christian world as deserving the execration of all friends of liberty, and of all influenced by the spirit of the Gospel of Jesus.
THOMAS DREW, Chairman.
Mr. DREW having left the chair, and the Rev. WILLIAM GIBSON being called thereto, it was moved by the Rev. Dr. EDGAR, and seconded by Rev. JOSIAS WILSON : -
That the warmest thanks of this meeting be returned to the Rev. THOS. DREW, for his very proper conduct in the chair.
WILLIAM GIBSON, Chairman.

Rev. Dr. Drew attended a number of meetings in Belfast where Frederick Douglass, the renowned African-American abolitionist and civil rights activist was the guest of honour and gave lectures. One of these took place on Friday 5 December 1845 and the following year, *The Northern Whig* of Thursday 9 July 1846 reported on another important gathering:

ANTI-SLAVERY MEETING
A MEETING was held, last night, in the Primitive Wesleyan Chapel, Donegal-place, to hear the fugitive slave, Mr. Frederick Douglass.
The Chair was taken by Doctor DREW.

On the platform were several Ministers and gentlemen of the Anti-Slavery Committee. Mr. DOUGLASS gave a most eloquent lecture, of nearly two hours, which was listened to with breathless attention. He demonstrated the imperative duty of every Church to refuse fellowship with men polluted with the sin of stealing their fellow-men, and holding them in hopeless bondage.

He especially alluded to the fact, that he the slave, and Dr. Smyth, of Charleston, the Minister, at least, of a slave-holding Church, should now meet in Belfast; and he challenged him to contradict any of his (Mr. Douglass's) statements, or convict him of falsehood. In America, he dared not challenge Dr. Smyth, he would soon be put down; but here, on the Belfast soil, under the protection of British law, the truth was not in danger. He trusted that the Irish General Assembly would do as the other sections of the Christian Church, and as the Evangelical Alliance had done, namely, refuse all fellowship with slaveholders; and concluded by expressing his delight at the spirit which seemed to pervade the General Assembly, during the debate on this subject, that morning.

The Rev. I. NELSON then moved a resolution, expressing the duty of all missionary Churches to take an interest in the melancholy condition of 3,000,000 of slaves in the Southern States of America, deprived of access to the Scriptures.

The Rev. Dr. EDGAR, of Armagh, seconded the resolution, in a speech of great power and argument, proving that the Sacred Scriptures gave no countenance to the interpretation attempted to be put upon them by the slaveholding Divines of America; that slaveholders, and buyers, and all engaged in the vile traffic, were ranked by the Apostle Paul as murderers of fathers and murderers of mothers, and they were just in such company as they were entitled to. The Rev. Speaker sat down amid much applause. The Rev. J. HODGENS was then called to the Chair, and a vote of thanks passed to Dr. Drew; after which, the meeting separated.

In July 2023, a statue of Frederick Douglass was unveiled at Lombard Street in Belfast to commemorate his important historical connection to the city.

19.
BLESSINGS, COURAGE AND LOVE

Here our stories are nearly at an end. The primary one of course is about George Henry Thompson, who may or may not have also been known as Henry Thompson, George Alexander Thompson and William Alexander Thompson. I have made many educated guesses to link them as the same person, but that is all they are - without a time travelling machine I doubt we will ever know for sure. What we do know is that George Henry Thompson *definitely* had an incredible time in Belfast. Fisticuffs in Townsend Street with Arthur McIntyre, treading the boards at McCormick's Show, and then, on August 18, with the town in tumult, his pièce de résistance, leading a 2,000 strong mob of Shankill Road fighting men with the immortal cry of "Come on ye sons of William!" Not to mention his encounter with Margaret and her young daughters in Crimea Street. This was followed by imprisonment and of course the overtly racist letters, editorials, articles and songs written about him in the press. That's quite something for *any* person let alone a Black person in the 1870s!

My gut feeling is that the George Alexander Thompson AKA William Alexander Thompson we find in England was the same person, and the adventures that took place there were almost as astonishing as those that took place in Belfast. If it *was* a different person, then he was remarkably similar to George Henry Thompson.

History should include those from all walks of life. It is not complete without it. Ideally it should be told honestly and without bias. Andrew Boyd started this journey off with his book *Holy War In Belfast*. On finding his account to be vastly different to what is written in the contemporary newspapers, which are the only sources available to researchers, I hope I have provided a more accurate account of George Henry Thompson and also that of Margaret Donaghy/Donegan.

The next Black man to make a big impression on the Shankill Road was the Reverend Gilbert Emmanuel McKenzie, a Presbyterian Missionary from the Church of Jamaica and Grand Cayman, now known as the United Church in Jamaica and the Cayman Islands, who arrived in

December 1976 as part of an exchange programme to work with the Shankill Road Mission Team Ministry. He got to work straight away, helping with a Christmas party for 350 older people which was followed a few days later by a community carol service where he was the preacher. Six feet tall, he liked to be known simply as Gilbert. He preached and spoke at meetings all over Northern Ireland and was also involved with youth work and hospital visits. In one newspaper interview he said:

> *"Being black - not coloured I must stress - has no problems for me. Indeed it's been an immense help in introducing myself to people. There are so few black men and women in Ireland that I stand out in any street and I've had some amusing encounters."*

In others he said he had been made very welcome in Northern Ireland and that the people were friendly, but joked that he was not so keen on the weather. He got on particularly well with the children of the area and said:

> *"I get on great with the kids in the Shankill. Some of the young ones had never seen a black person before, except on TV, and they wanted to touch me to see if I felt different. Children are very honest. It's much easier for an adult to be hypocritical."*

He liked to wear technicolour suits and enjoyed the music of Bob Marley. Gilbert also appeared on local television. He appeared on UTV's *Friday Night* show, a five minute programme, which aired on Friday 18 November 1977. Shortly after this, a BBC Spotlight offering called *A Little Bit of Colour* was shown on Wednesday 23 November at 9.25 pm. The Spotlight team had followed him around for a while recording his progress and this documentary was the result. The title was apparently taken from Gilbert himself saying he aimed "to bring a little bit of colour" to Belfast shortly after he arrived.

Born on 21 November 1942, from a young age he felt called to serve God, and this he would do, spending his entire adult life in ministry. He travelled the world and in his mid and later life, was the Minister at a number of Presbyterian churches in America. He died at his home in Denver, Colorado, USA, on 4 July 2022 after a lifetime of service. His obituary says that he always ended his meetings or signed off correspondence with the words "Blessings, courage, and love."

Nowadays we live in a globalised world. It is easier than ever for people to move vast distances and live and work in Western Europe. Human beings from all over the planet, of all faiths and none, have made all parts of the United Kingdom and the Republic of Ireland their home. The prophecy of the *South Wales Evening Telegram* of 17 July 1872 - albeit written sarcastically I suspect given what preceded it - seems to have come true:

> *But the time is rapidly approaching when growing intelligence will banish forever all the differences of race, caste, and colour, and when the inhabitants of the world shall be all cosmopolitans.*

If time travel *was* possible, and the esteemed and pioneering actor Ira Aldridge was to visit Coventry in 2025, he would no longer stand out in a crowd or be considered a curiosity - unless of course he decided to do a spot of impromptu acting, and if he did he would probably then wonder what the things in people's hands were that were pointing at him as he recited lines from Shakespeare, sang a song or two or gave a speech. Perhaps some of the audience would take selfies with him and tell him he was a "sick actor bro!," and then ask what "socials" he was on? Ira would no doubt be amazed at the diversity of the people in the city centre and the variety of languages spoken. He would see many Africans and those of African heritage, and also note that those who joyfully preach the Christian gospel in the shadow of the Lady Godiva statue and other places in the heart of the city to passers by are mainly Africans and those of African heritage. If he asked where the Theatre Royal was in Smithford Street, he would be greeted with blank expressions before being directed to The Belgrade Theatre in Corporation Street. Here he would see the stunning mural of himself in flowing orange robes gracing the outside wall. Maybe he would smile broadly and give a nod of appreciation.

Likewise, if George Henry Thompson was to warp to the Shankill in 2025, he might notice the African food and convenience stores near Carlisle Circus and also at Peter's Hill, not far from Townsend Street. Like Aldridge, he would not be considered a curiosity anymore and find that the Shankill is a diverse place and welcoming of those who contribute positively to society.

If he had been there on Saturday 28 June, to watch the annual Whiterock Parade - also known as the Shankill's 'mini-twelfth' - when the area puts its best foot forward, he would have seen among the members of the Orange Order that were marching a smiling young Black girl. Her name, of Yoruba origin, and meaning 'child of wealth' or 'child of honour,' was proudly displayed on her orange collarette which was worn over the top of a Linfield Football Club shirt. As the procession made its way under the impressive Military and Orange arches and along streets decorated with red, white and blue bunting and Union flags, he may also have noticed the young 'stick men' or junior drum majors leading the Shankill Sons of Ulster flute band onwards. One of them, skilfully twirling and throwing his drum stick in the air, was a Black boy. Perhaps on seeing these two youngsters freely embracing the proud traditions of the area, George may have raised an arm in the air, smiled wryly to himself and uttered an updated version of his legendary cry:

Come on ye sons and daughters of William!

REFERENCES

1: TALES FROM WALKER'S LANE

1. The Belfast News-Letter, 28 July 1840; The Vindicator, Belfast, 29 July 1840.
2. The Vindicator, Belfast, Wednesday 23 June 1847.
3. The Belfast News-Letter, 16 October 1849.
4. The Northern Whig, 16 January 1851.
5. The Belfast News-Letter, 30 June 1865; The Belfast Chronicle, 1 July 1865.
6. The Belfast News-Letter, 9 February 1865; The Northern Whig, 11 April 1865.

2: THE ATHENS OF IRELAND

1. The Belfast News-Letter, 30 May 1870.
2. The Ulster Echo, 1 June 1874.
3. The Belfast News-Letter, 1 June 1874.
4. The Belfast News-Letter, 10 June 1872.

3: THE ROAD TO RIOT

1. Belfast Riots - A Short History by John Dorney. The Irish Story (online).https://www.theirishstory.com/2013/01/09/belfast-riots-a-short-history/
2. The Daily Examiner, 1 June 1872.
3. The Belfast Weekly News, 13 July 1872.
4. The Daily Examiner, 13 July 1872.
5. The Belfast News-Letter, 5 August 1872.

4: FAITH AND FATHERLAND

1. Belfast Evening Telegraph, 13 August 1872.
2. Ulster Examiner and Northern Star, 22 April 1873.

3. The Belfast News-Letter, Morning, 15 August 1872.
4. The Belfast News-Letter, 16 August 1872.
5. The Belfast Weekly News, 24 August 1872.
6. The Daily Examiner, 2 October 1872.
7. The Belfast Weekly News, 7 September 1872.
8. Ulster Examiner and Northern Star, 29 March 1873.
9. Belfast Evening Telegraph, 24 August 1872.
10. The Evening Telegraph (Dublin), 26 August 1872.
11. The Northern Whig, 24 March 1873.
12. The Constabulary Gazette, 5 June 1920.
13. The Irish Weekly and Ulster Examiner, 5 June 1920.
14. The Freeman's Journal, 31 May 1920.
15. Belfast Weekly Telegraph, 12 April 1873.
16. The Newry Reporter, 17 August 1872.
17. The Newry Reporter, 22 March 1873.
18. Belfast Evening Telegraph, 22 August 1872.

7: THE SONS OF WILLIAM

1. The Belfast News-Letter, 15 November 1867.
2. The Belfast Morning News, 22 October 1869.
3. The Belfast Morning News, 10 January 1870.
4. The Belfast Morning News, 11 April 1870.
5. The Belfast Morning News, 4 July 1870.
6. The Weekly Examiner, 2 November 1872.
7. The Northern Whig, 27 February 1873.
8. The Daily Express, 18 August 1880. J. C. O'Donnell died on this day, not long after riots took place after the Lady Day procession of that year.

The account of the first hearing and beetle incident is sourced from the following newspapers:

Belfast Evening Telegraph, 12 September 1872.
Daily Examiner, Friday 13 September 1872.
The Belfast News-Letter, Morning. 13 September 1872.
The Northern Whig, 13 September 1872.

10: ALWAYS GRINNING AND LOOKING PLEASANT

Sources for the second hearing are:
The Daily Examiner, 20 September 1872.
Belfast Weekly News, 21 September 1872.

1. The Belfast Morning News, 9 July 1879.
2. The Belfast Weekly News, 5 April 1873.
3. The Newtownards Chronicle and County Down Observer, 8 November 1890.

11: ARTISTIC LICENCE

1. The Daily Examiner, 20 September 1872; Belfast Evening Telegraph, 14 March 1873.
2. Ancestry.com. Scotland, Select Marriages, 1561-1910 [database on-line].
3. The Limerick and Clare Examiner, 17 July 1852.
4. The Southern Reporter and Cork Commercial Courier, 5 August 1852.
5. The Belfast Morning News, 17 May 1862.
6. https://www.dib.ie/biography/dorrian-patrick-a2719 - Ambrose Macaulay.
7. Queensland State Archive; Chermside, QLD, Australia; Immigration Indexes, 1848-1972.
8. Belfast Evening Telegraph, 25 May 1905.
9. The Constabulary Gazette, Dublin. 10 August 1912.
10. https://adb.anu.edu.au/biography/cahill-william-geoffrey-5462
11. Sourced from various newspapers that covered the tragedy.
12. The Irish News and Belfast Morning News, 10 September 1908; The Ulster Echo, 12 October 1908; The Irish News and Belfast Morning News, 12 January 1909.

12: BORN IN THE USA?

1. The Northern Whig, Belfast, 20 March 1873.
2. Ulster Examiner and Northern Star, 21 October 1874.
3. Larne Times and Weekly Telegraph, Saturday 12 August 1911.

14: IS THE TRIAL READY FOR ME?

1. Ulster Examiner and Northern Star, 26 March 1873.
2. Ulster Examiner and Northern Star, 3 May 1873.
3. The People's Advocate, 15 December 1900.
4. The Weekly Examiner, 14 September 1872.
5. The Constitution (Cork), 7 April 1873.
6. The Flag of Ireland, 17 August 1872.
7. The Nation (Dublin), 1 January 1876.

15: WHITSUNTIDE IN COTTONOPOLIS

1. The Yorkshire Post and Leeds Intelligencer, 13 February 1874.
2. The Manchester Courier and Lancashire General Advertiser, 27 May 1874.

www.ingramcontent.com/pod-product-compliance
Ingram Content Group UK Ltd.
Pitfield, Milton Keynes, MK11 3LW, UK
UKHW041653220226
468232UK00003B/205

9 781836 156215